Messianic Judaism

A Rabbi's Journey
through Religious Change in America

CAROL HARRIS–SHAPIRO

Beacon Press
BOSTON

Beacon Press
25 Beacon Street
Boston, Massachusetts 02108-2892
www.beacon.org

Beacon Press books
are published under the auspices of
the Unitarian Universalist Association of Congregations.

05 04 03 02 01 00 99   8 7 6 5 4 3 2 1

This book is printed on recycled acid-free paper that contains at least
20 percent postconsumer waste and meets the uncoated paper ANSI/NISO
specifications for permanence as revised in 1992.

Text design by Elizabeth Elsas
Composition by Wilsted & Taylor Publishing Services

Library of Congress Cataloging-in-Publication Data

Harris-Shapiro, Carol.
    Messianic Judaism : a rabbi's journey through religious change in
    America / Carol Harris-Shapiro.
        p.   cm.
      ISBN 0-8070-1040-5
      1. Jewish Christians—United States.   I. Title.
    BR158.H37   1999
    289.9—dc21   98-54864

TO JON, WHO MADE ME COFFEE,
AND TO ARYEH,
WHO MADE ME SMILE.
THANKS, YOU GUYS.

CONTENTS

CHAPTER I

Studying the Messianic Jews

There is a joke about a Jewish peddler, hurriedly walking through the wild, dark woods of Russia to his next destination. He feared that in such an isolated spot he might meet with bandits, or, God forbid, wild beasts! His worst fears were realized when, out of the corner of his eye, he caught a glimpse of a large, dark shape. Whirling around, he saw it—a bear! He dropped his pack and prepared to run, but then he noticed a funny thing. The bear was wearing a *yarmulke!* The bear was wearing ritual fringes! And, strangest of all, the bear held a Hebrew book in his paw and appeared to be praying!

The peddler drew closer to this amazing sight—a Jewish bear! Could anything be more wonderful! He drew a big sigh of relief, feeling safe. And then he heard what the bear was praying—the blessing before a meal.

Messianic Judaism[1] is a largely American Jewish/Christian movement whose origins can be traced in the United States to Hebrew Christian missions to the Jews in the nineteenth and twentieth centuries, the Jesus people of the late 1960s and early 1970s, and the resurgence of American Jewish ethnicity during the same decades. Messianic Jewish congregations are composed of both those born Jewish who accept Jesus as their savior and their Gentile supporters who adopt a "Jewish lifestyle."

Known more popularly (but misleadingly) as "Jews for Jesus," Messianic Jews have a paradoxical identity: they take two identities which have represented "the Other" for one another and made them one. Jews have served Christians for centuries as the examples of "those who killed/rejected Christ," the bearers of values antithetical to Christianity, and even representatives of Satan himself (Ruether 1974, 117–183). In turn, Jewish literature used the figure of Esau as the carnal, violent, rather stupid brother of Jacob to portray Christians and their persecutions of the Jews (Liebman and Cohen 1990, 39). A Jew who accepted Christ as savior was assumed to have abandoned the Jewish people, and indeed during the medieval era Jews who converted to Christianity (apostates) were notorious for their activities against the Jewish community (Endelman 1987, 6). While in the last two centuries this mutual enmity has changed first to toleration, and now at times even to admiration, both groups still perceive the other as having a unique, separate identity.

Even today, the ineradicable distinction between Christianity and Judaism is a crucial boundary marker for American Jews. A group easily assimilable into the Christianized culture of the United States, as well as a group internally pluralistic in religious and ethnic practice, the Jewish community needs a sense of "who we are not" to maintain its group cohesion and integrity. The one surety for even the most inactive Jew is that "Jews are not Christians." Norman Mirsky makes the point: "In a world where Jews and Christians are presumed to be equal and in law are equal one of the few universally shared Jewish values is that Jews are not expected to believe in, or even to admire, Jesus" (Mirsky 1978, 5). Jews who cross the boundaries are seen to be traitors, almost violating a law of nature. One notes the journalist Susan Schwartz McDonald (1976) comparing a Messianic Jewish service to the "ambiguous sexuality" of Renee Richards, a sex-change recipient. Solomon Goren, the chief rabbi of the Israeli Defense Forces, called one who is Jewish by nationality and Gentile by religion a "hermaphroditic creature" (Litvin 1965, 47). In order to explain this anomaly, Messianic Judaism, almost since the group's inception, has been labeled a cult by the mainstream Jewish community, on the assumption that adherents have to be brainwashed into their assertion that one could believe in Jesus and remain Jewish.

American Christians view the matter somewhat differently. It would be more difficult, if not impossible, for Christians to make the counterclaim, "Christians are not Jews." After all, Jesus was a Jew, the early church was composed of Jewish disciples, and the Hebrew Scriptures are part of the Christian canon. The past four decades of dialogue have led both to a decrease in anti-Jewish rhetoric and to a renewed appreciation of the Jewish roots of Christianity. However, the existence of "Jewish Christianity" can be seen to threaten the unity in Christ promised in Galatians 3:28. Some liberal churches, uneasy with the evangelical slant of Messianic Judaism and supporting their Jewish dialogue partners, reject the religion as a deceptive hybrid (Kravitz 1996, 10). And, while many evangelical churches are openly supportive of Messianic Judaism, they treat it as an ethnic church squarely within evangelical Christianity,[2] rather than as a separate entity (Beiser 1995, 27; Quebedeaux 1978, 161–162).

As a result, Messianic Jews are looked upon with suspicion by liberal Christian churches, accepted only partially by some evangelical organizations, and are considered pariahs by the American Jewish community. It was this "taboo" organization that I set out to study.

I began my study of Congregation B'nai Mashiach (People of the Messiah), located in Liberty, a large East Coast city known for its Quaker origins and early toleration for all religions, in 1990–91. During that time I attended public services, Bible studies, international "Messiah" conferences, prayer meetings, concerts, social gatherings, and life-cycle events. I immersed myself in Messianic literature and tapes, interviewed twenty adherents formally (dozens informally), and visited other congregations in Maryland, Florida, and Israel. Through the 1990s I maintained my connection to the movement through literature, ongoing conversations and encounters, as well as follow-up visits. To preserve privacy, the names of all congregation members, the congregation, and the city, as well as minor biographical details, have been altered. This book falls under the category of "ethnography," a work based on the researcher entering a community as both an observer and, to an extent, a participant.

ENMESHMENT

It was a terrible day. The rain came down in sheets in the dark afternoon, with reports of flooding on the major highways. As I looked worriedly out of my den window, I was concerned about several things: an outright rejection for my proposed study, the assistant Messianic rabbi, Stewart, not showing up for our appointment, and, frankly, a car accident in this weather. When the weather let up slightly, a sign I took as a good omen, I set out for the Messianic synagogue, arriving with plenty of time to spare.

I had never actually been to the Messianic synagogue before, and didn't know the area well, but the neighborhood with its large Jewish population felt instantly familiar to me. Across a major highway from the regional Jewish community center, its narrow streets are lined with two-story row houses of a light grayish stone. The tiny front lawns, carefully tended, sport pink flamingos and little fences, and there are striped awnings over many of the windows. Small shops at every corner bear the names of discount clothing stores, delis, and shoe stores. If I didn't see the street names it would be easy to confuse this area with a neighborhood ten minutes away from my childhood home, all the way on the other side of the city. Even at three in the afternoon, the gloom was so deep many lights were on in the stores and homes, giving the neighborhood a warm, welcoming feeling.

The Messianic synagogue is located on a busy secondary artery, behind a car wash and right near a strip mall of stores and coffee shops. The building has a tall front of whitish stucco, smooth, with "Congregation B'nai Mashiach" in big letters across the front and a Jewish star. It is a tiny, rather shabby building at first glance, which looks as though it was built in the 1950s. A few children, apparently just out of school, were playing on a few pieces of playground equipment in the back parking lot. Despite the formality of the little girl's clothing (it was unusual to see a girl in a dress on monkey bars) the children seemed normally boisterous.

The "normality" of the children was indeed important to me. My tension stemmed from more than my need to get permission to study this community, although that was enough to give me butterflies. I had had my heart on this topic for eight years. However, I had more on my mind than a successful study. I had heard so much about this congregation as I was growing up in the Jewish community: how they brainwashed people, how they conned small children into their facility to be coerced into their religion, how they were deceptive and dangerous. I remembered all the jokes and even the fears that, despite the fact that I was a rabbi, I would end up in a zombie-like Messianic Jewish coma. Old conditioning dies hard; despite my intellectual conviction that these stories were ridiculous, I still felt as though I was visiting the bogeyman. Some Jews were hopeful that this study would unearth terrible secrets, not so much the skeleton in the Messianic Jewish closet but the fresh corpse in the basement! Even this initial contact made me feel both disloyal and daring. The nearby bagel shop, the kosher meat market, and the group of students walking by from the nearby Orthodox yeshivah all made me feel both comforted and embarrassed. What was a good Jew doing here?

The Rabbi and the Researcher

My own experience with Christians and Christianity has changed markedly over the years. I grew up in an almost all-Jewish neighborhood; all of my friends were Jewish. Christians were the Catholics on "the other side of the Boulevard," equivalent to "the wrong side of the tracks," separated from us culturally, socially, and economically. They were understood as the bearers of anti-Semitism, the attenders of remedial classes, the ones who smoked on the back steps of our high school. There were some exceptions: Catholic neighbors with whom my family was friendly, a Catholic classmate. Still, the categories were fairly firm—there was "us" and there was "them." Protestants didn't really exist; they were invisible, or honorary Jews.

At the state college that I attended, my horizons broadened considerably. My roommate and close friend was active in her Catholic parish and other good friends were church-going Lutherans and Methodists. I learned a lot from our conversations, and soon became rather fascinated with religious studies in general and Jewish-Christian relations in particular. As I entered graduate school and rabbinical school, I became involved in interfaith dialogues on a local and national level. I found relating to those who had once been considered my "enemy" both a liberating experience and a profound learning experience. I was taken with the imaginative process of interfaith encounter, putting myself in the shoes of my dialogue partner, temporarily exchanging my vision of the world for hers. Returning to my tradition, I could see its strengths with fresh eyes; my Judaism became deeper and more thoughtful as a result of each meeting.

After a time, however, polite dialogues with liberal Christians dissatisfied me. Liberal Jews and liberal Christians often have so much in common that dialogue sometimes felt like I was talking to myself! I found myself more and more interested in the "uncivil Christianity" of fundamentalism that dictates rather than discusses.

It was precisely that dogmatism that intrigued me. Indeed, as I spun through the dials of my radio or television, I sometimes stopped to hear Christian radio Bible studies and episodes of the *700 Club*. It was not the Christian theology that interested me, nor the specific content of these programs. It was the assertion of uncompromising truth, the language of certainty used about God, His workings in the world, even His desires for the individual, that I found (and find) compelling.

Their passion appealed to me, a person leading what could best be called an inconsistent approach to Judaism. When immersed in prayers or hearing the Torah read, I feel profoundly touched by the Transcendent, accepting of an active and personal God who has an intimate stake in the lives of the Jewish people and humanity. I can pray *to* this God, not *about* this God. Away from these moments of prayer and contemplation, these intuitions are eaten away by intellectual skepticism. What can we really know about God when the Bible and Talmud were written by fallible human beings, when the traditional Judaism which most strongly supports belief in God does not encourage or even allow me, as a woman, a way of practicing that belief apart from a highly segregated woman's role? The traditionalist part of me lives a fairly observant life by liberal standards, but the skeptical part of me mocks—does God really care if I turn on an electric light on Shabbat? I simultaneously immerse myself in and struggle with Judaism; in any case, I am irrevocably committed to it.

What would it be like to be so certain—certain of the Bible as the inerrant Word of God, certain of my progress toward Godliness with the indwelling of the Holy Spirit, certain of being cleansed from all sin and shortcomings through the death of Jesus, certain of a future already foretold in Scriptures? I could perceive the sense of purpose in such a worldview.

My curiosity was piqued further because fundamentalist Christianity is often perceived in Jewish circles as the direct antithesis of liberal Judaism. They are primitive, we are sophisticated; they are anti-intellectual, we think; they are prejudiced, we are enlightened; they seek to convert/eliminate the Jewish people through spiritual genocide, we bravely hold onto our traditions and refuse to succumb. I absorb these understandings as an American Jew, and am never free of them even as I challenge them.

If fundamentalist Christianity is in some way "the enemy" of Judaism in American Jewish categories, Messianic Jews are those traitors who have sold out and joined the enemy camp, only pretending to be

Jewish in order to lure prospective converts into their web. They are worse than adversaries; they are turncoats. They are the "Jewish bear" of the story above, ready to consume the too-trusting Jew into the ever-hungry maw of Christianity.

Throughout my teens and twenties I learned of the threat of the "Jews for Jesus" through conversations, articles in the local Jewish newspapers, and other encounters. These reports I evaluated with both the overweening cynicism and the inflated credulity of adolescence; I knew that this rhetoric was overheated (especially the unfortunate comparison with Nazis that seemed to set the tone for most discussions) but I also believed that there was something suspicious about the organization, an attitude that had been confirmed for me far earlier in a very personal way.

I was about eight years old, my cousin already in her mid-teens. I liked my cousin. She used to give me a lot of her old toys as presents: charms from gumball machines, a Ringo doll, and a great Indian leather headband I wore constantly until the laces broke.

Something about my cousin, however, created a lot of tension between my parents and my aunt. I gradually discovered that she'd gotten involved with "Jews for Jesus." At least, that's how my parents phrased it. One afternoon, as I was hanging out in her room, my cousin showed me Isaiah 53, and subsequently tried to talk to me about the Virgin Birth. I told her that this wasn't possible, that no one could still be a virgin and give birth. She simply replied, "If God can do anything, why not a virgin birth?" All my arguments to the contrary wouldn't sway her from that simple answer—I was getting more and more upset. Very confused, I returned home and told my mother, who declared, "I hope you weren't listening to that nonsense." I yelled out tearfully, "Maybe it isn't nonsense," and stomped upstairs. My first experience with proselytization! While my cousin has since moved on to more standard evangelical Christianity, her beliefs put a painful rift in the family.

The study of Messianic Judaism thus appealed to me on a number of different levels. Intellectually, I was drawn to the paradox the group represented, the oxymoronic identity of being Jewish and Christian at the same time. As a Jew, I sought to understand myself by understanding the Other, getting a better sense of my own Judaic commitments and Jewish communal loyalties when confronted with a group that seemed to embody the very opposite. As an individual, I wanted to understand the appeal of the Messianic movement for my cousin, to comprehend what had happened in my family. It was a study that satisfied the personal, religious, and intellectual parts of my psyche.

Being an "unsaved" Jew studying the Messianic movement has its own complications; certainly members would tirelessly try to persuade any such researcher that accepting Yeshua as savior was a superior course of action, bringing the person to a point both of discomfort and exhaustion. My additional role as rabbi added a new dimension of difficulty to what was already a complicated experience.

As a rabbi, I both knew and accepted the basic assessment of the Messianic movement prevalent in the Jewish community. What they practice is evangelical Christianity, not Judaism. They don't belong in our synagogues, our Hebrew schools, our Jewish organizations. I recognized that their gains were our losses, their successes were our failures. We were on opposite sides in the religious competition.

The Messianic community understands this competition well; they too would see any victory for "rabbinic Judaism" (normative Judaism) as a defeat for "true Biblical Judaism" (their version). To allow not just an unsaved Jew, but a rabbi in to study the community was a real risk on their part; as Stewart put it, it was akin to "letting the wolf in among the sheep." Would I try to convince members of the fallacies of their beliefs? Would I release names and addresses of members to "Jews for Judaism," the Jewish anti-missionary organization? These were questions that were raised explicitly to me. I'm sure they were just the tip of the iceberg.

Gaining entry to the congregation took several months, because of the congregation's suspicion concerning my motives and the potential harm such a study could do to the cause of Messianic Judaism. In fact, I just kept coming back, even though I was initially told "no" to the length of the study and "no" to the idea of interviews. After a while, when the members began to trust at least my good intentions, some of their fears seemed to subside. At one point, a woman leader said, quite openly, "I don't know why we are letting you do this." However, others had their own ideas. Several members told me that since at this time they were seeking legitimacy in the Jewish community, my study might prove useful.

Thus, the community clearly had a vested interest in making me think the community was wholly wonderful and warm, to influence me as a rabbi and a scholar as well as to approach me as an unsaved Jew. Some members remained distrustful; some who spoke to me frankly about the community seemed concerned about "repercussions" if the leadership knew about our conversations, even toward the end of my study. I certainly had more open relationships with newer members and Gentile members who did not experience direct rejection from the Jewish community. Under these circumstances, friendships with the more marginal and more accepting members of the congregation helped me to break through the group's "public persona."

One member who became a friend helped me to understand more of the inner workings of the community. I met Tom at a Messianic singles brunch I attended. He was artistic and well-spoken, and we discovered we lived very close to each other. New to B'nai Mashiach, he was trying to understand what the congregation called the "Messianic vision," the role of Jewishness, in his life as a believer. Having been raised Catholic, with a devoted Catholic mother and a completely non-practicing Jewish father in a small town, he knew very little about Judaism. It wasn't until he experienced anti-Semitism that he began to explore his Jewish identity, and, having already accepted Jesus as his savior, he found his niche at B'nai Mashiach. Regularly carpooling with Tom to services, I learned about the differing attitudes the congregation showed to Jew and Gentile, even to African-American and white members. I learned how an outsider might see the emphasis on Jewishness in the congregation as ethnocentric, even too fearful of Jewish approval. I learned from his encounters with leadership how far freethinking might be allowed in the group, and how much they were willing to tolerate in order to include a marriageable young Jewish male with a good job. And I learned how someone who was highly intelligent could nonetheless be fascinated with Biblical prophecy, uncritically pointing to dissociated verses to prove, for example, that the nuclear accident at Chernobyl was foretold in the Scriptures. It was friendships with people like Tom that enabled me to really see the congregation in some depth.

As a Reconstructionist[3] rabbi, I was not only under suspicion but came to be seen as the representative and supposed defender of organized Jewry. People went out of their way to express their scorn for the Reconstructionist movement's acceptance of homosexuality or the presence of a supposed witch among the movement's rabbinical students, as well as the shortcomings of the Jewish community, from the "deadness" in synagogues to the inadequate training of rabbis to the occult beliefs of some Hasidim. Despite this interaction, ranging from good-natured teasing to angry accusations, I consciously attempted to be a better listener than a reactor. At the same time, because I was a rabbi, few tried the traditional prooftexting approach to convince me of the truth of Yeshua; they expected I would have ready answers to their gambits. The conversations we did have were more general and more gratifying: on the nature of God, of faith, and of the role and destiny of the Jewish people. While Biblical passages were involved and sometimes disputed in these discussions, we often were able to get far beyond quarreling over well-worn ground. Some even asked me for the correct translation of a Hebrew word or document. This was a part of the study I enjoyed, one which my rabbinical title may have helped facilitate.

My identity as a Jew and a rabbi certainly prevented me from immersing myself in the movement as a full participant in the participant-observation process. To be a full participant I would have had to believe that Jesus was the Messiah and the son of God. While I took their religious claims seriously, and carefully researched the Bible once more to understand their perspective, I was no more convinced than I had been before. However, while I was certainly not a "born-again" believer, I did try to speak to them seriously about their beliefs. My openness to such discussions and to other activities (such as being prayed over) continually surprised members of the community.

Indeed, I believe that some members were actually quite concerned about my unsaved state. At an international Messianic conference I attended, there was a workshop on the gifts of the Holy Spirit. The large room was filled with people with upraised hands, chanting or shouting or whispering unintelligible syllables. A long line of Messianic rabbis and elders was arrayed in the front of the room, praying intensely for the middle-aged and elderly members flocking to the front. Every few seconds, a person, stiff as a board or collapsing in the middle, would be laid gently down on the floor, where he or she would laugh out loud, cry, or repeat over and over again, "Thank you! Thank you!" while another person prone at another section of the room would get up, straighten her clothes, and walk quietly out of the room.

I was already somewhat unnerved by the largest display of charismatic worship I had ever seen. When the Messianic rabbi encouraged each of us to pray for someone else, Annie, one of the women in leadership at B'nai Mashiach with whom I felt I had a friendly relationship, asked me if I minded if she prayed over me. I was really curious to see the result, so I agreed. She began to pray quietly, her hands on mine. Suddenly she began to shake uncontrollably and cry. Her hands gnarled up like claws as they withdrew from me; it was as if some chemical in my body had poisoned her! I felt guilty, as if I had really done something to her. Suddenly, Lisa, Stewart's wife was there, also laying hands on me and praying, interweaving Biblical verses on salvation with fervent words. She too began to cry. After about twenty minutes they both stopped, and Lisa said, "God loves you very very much." I asked Annie what happened, and she seemed reluctant to tell me at first. Finally she said, circuitously, that sometimes "something" blocks the ability to know God. After some prompting on my part, it became clear to me that she felt that Satan had a hold on me. Their compassion and concern shone out of their eyes. They asked me to keep praying to know the truth. They left together, and it was only after they left that I could process the emotional experience. I realized that the interpretation of Satanic oppression made sense. After all, here I was, an open, interested person as yet unconvinced of the evident truth of Messianic Judaism. I'm sure that they really would have liked to save me, and couldn't understand why I was so blind to the truth.

While my beliefs and status in some ways separated me from the Messianic community, my knowledge of the Jewish community was at times an invaluable asset. I was a *partial* participant in a wholly different way. I grew up in the same kind of Jewish environment that many of the Messianic Jews experienced. I shared the same languages about growing up Jewish in America, and in fact shared some of their assessments of the established Jewish community. I also felt very close to individuals as they spoke about their religious quest, as I experienced the same search in high school, and shared their passion for "ultimate things." In fact, as I spoke with more and more people, I realized that if someone from that group had approached me when I was eighteen or nineteen years old, before I came to terms with my own community, I might very well be a member of the congregation instead of studying the congregation. In that sense, I could call myself a "partial native."

I was certainly *not* a fly on the wall. My constant note-taking bothered a lot of members (although I tried to avoid such activity in inappropriate situations) and reminded them exactly what I was doing there. After I asked Stewart why they prayed for Russian Jews and not Ethiopian Jews, at the very next public service he included a prayer for Ethiopian Jews. After one service where I sang the songs I felt I could sing (songs that didn't refer to Jesus) with great gusto, one person approached me and said, "We saw you singing and enjoying yourself. Watch out, you could become one of us." I was even asked to write an article for a newsletter coming out of the Messianic Jewish Alliance of America (I declined). Certainly, any researcher entering a group ethically and openly can expect to influence a group under study, but these very changes provided even greater insight into the members' values and ideals.

My identity as rabbi therefore highlighted my presence and shaped this book in different ways than a non-Jewish or nonrabbinic investigator would have experienced. My own reactions, too, were strongly determined by my background. As a rabbi, I admired the central role God played in the life of the community, the unabashed ability of members to invoke God in everyday conversations, and the warmth and delight they took in worship, prayer, and Bible study. The most fervent among them saw God's presence and care shining through even the most mundane daily events. At the same time, as a rabbi and an informed Jew, I was often furious with them, at their misunderstandings of Judaism, their reductionistic answers to complex issues, and was even frightened at their successes. When their altar calls went by with nary a response, I was pleased. When a new person of Jewish birth "came to the Lord," I grieved. Clearly, there were times when *I* would have liked to have changed *their* minds and "bring them back to the fold," much as they were trying to do with me.

Does this emotional involvement invalidate my work? I don't think so. As Barbara Myerhoff rightly pointed out, anger is a form of attachment (Myerhoff 1980, 184–185). In some ways, my anger, as well as my more positive emotional feelings, shows my engagement with the group. The opposite of love is indifference, and that was one feeling I *never* had. One great fear a member expressed to me early on was that I'd be examining them as a microbiologist looks at slides. That, I think, rather than emotional engagement, is the great danger to ethnography. I can say that although I only occasionally approved, I often felt that I understood.

My position as a rabbi investigating Messianic Jews spilled over to my own Jewish community. Many Jews were fascinated with my research topic. Questions such as "What do they *do* for Yom Kippur?" "Are there a lot of non-Jews in the group?" and "How can they say they are Jews when they accept Jesus as God?" were frequently asked. Especially in the early months of my research, it was as if I were investigating the seamy underworld; my study had for my Jewish circle the fascination of the mysterious, the forbidden, the feared.

However, like my experience with the Messianic community, the experience with the Jewish community has had its share of frustrations. Accustomed to a certain "party line" regarding the Messianic community, laypersons and rabbis alike have expressed concern that, because I do not regard the Messianic movement as evil or cunning, I am either hoodwinked or pandering to the greatest spiritual threat in Jewish history. Even more threatening to some is the topic of my last chapter, when I point out that the Messianic movement, like heretical movements in general, can be especially perceptive in its evaluation of the faults of the "parent" organization. Accepting some of the Messianic movement's trenchant critiques of the American Jewish community, however, is far from personally accepting Messianic Judaism. I hope that in this work I make that distinction clear.

There is no escaping the fact that the topic of Messianic Judaism is inescapably meshed in an ongoing power struggle to establish the character and future of the Jewish community, a power struggle with which, by virtue of my being a Jew, a rabbi, and a researcher, I am intimately involved. In this place, there is no neutral ground.

QUESTIONS OF IDENTITY

How can Messianic Jews claim to be both Jewish and Christian? Like all language, this question takes its meaning not so much from the words as from their inflection. I ask and answer this question in two ways. The first is the question of an intrigued researcher, and can be rephrased, "What are the processes that holds this unique identity together, despite its ever-present disconfirmation in the structure of American religious culture?" The second is the reaction of an uneasy Jew, which can be rephrased, "How do Messianic Jews have the temerity to call themselves Jewish and believe in Jesus?" I own both of these inflections; I am both the intrigued researcher and the uneasy Jew.

Thus, I seek here first to illuminate the process by which these Messianic Jews are able to construct a coherent identity out of two identities which have long been seen as mutually exclusive—Jewish and Christian—and, second, to examine the import this identity claim carries for the American Jewish community. Just as this study challenges Messianic Jewish reporting of its identity as "pure," providing the true faith devoid of internal conflict or complication, the Messianic Jews in turn challenge American Judaism's picture of itself as "pure," holding a shared true Jewish identity handed down continuously through the millennia, invulnerable to Messianic Jewish claims.

The Challenge for the Messianic Movement

Adherents claim that Messianic Judaism resolved many contradictions in their lives and provided an answer to their prayers and problems. However, their proud assertions of authenticity coincided with some difficult contradictions. The conflicts Messianic believers face are not only with the American Jewish mainstream community and Christian churches, but also with the two contradictory cultural contexts—American Judaism and Spirit-filled Protestantism—that shape the ever-present internal process of Messianic believers to construct and maintain a "new thing," Messianic Jewish identity.[4]

Possibly what engenders the most conscious sense of tension among Messianic Jews is that they refuse to call their religious movement a "blend" of Judaism and Christianity. The self-appointed task of Messianic believers is to claim an ongoing *Jewish* identity, despite their belief in the divinity and saving power of Jesus of Nazareth. Herein lies the greatest struggle of all. As we will see, this identity claim is clearly contestable by both the Jewish and Christian communities, and thus the congregation continually works to re-create and re-establish this identity claim in sermons, music, dance, conversation, and even dress.

This does not mean that Messianic Jews uncritically accept the definitions proffered by the American Jewish establishment. Messianic Jews want not merely to legitimate their perceived Jewish identity, but to *change* this identity. As "saved" people, they understand themselves to be fundamentally different from "unsaved" Jews. Thus, Messianic Jews seek to actuate two messages: "We are *Jews!*" "We are *Messianic* Jews!" The different emphases, on "Jew" and "Messianic," describe the tension that leads not just to an affirmation of American Jewish identity, but also to a transformation of that identity to fit the new image of a "saved" Jew.

However, not all Messianic believers *are* Jews. Nothing is as problematic as the large numbers of Messianic Gentiles in the movement. To claim Jewish identity when one is not Jewish oneself adds another layer of struggle: "We are *Jews!*" "We are *Messianic* Jews!" "We are Messianic *Gentiles/spiritual* Jews!"

A last complication arises, that of the hostility of the American Jewish community. While Messianic believers consider it their special calling to convert Jews, American Jews for the most part consider Messianic Jews not only traitors for leaving the fold but also liars for claiming they are Jewish, not Christian. This adds a fourth and fifth claim: "We are *Jews!*" "We are *Messianic* Jews!" "We are Messianic *Gentiles/spiritual* Jews!" "The Jews are *our responsibility!*" "The Jews are *our enemies!*" This complication leads to both romanticization and villainization of different aspects of Jewish life. Each of these claims, each of these evocations, pulls in and re-shapes two cultural contexts from which the community draws.

In this study, I uncover the tensions and conflicts inherent in an identity others see as a simple synthesis. What might appear on the surface as the smooth semblence of salvation is the result of selective attention, well-chosen silences, and an ongoing re-creation. The identity of belonging to Jesus *and* the Jewish people, being part of the "saved" and part of the "chosen," must be continually negotiated.

It is not only the Messianic believers who negotiate partial and shifting identifications. In a world replete with choices, with little identity structure that is "given," all of our identities by necessity become pastiches composed of fragments gleaned from multiple cultural contexts. We operate in different spheres (work, family, religion, leisure) that create various, often conflicting identity expectations; we come from backgrounds (ethnic, racial, religious, gender, regional, national) that provide us with a wealth of different cultural symbols to draw upon and different loyalties to express. Even cultures that appear unified contain instead jostling discourses that are always in flux, reshaped to the needs of the moment (Bowen 1992; Heath 1992).

Some believe religion helps us to escape all of our multiple confusions, to find one identity that cannot be doubted, questioned or denied (Bell 1992, 20; Weigert 1991, 5). However, "it would be wrong to suggest that everybody actually makes such a choice to the exclusion of other world views. . . . The creative bricolage, experimentation, alternation, revision and special pleading which partly characterize our everyday reasoning are a significant element in religious thought and feeling" (Beckford 1983, 14). Even those in our society attaining seeming identity closure through a deeply felt religious identity are always in active parley with elements of an attractive and menacing modernity (Carlson 1992; Heilman 1977; Hunter 1983; Thumma 1991). All of our identifications are partial, positioned, and transitory; even as we speak the language of continuity, we change in profound ways.

The Challenge of the Messianic Movement

Ironically, the group that might best be able to empathize with the Messianic attempt to bring together two incommensurate cultures is the group that has out-and-out rejected Messianic Judaism—the American Jewish community. For centuries, for millennia, Jews have negotiated Judaism with Hellenism, with Christianity, with Islam, with secularism, with socialism, with the American way of life. In each of these cases Jews have created and been created by the interactions between Judaism and these systems, as Judaism adopted certain elements of the dominant culture into its own expressions. Thus, the Jewish community, like all communities, has shared in some degree the same conflictual identity process as have the Messianic believers.

However, it is precisely that fragility that causes much of the Jewish resentment of the Messianic movement. It serves as an uncomfortable reminder of the recent imbalance in the balancing act between the Jewish and American worlds—increasing assimilation, the rising intermarriage rate, the fact of Jewish grandparents and Christian grandchildren. Because Messianic members are visible and enthusiastic missionaries, they become the feared symbol of seductive Christianity and disappearing Judaism.

Moreover, as a result of Judaism's encounter with modern culture, Jewish identity has fragmented; "Who is a Jew?" has become a question with an ever-increasing number of answers. Because of this diversity, Messianic believers challenge the notion that they are apostates from some sort of "true Judaism." Under Messianic Jewish scrutiny, the American Jewish reasoning that accepts secular Jews as Jews but not Christian Jews as Jews, practicing Christian spouses of Jews as members of liberal synagogues but not Messianic Jews as members of liberal synagogues can appear fragile, fuzzy, even self-contradictory. Just as this study uncovers the struggles within the coherent identity expressed by Messianic Jews, Messianic Jews uncover the confusion within the coherent Jewish identity professed by American Jews. Therefore, the second goal of the study is to examine this Messianic Jewish critique of American Judaism's self-definition(s), a critique that bitingly contests long-held assumptions of the American Jewish community.

CHAPTER 2

What Is Messianic Judaism?

Jewish Jesus-believers are hardly a new phenomenon. After all, Christianity began as a sect within Judaism. Jesus was born a Jew, his disciples were all born Jewish, and Paul, that great formulator of Christian doctrine, states his own identification as a Jew in Acts 22:3. Jewish Christians were expected to follow Torah laws, and even Paul's Gentile additions to the new church were not completely out of the Jewish sphere, since they followed rabbinic laws appropriate to righteous Gentiles (Segal 1992). For approximately one hundred years, accepting Christian doctrine did not necessarily remove one who was born Jewish from the Jewish community. A definitive break between Judaism and Christianity did not come until 70 CE, and perhaps as late as the Bar Kochba revolt of 135 CE (S. T. Katz 1984), as the rapidly increasing Gentile constituency fundamentally changed the practices and theology of the early Christian movement (Wilson 1995, 168). Although after the schism between the two groups there was positive religious interaction between the Jewish and Christian communities as well as Jewish Christians trying to stand a "middle ground" between Judaism and Christianity,[1] by the seventh century organized Jewish Christianity had all but disappeared (Fruchtenbaum 1983, 47).

Further historical evidence for manifestations of Jewish Christian identity throughout the Middle Ages highlights its sporadic character (J. Katz 1961, 74–75). In medieval Germany of the twelfth and thirteenth centuries, Jewish converts to Christianity attempted to retain ties to Jewish life, contributing to Jewish charity and wanting to be owners or part-owners of the scroll of the Torah used in the synagogue service. After the conversions of Jews to Christianity in Spain and Portugal during the fourteenth and fifteenth centuries, some

"New Christians" and their descendants merged elements of their Jewish background with their Christian practice, liberalizing or re-forming Christianity along the way. A group of Jewish converts to Christianity in Italy actually recreated a full-blown form of Jewish Christianity—accepting Christian theology but practicing Jewish law.[2] However, none of these provide a historical link between the Jesus movement and the present day; it was the Protestant missions movement that re-created, rather than inherited, Jewish Christianity.

THE MISSIONS MOVEMENT

For much of Christian history, conversions of Jews had been viewed as victorious battles in a war waged against a theological enemy. Beginning with the early Church Fathers, the Jews were vilified for their supposed lustful, carnal ways, their killing of Christ, and their consorting with the Devil. The fact that Christianity became the state religion and the Church's influence spread to many parts of the world led to the activation of this anti-Jewish ideology in practice. Conversion to Christianity was a result of force, either the direct threat of violence upon Jews or the indirect promise of oppression and economic misery lifted upon acceptance of baptism (Ruether 1974, 183–225).

With the development of Christian humanism and the Protestant Reformation, more positive evaluations of Jews and Judaism entered Christian discourse. Protestant leaders, learning the Bible from Hebrew scholars and Jewish commentaries, developed a renewed interest in the Hebrew language and Jewish customs (J. Friedman 1994). The "sword for the Lord" proselytizing diminished in Protestant lands, to be replaced by a renewed confidence in the art of persuasion. Surely, Protestants asserted, Jews could be convinced of the truth of Christianity through the right words. While a non-violent Protestant effort to evangelize the Jews was beginning to emerge in Europe and America of the eighteenth century, the nineteenth century saw the real development of organized missionary activities to the Jews in England and in the United States.

There are a number of reasons for this upsurge in evangelism. Connected with an expectation of the imminent return of Christ was an interest in the Jews, who were expected to return to Israel and come to Christianity as a sign of the Messiah's return (Sandeen 1970, 3–21). This expansion of Jewish missions work was part of a much wider movement to "civilize and Christianize" the world in the nineteenth century (Evearitt 1989, 90); the large urban concentrations of Eastern European immigrants to the United States and Western Europe in the nineteenth and early twentieth centuries gave missionaries a fruitful field of endeavor. The "culturally sensitive" approach used in China and India was also employed in these Jewish neighborhoods, where Jewish-born evangelists encouraged Jews to retain elements of their culture. Thus, a Jew accepting Christianity was referred to by these missions as "completed" rather than "converted." The traditional missions approach, offering job training and schooling as a prelude to salvation, was even more attractive for new immigrants seeking to better themselves in America.

The widespread acceptance of premillennial dispensationalism among conservative evangelicals added impetus to the renewed effort to convert Jews (Rausch 1979, 71–72). Formulated by John Nelson Darby in Great Britain and popularized in the United States by C. I. Scofield in his *Reference Bible*, dispensationalism theorized a pattern of historic change that informed Biblical interpretation and placed all of human history under the sweeping supernatural hand of God. Each dispensation, or age, was characterized by a mode of relationship between God and humanity, one which humanity failed to keep. For example, the age of Adam and Eve was one of an innocent humanity, which ended when Adam and Eve ate the forbidden fruit. Each subsequent age was marked by similar failure; at the end of each epoch humankind disappointed a loving God (Marsden, 1980, 64–66). According to the dispensational map, the time from Abraham to the year 70 CE constituted the "Times of the Jews"; after the Jews rejected Jesus and the Second Temple was destroyed, God turned to the Gentiles to bring them into relationship with Him through Jesus. This shift indefinitely postponed Jesus' Second Coming (Weber 1983, 19). However, ancient Biblical promises to the Jews would be fulfilled. Israel would begin to come back to the Land of Israel "in unbelief," signaling the end of the dispensational lacuna and the beginning of the Last Days. Soon the Antichrist would grip the world in a seven-and-a-half-year period of persecution known as the Great Tribulation, culminating in a decisive Middle Eastern battle between the forces of good and evil (the Battle of Armageddon) and resulting in Jesus' Second Coming, the coming of the Jewish people to faith in Jesus, and to the Jewish rule of a peaceful world from Jerusalem for a one-thousand-year reign.

Those Bible conferences and Bible schools (for example, the Moody Bible Institute in Chicago) based on this theology supported Zionism as the instrument of God's will and the harbinger of the End of Days; each battle fought on Israel's soil was viewed through an eschatological lens (Rausch 1979, 296–297). Jews would certainly be more open to a salvation message that affirmed a central role for the Jewish people and their unbroken legacy of the Land of Israel (Weber 1983, 141–142). As Timothy Weber pointed out, "Eventually, nearly every major American city that had a substantial Jewish population had some kind of evangelistic witness to the Jews, most of whom were either founded or at least heavily supported by premillennialists" (Weber 1983, 144). Those Jews who converted to Christianity became exemplars of the saved Jew who would take the lead spiritual role during the Millennium. (Rausch 1979, 307). Many of these outreach efforts eventually evolved into what would become the Hebrew Christian movement.

A number of organizations crucial to the development of Hebrew Christianity emerged at this time. The American Board of Mission to the Jews (ABMJ) was one of the most successful, and certainly one of the longest lived of the missionary enterprises; it was begun by Leopold Cohn, a Jewish convert, in Brownsville and Williamsburg. Providing social services in areas not yet covered by Jewish organizations Cohn was rather successful (Gutwirth 1987, 28). By 1937, the year of Cohn's death, Cohn estimated he had converted over one thousand Jews and funneled them into existing churches (Pruter 1987, 61). Setting up a separate Hebrew-Christian denomination was not his goal, at least in part because the ABMJ was funded by fundamentalist/evangelical churches that frowned on the "wall of partition."

Despite this reluctance of the ABMJ to encourage a separate denomination, new Christians of Jewish origin were still faced with a choice: to assimilate or to remain distinct. Structurally, because of anti-Semitism in the churches and the anger of the American Jewish community against them as traitors and apostates, they could not blend into either mainstream churches or mainstream synagogues. Furthermore, although the Christian evangelical community feared the partition of Jew and Gentile, it often urged Hebrew Christians to serve their own people as their only effective missionaries, and indeed needed Jews to differentiate themselves. How could saved Jews retain the promises of a physical Israel and return to the Land if conversion eradicated their Jewish identity? Thus, accepting the need to stand separate, Hebrew Christians created an organization to provide support and help retain their identity. This was the Hebrew Christian Alliance of America (HCAA).

The Hebrew Christian Alliance of America
One of the earliest mutual aid societies was The Hebrew Christian Union, formed in London in 1865 by Dr. C. Schwartz, to "stir up and stimulate one another in the endeavor of uniting with and caring for our brethren" (Sobel 1974, 178–179). In the United States, a similar group formed with the same dual purposes of fellowship and evangelism. As a result of a conference of Hebrew Christians, spearheaded by Mark Levy, an English convert of Jewish origin, and Dr. Edward Niles, a Gentile dentist, interest was sparked in a Hebrew Christian Alliance, which was formally established in 1915 (Winer 1990, 57).

To promote the "Good News" among the Jewish community, various evangelistic endeavors were attempted and important institutional ties created with groups interested in Jewish evangelism. Many of the members and activities of the HCAA were connected to Gentile missions to the Jews.[3] However, during a lull in missions activities in the 1920s, when Jews were wealthier and thus less responsive to the traditional missions approach (Gutwirth 1987, 33–34), the group shifted its emphasis to creating and preserving a unique Hebrew Christian identity among its membership, an emphasis that remained steady even as it re-entered the missions field in later decades.

The Congregational Movement
Along with an Alliance to help support Hebrew Christians, attempts to create separate Hebrew Christian congregations can be seen in the Jewish missions movement since its inception, although many of these early attempts were ephemeral. The first autonomous "Hebrew Christian Society" began in 1813 in England. Meeting at the Jews Chapel in Spitfall, forty-one converted Jews formed the congregation Beni Abraham for prayer and the spiritual welfare of their brothers (Eichhorn 1978, 23–25). Joseph Rabinovich, a former *maskil*

(member of the Jewish Enlightenment) who converted to Christianity, started a group in Kishinev, Russia, in 1884 called the New Israelites, meeting in a "synagogue" supported by the contributions of English and Scottish Protestants. His was but one of several Jewish Christian fellowships in Russia during this period, including The Biblical Brotherhood and the New Israel. Unlike the latter two organizations, the New Israelites believed in Jewish distinctiveness, which included observing circumcision, the Jewish Sabbath, and Passover while rejecting the Trinity. However, after Rabinovich died in 1899, the congregation disbanded (Rausch 1982, 93–98; Zipperstein 1987, 216–226). While Jacob Freshman, a missionary, opened the First Hebrew Christian Church in New York City in 1885, it too disappeared by the turn of the century (Evearitt 1989, 278–285). Even in Cohn's ABMJ, some of his Jewish believers apparently met for worship separately (Evearitt 1989, 220–221).

While independent Jewish expression was contested over fears of "Judaizing" (Winer 1990, 20–22), congregational development continued to accelerate in the twentieth century. John Zacker, a Hebrew Christian, founded The Hebrew Christian Synagogue of Philadelphia in 1922 in order to increase evangelistic effectiveness, to gain Hebrew Christian independence from Gentile denominational control, and to challenge the Jewish community by creating strong Hebrew Christian parallel institutions (Winer 1990, 106–112). David Bronstein, a Hebrew Christian and Presbyterian minister, got permission from the Presbyterians to open The First Hebrew Christian Church of Chicago under their auspices (Rausch 1982, 99–102). By the 1950s, about seventy Jewish converts attended the church weekly. Two other congregations had been "planted" by the Presbyterian church in the 1950s: Beth Messiah in Philadelphia and Beth Emmanuel in Baltimore (Schiffman 1990, 32–33). Edward Brotsky in the 1960s began a small Hebrew Christian congregation in Philadelphia, The Congregation of the Messiah (Rausch 1982, 102; Winer 1990, 41–42). Besides congregational worship, the HCAA held some separate "Jewish worship" in their local branches, including Seders and a Yom Kippur service (Gutwirth 1987, 37).

These congregations maintained a primarily Protestant form of worship, including hymn singing and the taking of communion. However, most used nominal Jewish iconography, such as seven-branched menorahs and the words *Yeshua Ha-Mashiach* ("Jesus the Messiah" in Hebrew), written on walls and podiums (Gutwirth 1987, 36; Winer 1990, 23). Here Hebrew Christians could be themselves, expressing their novel identity in relative comfort.

Despite these continual efforts at self-definition, the Hebrew Christian movement was not dynamic. The average age of the people involved was one factor (about fifty to fifty-five years old). A second factor was the generation to which they belonged. In the history of American Judaism, the second generation of immigrants was often more assimilated, eschewing the old-world religion of their parents and choosing more secular routes to Jewish identity. The fact that the majority of Hebrew Christians in 1965 were of that generation meant they shared in the "melting pot" philosophy of their Jewish contemporaries; it was good to be Jewish, but not "too Jewish" (Gutwirth 1987, 38). It was against this ethos that young American Hebrew Christians rebelled, as did young American Jews.

THE COUNTERCULTURE AND MESSIANIC JUDAISM

The 1960s were a time of enormous upheaval, both in the American milieu at large and certainly in the American Jewish community. In the mid to late 1960s students and young people thronged to counter-cultural alternatives: radical politics, hippie lifestyles, and drug sub-cultures. Because of the baby boom, the affluence in the United States after the Second World War, and extended childhoods due to college enrollment, many persons aged eighteen to twenty-two were available for the kinds of experimentation that occurred in the late 60s and early 70s (Wuthnow 1978, 29–35). A new cultural pluralism emerged through the rise in ethnic and Black power movements (Glazer 1972, 150–152). While many people turned to alternative lifestyles such as communes to create an intensive, egalitarian, experiential lifestyle, others found themselves attracted to unusual religions such as the Hare Krishna, Mahara Ji, Jesus movements, fundamentalist churches, and youth movements in Catholic, Episcopal, and Presbyterian churches. One of these new groups was the Jesus people, a loosely connected group of young people who combined fundamentalism and a dedication to evangelism with a countercultural style (Lipson 1990, 2). Many of the Jesus people also practiced Spirit-filled or Charismatic Christianity, a form of Christian belief and worship that believes the New Testament "gifts of the Spirit" can be exercised to-day, such as healing the sick through prayer, speaking in tongues, and receiving direct prophecies from God. Accompanying Christian re-vival movements in the eighteenth and nineteenth centuries (Al-banese 1981, 264–269), these charismatic practices, emphasizing the individual's experience of the immediacy of God, in the twentieth century became the cornerstone of the Pentecostal movement and the Charismatic Catholic movement as well as the Protestant "Jesus movement" (Neitz 1987; Poloma 1982; Quebedeaux 1983). Jesus people communities often exercised charismatic gifts and felt the power of such personal "miracles" in their lives (Ellwood 1973, 84; Quebedeaux 1983, 130, 230–231).

A contributing factor to the Jesus people upsurge was the evangel-ical response to the 1967 Arab-Israeli war. For many evangelical Christians, the Israeli victory seemed to confirm prophetic expecta-tions about Israel, and the time seemed at hand for the 144,000 Jewish evangelists (foretold in Scripture) to make their appearance and ac-tively work to convert the Jews. Thus, for a segment of evangelical Christians, there was a new interest in the Jewish people. Tied to end-time prophecies, this interest was part of the Jesus people revival (Rausch 1982, 73). Popular Biblical prophecy books, such as *The Late Great Planet Earth*, put Israel at the center of prophetic events.

American Jews were also deeply affected by the Arab-Israeli war and the counterculture. The war encouraged new loyalties to Israel and Jewish peoplehood, as former Leftist allies spurned Israel's cause as "imperialist." The countercultural ethos of authenticity, as well as the example of the Black Power movement, encouraged some to re-ject the "gray-flannel-suit Judaism" of their parents and seek their true Jewish self in ethnic re-creation based on the food, music, and folkways of earlier generations (Glazer 1972, 151–152). For some, the search for genuine Jewishness led to a new commitment to Jewish religion either through informal Jewish *havurot* (spiritual and social fellowships) (Prell 1989, 69–100) or by entering Orthodox Judaism (Danziger 1989, 71–95).

Given the large numbers of Jewish youth seeking religious mean-ing, their new sensitivity to Jewishness due to the Six-Day War, and the evangelical foregrounding of that same war, it is hardly a surprise that a group such as "Jews for Jesus" (Hineni Ministries) was formed.

Martin "Moishe" Rosen, a former missionary for the ABMJ and himself a Jewish convert, found his methods of outreach outdated in the hotbed of countercultural activity of San Francisco. Rosen adopted the "up-front" evangelistic style of the Jesus people, and by 1970 set up a full street outreach, based on the premise that one could believe in Jesus and retain a Jewish cultural identity. Adherents often wore T-shirts proclaiming "Jesus made me kosher," wore *kippot* (skullcaps), and created Jewish-sounding music with a Jesus message (Lipson 1990, 19–22). Rosen's tactics of noisily confronting the Jewish community added to the publicity of the movement (Lipson 1990, 66–75). Given the rise in peoplehood consciousness among many young American Jews, it was clear that Rosen had hit upon a workable approach.

The youth revival touched Hebrew Christianity in other ways. Beginning in 1965, a youth branch of the HCAA begun by Manny Brotman, a young Spirit-filled Hebrew Christian, grew rapidly as more and more Jews who accepted Jesus through the youth movement entered into the organization. In 1967, Manny Brotman attracted third-generation Jewish federal employees and professionals to Hebrew Christianity in the Washington, D.C., area. For the first time, Hebrew Christianity was having an unqualified success reaching Jews (Gutwirth 1987, 40; Winer 1990, 47). Other areas of the country, notably Philadelphia and Cincinnati, were also experiencing a Young Hebrew Christian renaissance.

In June 1970, the Young Hebrew Christian Alliance (YHCA) held its first independent conference at Messiah College in Grantham, Pennsylvania. Here the youth orientation expressed itself fully: the prayer meetings were Spirit-filled, including speaking in tongues and faith healing, the name "Yeshua" rather than Jesus was used frequently, and the young people seemed more interested in Jewish cultural practices than their elders had been (Gutwirth 1987, 40). As more and more Jewish practices were incorporated, traditional Christian denominations became more uncomfortable, which only added an impetus to create a new, more autonomous movement.

Because of the younger membership, the more aggressive stance toward Jewish culture, and the example of "Jews for Jesus," the younger contingent of the Hebrew Christian Alliance sought a name that would reflect their desire to be identified more strongly as Jews.

An earlier attempt in 1973 to change the name was narrowly defeated; in June 1975 it passed. The organization would now be called the Messianic Jewish Alliance of America (MJAA), the youth movement was now called the Young Messianic Jewish Alliance (YMJA), and the quarterly journal changed its name to *The American Messianic Jewish Quarterly* (Winer 1990, 51).

As David Rausch pointed out, this term was not new. In March 1895, the subtitle of the ninth issue of *Our Hope*, a Hebrew Christian publication, was changed to "A Monthly Devoted to the Study of Prophecy and Messianic Judaism" (Rausch 1982, 55). One Messianic leader, however, claimed to have gotten the name from a vision from God Himself. In a February 1980 bulletin from Congregation B'nai Mashiach, this vision is described under the heading "Pastor's Perspective":

> As I was meditating more than four years ago, suddenly I had a vision. As I looked up to the sky, I saw these two words: "Messianic Judaism." They were evidently miles high. As I kept looking at it I began to ask God what it might mean. He impressed on me strongly that this was the Last Day Revival which was soon coming. Our Jewish people would be in the center of it, just as in Acts 2. And I should also expect tens of thousands of our Jewish people to suddenly be moved by the Spirit of God to consider the claims of the Messiah and to accept Him!

While the name change hardly amounted to an acceptance of rabbinic Judaism, there was a definite move among these Messianic Jews to free themselves from being associated with Christian denominations both in overt funding and in ideological control.[4] This transition was met with some resistance. Older members of the Alliance were displeased with the name change and its emphasis on Jewish identity, while traditional missions to the Jews also reacted negatively to this "re-Judaizing" movement (Rausch 1982, 77–79; Winer 1990, 53–54).

Starting in the early 1970s, Hebrew Christian fellowships and congregations (now called Messianic synagogues) began to flourish. According to a leader at B'nai Mashiach, there were key leaders who, raised nominally Jewish, began to go "overboard" on Jewish practices: using *tefillin* (phylacteries), wearing *tzitzit* (ritual fringes), and conducting services entirely in Hebrew. These leaders believed this was the appropriate direction of the movement, and left to form their own congregational organization. In 1996 the Union of Messianic Jewish Congregations (UMJC), which resulted from the split, included 78 congregations, each with an average of fifty to one hundred members, approximately half of whom are Jewish.

Catching up, the MJAA formed the International Alliance of Messianic Congregations and Synagogues (IAMCS) under its auspices in the spring of 1986. Beginning with 15 congregations, as of April 1996 it had over 159 congregations worldwide. Both the UMJC and the IAMCS have institutes that train Messianic Rabbis to serve these communities (Winer 1990, 64–66).[5] These organizations have grown much closer since 1993, when a formal reconciliation took place; it is not unusual to see UMJC rabbis at MJAA conferences, and during the 1995 MJAA international conference many overt statements were made about the joy of unity between the two formerly antagonistic organizations.

These two organizations form the bulk of Messianic congregational membership, establishing its character as emphatically charismatic and moderate in Jewish-style practices. However, smaller congregational alternatives mark the present edges of the Messianic movement. On February 25, 1986, a national forum of twelve Messianic Jewish leaders formed the Fellowship of Messianic Congregations (FMC), a noncharismatic group. The reason given for this development is to promote unity by achieving "spiritual and doctrinal stability" and to allow the Messianic movement to retain its "New Testament," rather than a rabbinic Jewish orientation (Lapides 1987). Consisting of 10 congregations in 1996, the FMC congregations put their emphasis on doctrine rather than the gifts of the Spirit. "We are the few, the proud, and the eggheads," as one leader facetiously put it. A second organization, the Association of Torah-Observant Messianics, with 6 member congregations, follows Jewish practices not as part of a cultural heritage, but as laws ordained by God, not necessary for salvation but for holy living. Unlike most Messianics, many follow rabbinic *kashrut* (dietary laws, including separation of milk and meat), men wear *tzitzit*, and married women even debate wearing headcoverings. Seen as both Judaizing and even hypocritical by some Messianics (because they claim to follow the Law but do not adhere to every stricture of Orthodox Jewish practice), they nonetheless feel their commitment adds a significant dimension to Messianic practice.[6] A third organization, recently formed, appeals to the Sephardic background of its leadership. The International Federation of Messianic Jews, "promoting the Jewish Messiah and Torah Observance," looks to integrate Sephardic, rather than Ashkenazic Jewish practice into Messianic beliefs. These Messianic margins point to the existence of increasing diversity in the movement, while their small numbers highlight the strength of the mainstream expression of Messianic Judaism.

The total number of Messianic Jews is difficult to ascertain. One Messianic Jewish leader claimed in 1991 that there were over 120 Messianic Jewish congregations in the United States, including Messianic Jewish congregations still affiliated with Protestant denominations (Stern 1991, 198). In the next four years this number had almost doubled, to 207 (Beiser 1995, 28). The size of each congregation varies widely, from fewer than ten members in some congregations to four hundred adult members in others. If one assumed that each of the 207 congregations were of the size and composition of an average UMJC congregation, at one hundred members, with fifty born Jewish members, there would be a little over ten thousand Jewish adults in this movement. While this number contrasts sharply with the one hundred fifty thousand Messianic Jews claimed by the movement, the large discrepancy can be explained by the vagueness of the definition of who is a Messianic Jew. That figure would reflect the number of people of Jewish origin now calling themselves Christian by religion, whether they belong to a Messianic congregation or are members of mainstream Christian denominations (Stern 1991, 197–198). Also, because the movement generally recognizes a person born of a Jewish father and Gentile mother as Jewish, Conservative and Orthodox individuals who accept only matrilineal descent may find far fewer born Jews in the movement than the Messianics claim.

There are some, however, who protest that any distinction made between Jews found in standard Christian churches and in Messianic synagogues is moot; they cite the powerful ties that bind the Messianic movement to Gentile Christianity. Many of the individuals who later became leaders in the Messianic movement were educated in evangelical or fundamentalist Bible schools, were ordained by Christian denominations, and had conducted some form of Jewish missions work funded by Christian denominations (Schiffman 1990, 113). Some congregations have been and continue to be planted or funded by "independent" missions to the Jews (funded by Gentile Christians and Gentile Christian organizations, although not tied specifically to any one group), while others continue to be planted or funded by denominations (Sevener 1989, 69). Even in 1987, almost 25 percent of congregations surveyed were affiliated with Christian denominations such as the Assemblies of God, the Presbyterian Church in the USA, the North American Baptist, and the Evangelical Free Church of America (Schiffman 1990, 131–132). Many are given meeting facilities in friendly churches, whose members are often exhorted to financially support the enterprise (Schiffman 1990, 130).

These connections were vividly displayed in 1996, when the thirty-congregation Southern Baptist Messianic Fellowship, begun in 1985 by Gus Elowitz, congregational leader at Beth Yeshua Ha-Mashiach in Houston, Texas, entered the national news (News and Notes 1996, 23). In June 1996, the Southern Baptist Convention, with the urging of the Fellowship, passed a resolution stating their support of Jewish evangelism. The Jewish community responded with alarm, believing that this resolution gave the green light to a horde of well-prepared, well-financed Christian evangelists to descend upon them (Anderson 1996, August 8, 51).

This Southern Baptist brand of Messianic Judaism points to a phenomenon within the Messianic movement: a growing toleration of the idea of Messianic congregations exists among evangelical Christians, along with verbal and financial recognition of their success in bringing people to the Lord, and a concomitant overt strengthening of Messianic-Gentile bonds. The celebrated independence from denominational control that Messianic Judaism represented to its followers may be belied by increased acceptance of Messianic Jewish practice among those very denominations.

B'NAI MASHIACH: A HISTORY OF THE CONGREGATION

The history of B'nai Mashiach in Liberty is a microcosm of the history of Messianic Judaism. The congregation brought together the leaders of the Messianic Jewish movement, the Chazan family, with two of the most important Hebrew Christian youth workers of the late 1960s and the early 1970s, the Feinbergs. B'nai Mashiach, even today, is clearly the congregation in leadership of the Messianic Jewish Alliance of America and possibly the Messianic Jewish movement as a whole. Like the history of the movement in general, particular experiences in the congregation have shaped the present-day expressions of Messianic Jewish identity.

Many of the young Hebrew Christians who revitalized the movement in the late 1960s and early 1970s were brought in by Jim and Darlene Feinberg. The Feinbergs, born Jewish, were raised in a Jewish neighborhood. While Darlene did not go to Hebrew school and only attended a Conservative synagogue on High Holidays, Jim attended Hebrew school at a Reform synagogue until he was fourteen. Both Darlene and Jim, however, had Jewish friends and grew up in a culturally Jewish environment.

After discussions with a Christian missionary who ran a sports program for youth, Darlene and Jim were saved in their late teens. Despite strong parental disapproval, they maintained their beliefs and, after they were married, began to have a Bible study in their home. During the late 1960s, this Bible study became known as "Fein's Zoo," where young people troubled by drugs or those just searching could stay in their home and "hear the Word." The Feinbergs, like many involved in the Jesus movement, were willing to experiment with the gifts of the Spirit; Darlene narrated two incidents in which they tried to invoke healing through the use of holy oil and prayer, once for a drug addict experiencing a flashback and once for Darlene's hand, burned badly in a chicken soup accident. Both healings were not only successful, but also convinced formerly skeptical hangers-on of the truth of Jesus and the New Testament.

Jim and Darlene also conducted outreach work. Jim, executive director of the national YHCA from 1972–1975, was involved in the local Liberty branch as well (Winer 1990, 72, 127). The YHCA held monthly Saturday-night get-togethers with half a dozen people, all of whom would attend church on Sundays. The YHCA sponsored Hebrew Christian Passover Seders and also put together programs for local churches. A flyer from those early years advertises a "Jewish Youth Night" held on May 19, 1973, at a Baptist church with "[Jim Feinberg]: Music with guitar and singers from the Young Hebrew Christian Alliance."

One of those searchers at Fein's Zoo was my cousin. Six months after my study began, Darlene Feinberg offered to show me her old pictures from the congregation in its infancy. After lunch at her house, we looked at the photo album, chuckling over pictures of members of the congregation in hippie garb, absurdly young. Suddenly, a face came up that I thought I recognized, a teenager sitting in a rocking chair with a granny dress and shawl on. I asked Darlene who that was. "Oh, she didn't stay with us long," Darlene replied. "She was into astrology, witchcraft, all sorts of stuff." Still not sure, I asked her name. Sure enough, it was my cousin, which I promptly told Darlene. A look of disbelief mixed with suspicion crossed her face. "Really?" I replied that I had hardly recognized her, it had been so long since I had seen her. Indeed, while I knew she was involved in "Jews for Jesus," I had no idea that it was this particular group. Darlene reiterated that the young woman was "mixed up, confused, involved with drugs." Both of us hastened to cover our surprise and continued with the pictures with a loud "Anyway . . . " I was jolted. Expecting to retain my professional neutrality in a subject as secure and objective as a historical survey, I was once again mired in tumultuous feelings. The incident reminded me once again that no area of this study was "safe," "easy," or disengaged from emotional involvement. Everything about this group seemed to touch me personally. Had my cousin remained, she might have been one of the leaders of B'nai Mashiac. I might have been interviewing her, rather than Darlene, on the history of the congregation that formed shortly after my cousin's departure.

Darlene and Jim, with a group of twenty to thirty young people, began searching for a place to worship beyond the Bible studies that they had in their home. The group joined Beth Messiah, a Hebrew Christian congregation under Presbyterian auspices, but ended up leaving in November 1974. Darlene gives this reason:

> Actually we did spend a while at the downtown Messianic Jewish congregation. There arose a problem as the congregation got larger and we began to have a more Jewish kind of worship. We also found out that the congregation was more attached to the Presbyterian church than we knew. [The pastor] received a letter from the Presbyterian Board. Most of us knew very little about them. They wrote to us that we were not independent, that we could not appoint our own elders, our tithes were not under our own supervision, but under control of the board. It was not a scriptural way to run a congregation. Also, we didn't want to be Presbyterians. The letter said, "Either you become good Presbyterians or forget it." I don't even know how aware even [the pastor] was about this. Some people decided to stay there. [The pastor]'s decision was his own personal

choice. Our group wasn't terribly large, and he was receiving a salary there, and he had children, so he stayed there. No big animosity or anything. It was just the case of a group that decided to have their own congregation. . . .

The [Chazans] gave us the inspiration for the independent congregation. Many of the people around us in the early time were just off of drugs, and didn't have jobs yet, so the first job of an independent congregation was to first financially support a leader. It took these people a while to get their lives straightened out, get jobs, since they were just off of alcohol or drugs. (Telephone interview, April 18, 1991)

Michael Chazan was one of the first "old-time" Hebrew Christians to harness and develop the energy of this young Messianic Jewish movement. Working during the 1940s and 1950s for various Jewish mission organizations, he was trying to break away from his missions work for the American Association for Jewish Evangelism to start an independent congregation. In the Midwest, Chazan and his wife Jackie ministered to a small group of approximately thirty believers. During the late 1960s and early 1970s, young Jesus people began to flock to the congregation, swelling its ranks to over one hundred adherents. The Chazans, though taken aback at first, were unusual among their generation by accepting and even fostering this revival. Partly due to this growth, Michael Chazan was able to go fully independent with his congregation in 1970. The youth influence hastened the development of a Jewish style in the group; while still singing hymns and celebrating Christmas and Easter, the congregation began to learn about Jewish history, holidays, and Yiddish.

The small group in Liberty invited the Chazan family to lead their new congregation. Shortly after the Chazans left the Midwest and came to Liberty, the congregation swelled. The rapid early growth of the group came from young Messianic Jews, in Darlene's words "very aggressive and out front and revolutionary," already saved, moving from other parts of the country to be involved in this vibrant new congregation. This is what one member called "the first *aliyah*."

Michael and Jackie provided a kind of parental guidance for some of these young people who needed the stability of an older generation. One Messianic believer, remembering the early days, said that Michael told them they'd have to get a job or go to school, that they couldn't just sit around reading the Bible all day. One adherent put it this way:

In the early burst, in the seventies, when God poured out His spirit in this first wave of revival, what did he have to pour it out on? A bunch of crazy, untaught teenagers. The Jesus movement. People didn't know what they were doing, where they were going. There were only a few tiny nests of Jewish people, Jewish believers, who really had solid teaching. . . . I was a part of a young, untaught group that had no stable pastoring. I mean, I get down on my knees every day and say, "Thank God" for pastors like the ones that we have and the others in the Messianic movement who are stable and who can take the tremendous dynamite of spiritual fire that God is unleashing and channel it and guide us in it and be determined to see God do the real thing rather than watch us go off the wall, left and right, untaught, unmanaged, unguided. (Tape, "Messianic Judaism, Part I," April 14, 1985)

In the beginning, the new congregation created an intensive communal experience. This young group, composed of students and single people mainly in their twenties, shared apartments, went out in groups of twenty or thirty for movies or dinner, and engaged in campus evangelism and street theater. One member of the congregation, recalling those times, said she felt like she was really part of something. "We were brave and doing all these things for the Lord!" Activities included Messianic Judaism on Campus, an outreach organization run by Daniel Chazan, Michael's son, under Michael's supervision, and staffed by members of the congregation who were attending college at the time. A sisterhood existed (now disbanded), along with a proliferation of "cell groups" to socialize new members (originally as many as twelve to thirteen groups), recreational and leisure activities, evangelization excursions, and, of course, weekly and holiday services. Members were strongly encouraged to buy houses in Brookside Terrace, the same area in which the Chazans and Feinbergs were living.

The excitement and intensity carried over to the training of children. The congregation started a day school, Talmidim (students), in 1977, that met in people's homes. According to one school pamphlet, "In August of 1977 the Jewish believers of [Liberty's] Messianic community began to discuss the formation of a private day school for our students. At the time the impetus was impending strikes, lack of quality academic opportunities available in the public school system and the increasingly powerful political base for the teaching of secular humanism, situational ethics, and decadent sexual mores."

Because there were only twelve children in Talmidim from the ages of three to eleven in 1979 (Finkelstein 1979), and because of the generally young age of the congregation, the way that children were handled within the congregation occasionally showed more enthusiasm than wisdom. From one young man, Paul, who went through the school system:

> Paul: It was too intense. We used to use words to describe that ourselves. "If we were in a normal school," in other words, we were in an abnormal school. It was like a pressure cooker. They used to say "It's too hot in here, I can't deal with this, I need some fresh air."
>
> C. H.-S.: What's too intense? Is it the movement, the God talk?
>
> Paul: That's all part of it. One aspect is space. I like to give it because it's a great visual aid. Where [Talmidim] met, there was no ventilation, no windows, no light from outside; if some kid had an accident in the bathroom, it didn't diffuse really well. . . . We didn't change classrooms a lot, we had the same teachers. . . .
>
> C. H.-S.: And you would see them at services.
>
> Paul: That's why we called it a pressure cooker. It tended to polarize people. If you would do anything bad, you were afraid people would find out about it and what they would think of you. It kind of became this obsessive fear with this one guy, because he was consistently doing this one thing that was not acceptable to his parents and therefore to the community because his parents strictly forbid it and he really became obsessed with it, now he is better, but there is this communal aesthetic, and if you deviated from it, people would know, and so if you were doing something wrong, you were always in the light, and people didn't like that, and if you were bad, people knew you for that, your reputation was a really big thing. . . .
>
> Either you were a believer or you weren't, because either you were living it or you weren't, and I think that it wasn't done intentionally, but it made it really harsh. Maybe kids were made to feel like maybe the same standards were being applied to kids as were applied to adults, who were fully grown and able to make a decision and go with it. Even some adults don't do that. Sometimes I think there was this sense, you were either this or that, saved or unsaved.

This "pressure cooker" environment helps to explain some of the "defections" back to Judaism among what are now young adults, including the child of an important leadership couple in the congregation.

This type of strong authority characterized, and continues to distinguish, B'nai Mashiach. Like many charismatic churches (Boone 1989, 85–97; Quebedeaux 1983, 90–94, 135–142), the congregation is seen as a rather authoritarian family; although elders advise, and consensus is attempted, Daniel, the leader appointed by God, is the "father" with the final household say in matters of congregational worship and structure. Moreover, the leadership has strongly intervened in personal relationships, breaking up seemingly unsuitable couples or offering unsolicited marriage advice. Quiet resistance seems to be the main method of disagreement; open complaint or disregard of boundaries can lead to expulsion. While congregants still hold the power of the purse and the feet—a popular way of showing disapproval is through lackluster giving, spotty attendance, or switching affiliation—this pattern of power seemed unusually strong to me, raised in a liberal community. Leadership control was even stronger in the early years of the community, given the youth of its membership.

It is thus not very surprising that the Liberty Jewish community, which saw Jewish adolescents suddenly accepting the "irrational" beliefs of fundamentalist Christianity while proclaiming their Jewishness, moving into Brookside Terrace, accepting Michael and Jackie's guidance about jobs, education and relationships, and engaging in intense worship and outreach practices, understood B'nai Mashiach as a highly organized and sinister group duping and deceiving the most innocent and vulnerable of the Jewish population into a mind-controlling cult. While the activities of the Feinbergs had been noted by Jewish organizations since the early 1970s, there was little more than curiosity until a few years later. Congregation members participated in Jewish Defense League activities, and a singing group of the congregation performed several times in area synagogues. They even went to a Jewish senior-citizen's project regularly, giving them music, food, and "spiritual sustenance." Other congregation members joined Hadassah, a Jewish women's organization that supports Israel. Slowly, as they began to share their faith within these organizations, there developed within the mainstream Jewish community a suspicion that these people were deliberately infiltrating mainstream Jewish organizations for the purposes of conversion.

As the congregation grew and tried to find places to meet, it chose controversial spots, first next to an Orthodox synagogue and then in a largely Jewish apartment house. As the group moved from location to location, gaining an ever higher profile, its membership increased to over one hundred people, adding to the brewing controversy in the Jewish community.

The height of the conflict, reached from 1979 to 1984, was inaugurated by the congregation's attempt to buy a building near a Hebrew high school. This building, a large estate, needed to be rezoned to be used for the congregation and the day school. People from the neighborhood were up in arms, especially the Jewish families, and legal steps were taken to prevent the rezoning measures. Because litigation threatened to drag out expensively, the congregation had to drop the purchase attempt (Wohl 1979). The group still sought a building, and in April 1981 purchased an abandoned restaurant in a heavily Jewish area of Brookside Terrace under the name of one of their adherents (Loyd 1981).

The organized Jewish community, unable to block the purchase, began organizing various countermeasures. Perhaps the most dramatic was a series of demonstrations during the summer of 1984, culminating in a nine-hundred-person demonstration against the congregation on September 30 (Conway 1984; Silver 1984). Another point of controversy arose after Michael Chazan died in 1985. The Jewish cemetery that had agreed to take Chazan discovered his religious beliefs and refused to allow his burial (Schaffer 1985). Daniel Chazan, who had been the assistant pastor for many years, took over as the Messianic pastor/rabbi, and a new assistant was found. By this time, most of the Messianic Jews in mainstream Jewish organizations were made unwelcome, and these organizations began to recognize B'nai Mashiach members on sight.

In the stories that Messianic Jews told me, and in their approach to the media at the time, they pictured "the opposition" as a small group of leaders stirring up an otherwise peaceful populace. In stories told about getting kicked out of Jewish organizations, movement members said over and over again that it was only "a few leaders" that did it and that "the people" in general liked them.

This is not the whole story, however. In fact, internal evidence from Jewish organizations shows a very frustrated local populace advocating actions, such as mass demonstrations and even violence, that were not approved of by some Jewish community leaders. Unable to afford to move from an area that was becoming racially mixed and perceived as increasingly dangerous, the largely lower-middle-class Jews of Brookside Terrace interpreted the Messianic synagogue as another powerful threat to their vulnerable and beleaguered community (Yancey 1984). The fear grew so great that Jews in Brookside Terrace who looked traditionally Jewish or hung signs of Jewish interest in their shops were suspected of being Messianic Jews. After a pro–Messianic Jewish letter signed by a member of B'nai Mashiach was printed in a local newspaper, a man with a similar name who owned an area business had to put a large ad in the same paper to disclaim identity with the B'nai Mashiach member. Rumors ran rampant of Messianic Jews "snatching children" and trying to indoctrinate them, running supposedly Jewish day-care centers under false pretenses, and taking advantage of helpless Jews. These led to real anger, fear, and panic in a neighborhood that already felt outside the core of Jewish community concern.

Organizations within the Jewish community, trying to stem this problem, tried a number of different approaches, not always in conjunction with one another, or approved by all segments of the Jewish community. The angriest individuals tried to put intense pressure on B'nai Mashiach through large demonstrations or infiltrations of the congregation to gain hidden information. Other individuals and agencies tried to make psychological services available to adherents and their parents. Some, believing that B'nai Mashiach's attraction was the social services they provided, tried hard to get people into establishment Jewish facilities to help them with practical needs. Others, through public celebrations of Jewish holidays, attempted to present the joy of Jewish festivals in the same public way that B'nai Mashiach members celebrated their holidays (for example, the Jewish community sponsored city-wide Sukkot parties in the 1980s). Synagogues and Jewish centers, believing that Jews joined this movement out of ignorance of their own tradition, ran classes on Judaism. Orthodox members of the Jewish community offered entry into their own strongly religious communities.

Responding to the controversy, some mainline churches also openly disagreed with the Messianic Jewish approach. An open letter to the congregation, signed by the executive director of the Metropolitan Christian Council, the Executive Director of the Cardinal's Commission on Human Relations, Coordinator of Ecumenical and Religious Affairs, and the pastor of a local Presbyterian church, stated that the group was fraudulent. "[B'nai Mashiach] cannot be considered a part of Judaism or legitimately represent itself as such. . . . The vague references to bread and wine, the lack of the symbol of the cross, the total anonymity of the building indicate to us a manufactured religion of human invention which misuses Christian symbols and attempts to create good feelings through the irresponsible use of Jewish and Christian symbols and customs in whatever way the leadership may determine" (Christian leaders . . . 1985).

Beyond the local efforts, Jewish organizations with national scope attempted to disseminate information about and directly challenge Messianic Judaism. The best-known organization for this purpose, Jews for Judaism, was established in 1975. With several full-time workers, it provides counseling services for Messianic Jews and their families, outreach programs to unaffiliated Jews, information to Jews about the dangers of Messianic Judaism, and a range of books and video materials. It is famous within Messianic Jewish circles for being confrontational and somewhat threatening to Messianic Jewish belief; new and inexperienced believers are advised to avoid the conspicuous "Jews for Judaism" van parked outside every major Messianic Jewish conference. According to its site on the World-Wide Web, it has reached over two hundred thousand Jews in over twenty years of operations. Another organization with a national audience is the Task Force on Missionaries and Cults within the Jewish Community Relations Council of New York. The fact that both missionaries and cults are in the purview of Jews for Judaism and the Task Force points out the prevailing belief in American Jewish circles that both cults and Messianic Judaism illegitimately change aspects of a convert's personality to conform to the authority of leadership (although more recently there has been a recognition that the extent of this "brainwashing" has been overstated). However, both these organizations are frustrated with their limited budgets compared to the Messianic movement itself. Dr. Phillip Abramowitz, head of the Task Force, estimates that the current budget for all anti-missionary efforts, including Jews for Judaism, is probably less than two hundred thousand dollars, compared to the estimated one hundred and fifty million spent on Messianic Jewish outreach (Interview, Nov. 20, 1995).

Although the disapproval of Jewish and some mainline Christian groups discouraged more timid persons from membership, the congregation continued to grow. Part of this was due to its strong alliance to evangelical Christianity; Michael Chazan appeared at the "Washington for Jesus" rally in 1980 and members worked for Pat Robertson's election campaign (Goldwyn 1987). In turn, evangelical churches and organizations such as the 700 Club sent born Jews who had accepted Christ to the congregation. Others born Jewish found their way to B'nai Mashiach by way of churches, college Bible studies, even through Bible radio broadcasts. Evangelical outreach thus paved the way; many, perhaps most born Jews at B'nai Mashiach had already accepted Jesus before joining (Gutwirth 1987, 143).

By dint of its own outreach efforts and the help of evangelical institutions, B'nai Mashiach reached its peak in 1984 with approximately 350 members, a number unchanged six years later. In 1991, the congregation was headed by Daniel Chazan as the Messianic rabbi, with an assistant Messianic Rabbi, five elders and thirteen *shammashim* (under-shepherds). The congregation had two singing groups, both of professional quality. One singing group was associated with the outreach arm of the congregation, which also sponsored a radio program, college outreach, literature distribution, and a discipleship program, among other things, funded in part by donations from Gentile Christians. Both singing groups performed concerts both in the synagogue and outside of it. The congregation had a regular Friday evening and Sunday morning service, and a Friday night Shabbat service and Sunday morning Bible study for children in addition to Talmidim. There were three ongoing satellite fellowships in areas at least forty-five minutes away from the congregation, and one cell group in Brookside Terrace, each meeting once every other week. In addition to regular and holiday services, there were separate congregational prayer meetings on Saturday mornings, other prayer meetings called throughout the month, and healing and deliverance meetings, where the gifts of the Spirit were exercised. Social events included monthly women's fellowship meetings, men's fellowship activities, a couples club, picnics and parties, and teens and college-age activities.

Families made up a majority of congregation members, with new babies being born almost every month. Both singles and families tended to be solidly middle-class, working in careers such as desktop publishing, sales, marketing, and teaching. Those members struggling with unemployment were given encouragement, advice, and often jobs by the other believers. Careers held by leadership helped to create the ideal of success; leaders were often professionals (psychiatrists, lawyers, family doctors) or very successful business people (one elder employed several other congregants in his business).

The past few years have brought about some interesting changes in Congregation B'nai Mashiach. While the membership numbers have remained stable (about 300 active members), a certain shift in membership appears to have taken place. Key leadership families have departed to begin their own congregations in central New Jersey, Manhattan, and Toronto; Stewart, the assistant rabbi, left, to be replaced in February 1996 by Jim Feinberg. New Gentile members have joined (according to Daniel, as many as 150!) who have added to the spiritual strength of the congregation.

The community itself is in the midst of an identity change. Five years ago, most core members lived close to Brookside Terrace or in Brookside Terrace itself, often within walking distance of the congregation. One's nearest neighbor was often a Messianic member; such physical closeness engendered warm personal contacts and a sense of community. New members were often encouraged to move into Brookside Terrace for this very reason.

Because of increasing crime and a "changing neighborhood," (usually a code phrase for an increased African-American presence, although no member said so specifically to me), members have been moving out of the neighborhood to nearby suburbs; the Messianic neighborhood is slowly disappearing. At the same time, membership has been growing in far-flung neighborhoods as far as an hour's drive away. Bi-weekly havurah groups meet both at B'nai Mashiach and in the area communities to provide fellowship and spiritual support; most of these are population-specific (singles, young marrieds, seniors).

As a result of the ever-spreading Messianic community and the inadequacy of the present building to meet their needs (the enrollment of Talmidim has "topped out" at 65; Daniel estimates there could be 100 students in larger facilities), the congregation is seeking to purchase land to build their version of "a shul with a pool," a Messianic Jewish community center that would house the day school, recreational and leisure facilities, and, of course, worship. Such a community center would compensate for the thinning of community now happening at B'nai Mashiach.

This may have the paradoxical effect of further distancing the Messianic community from the Jewish community. While the dispersion of Messianic homes places more Messianic members in predominantly Jewish neighborhoods, thus providing more opportunities to proselytize, a Messianic community center pulls Messianics from the Jewish community centers, which are particularly fruitful sites for "sharing." Members of the Messianic community have long been members of local Jewish community centers (JCCs), and, because of the non-sectarian membership policy of most JCCs, it becomes especially difficult to remove Messianic believers from the community center environment even when their beliefs become known. Going to a separate community center may limit opportunities to share with unsaved Jews.

As the congregation's average age moves to the mid-forties, its character is changing dramatically from the intense early years. As more and more congregants are having babies, the education of the second generation is taking greater priority, and the congregation faces the challenge of maintaining the fervor of the early years in the face of the increasing institutionalization of the movement and the increasing demands of family life. As the congregation changes, so does its expression and presentation of Messianic Jewish identity. Shaped by the controversies and experiences of the past, the struggle for Messianic Jewish identity continues to engage the members of B'nai Mashiach.

CHAPTER 3

The Messianic Jewish Self

FOUR TESTIMONIES

Joan

Joan is a Messianic Jew, an attractive, single, very articulate woman in her twenties, living in Brookside Terrace. Her parents are both born Jewish. While her grandparents are traditionally Jewish, keeping kosher and observing holidays, her parents were less observant, possibly because her mother hated organized religion. However, at least while the children were younger, the family did light Sabbath candles, celebrated Jewish holidays (including Sukkot and Shavuot) by attending the Conservative synagogue to which they belonged, lit candles through the eight days of Hanukkah, and attended a yearly family Seder. As the children became teenagers, her parents let their synagogue membership lapse, and the children were expected to make their own decisions about Jewish observance.

Joan herself attended Hebrew school until confirmation, even after her bat mitzvah. While she strongly disliked the other students in Hebrew School, as they were mean and snobbish, she took both Hebrew school and Judaism seriously, excelling in Hebrew school and even bringing Shabbat candlesticks on a vacation to Florida.

From a young age, her mind turned to "ultimate things." She believed in God, and used to pray and keep diaries that she referred to as "God books." Her quest for God was enhanced by her puzzled feelings about the world. Even as a young teenager Joan had problems reconciling the problems in the world and the evil of humanity with the existence of God. She saw people lying, cheating, and being hypocritical, and she couldn't stop herself from similar actions. Describing herself as "twelve going on thirty," she worried not only about the fickle nature of friends but also the plight of the poor and the old; who is supposed to take care of them, whose responsibility is it? Nobody at Hebrew school seemed to "know God"; even the rabbi couldn't or wouldn't answer her questions about why the world was so bad or people so false. In fact, since people in her synagogue gossiped and talked during services, yet (as she said sarcastically) "they were there, so that made them great Jews," they presented further examples of hypocrisy.

She went through different phases as a young teenager, trying to find an answer through astrology, Shirley MacLaine, and reincarnation; she finally decided, with a good friend, that they were both atheists. When that friend tried to commit suicide, Joan abandoned her atheist stance, but believing there was a God still gave her no way to reach God.

In college, the subject came up again. Her big sister in the sorority was saved, and brought her to a "Jews for Jesus" presentation of "Messiah in the Passover." Joan felt uneasy about the idea of Jesus, but she was impressed with the parallels made between the Seder service and the crucifixion of Jesus, such as the middle matzah being broken to represent Christ's broken body. After this event, Joan tried to attend church. Yet the church environment made her uncomfortable, with a "TV evangelist type of guy" and "everyone shouting Halleluyah," so she decided to "back off."

Still, she had received some Christian literature and decided to explore it intellectually. "I never wanted to be this type of people that someone could say, 'Oh, you believed as a crutch. You were miserable in your life, so you needed something as a crutch, so that's why you believed in that Jesus stuff.' I said, 'No way, that's not gonna be me. It's got to make sense to me.'" She was then given a book by her believing friends called *Mere Christianity* by C. S. Lewis. These friends explained to her that "Christianity" is something different than the Catholicism or Protestantism she had been exposed to as a child, and made the book acceptable for her to read as a "Jewish person." She finally understood the problems of mankind because of Lewis's book, since he explained the sinful nature of man and the need for atonement. "This made total sense of what mankind is like. I mean, this was the answer."

Her sister had noticed Joan's book on a visit home, and during a phone conversation asked how she liked the book. Knowing her sister attended synagogue regularly, she was afraid that "Miss Judaism" would disapprove. However, during that conversation Joan discovered that *her sister* was saved and attending B'nai Mashiach. She visited her sister, met a number of people in the congregation, and was urged to accept the Lord in her heart, but she still didn't feel ready or worthy to do that.

B'nai Mashiach allowed her to explore Christian beliefs in a way that was not "foreign to me." For example, she had always believed that Christians had three gods and Jews had one, but when the "one God" of the Shema (the Jewish credo) was explained as a "complex unity," suggesting the Trinity, she suddenly understood. She was equally impressed by the Bible, which she hadn't really studied before, especially Jeremiah's mention of a "new covenant." After reading a booklet put out by B'nai Mashiach, "I said, 'This makes sense' and I thought, 'This is what I need to do,' because obviously nothing else was working, you know?" She prayed the prayer to accept the Lord into her life, and while "I didn't have any kind of lightening bolt or vision or anything like that," she did have a sense that she had discovered the truth.

As a "baby believer" she found a local church near her work which she now calls a cult, since they didn't believe in maintaining Jewish identity and insisted that believers, rather than God, can usher in the Kingdom of God. They took a good deal of her money and her time. After visiting B'nai Mashiach again, and after leadership showed her scriptures that proved the Messianic Jewish way was right, she decided to move down and join the community.

Her relatives have been very supportive. "I was lucky." While her father is happy for his children, he himself is not a believer, while her mother has recently become a believer. Even her traditional Jewish grandparents have sent her a "Happy Easter" card. (Joan smiled at this, saying that they just didn't understand Messianic Judaism, which does not commemorate Easter). And despite other relatives' disapproval, they have made it clear to her that they still consider her family.

Todd

"I've always had a sense . . . that there was something more to be had in this life that went beyond the bounds of personal relationships with people, places to go, things to do." "Todd" is a Messianic Jew in his mid-thirties, soft-spoken, articulate, a teacher by vocation. He lives with his Messianic Jewish wife in a Brookside Terrace row house.

One of four children, he remembers a happy childhood, although his family moved frequently. Receiving fame and popularity as a student athelete still left him hungry for a larger meaning and purpose. His Jewish upbringing didn't answer that for him. While his family belonged to a Jewish recreational center, he didn't have a bar mitzvah, and his family didn't celebrate anything Jewish at home. They had no strong connection to Jewish organizations or to Israel. His only really "Jewish memories" were of his grandmother making Jewish food, and he calls his upbringing "religiously neutral." His Jewish friends' experiences in synagogue didn't attract him to that as a source for meaning. "Their experience with synagogue, unfortunately, was not all that positive. It was more cultural. . . . And for me, that wasn't like a place that I felt I was going to find something, unfortunately."

As a teenager and college student Todd read religion, philosophy, and even the Bible. He too had a question about God in the world; when he read in the Bible about the Jewish people in bondage in Egypt, he wondered how God could let that happen. He became friends with believers in college, and was impressed with their behavior. "People can say anything, words are cheap," but they had "a rootedness, a groundedness to them that went beyond circumstances, which is really something I was looking for." Even when he became confrontational with them about their beliefs, they behaved in a patient and loving way. In comparison to their more spiritual way of solving problems, with love and compassion, Todd remembers himself as being more selfish, more interested in "what's in it for me."

Finally, in graduate school, still not really understanding these beliefs, he asked God one night, "God, are you for real?" Right after he asked this, he recalls, "I just knew that God was alive and well and he was for real. And almost intuitively, not that anybody really told me, I asked, 'God, is Yeshua your son?' and the same type of response. It was so clear to me that the answer was 'Yes.' And almost immediately I asked the Lord into my life. And I can tell you that it was a genuine spiritual experience, where I knew something significant had taken place in my life, something that had never happened to me before." When he awoke the next day, he was "dying to read the Bible." The doorbell rang, and miraculously two of his believing friends presented him with a Bible. Immediately Todd began to read it. "I didn't know what I was reading, I just knew this is where I was supposed to be, this is where I connected with God." He found out about the Messianic synagogue from his Gentile believer friends, and four months after he was saved, he moved to Brookside Terrace. "I felt in the center of my heart, like a boom box, you're at home."

Ralph

Ralph is a member of another Messianic synagogue. While he said he was in his forties, he looked a good deal older, with missing teeth and hair slicked back, dressed in a suit coat and casual shirt for our interview. Ralph has a strong New York accent, and a dynamic, marvelous way of telling a story. At one point he said, "You could write a book on me, young lady." I think he's right.

Ralph was brought up with a distant Puerto Rican mother and a German father who died when he was sixteen and with whom he had a love-hate relationship. While his family had had money in Puerto Rico, it was long since gone. Raised in the Bronx, Ralph soon learned to be a street fighter; he explains the missing teeth and scars on his hands as a result of fighting with bottles and bricks. Raised as a Catholic, he quickly became disgusted with it because "the priests would fondle the altar boys." Still, there was a spiritual component in his childhood, as his grandmother practiced spells and believed in demons, and when he was a teenager his dead father's image appeared to him at the foot of the bed.

One of Ralph's best memories was that of his mother's best friend, a Jewish woman who partly raised him, and the Jewish girls in his neighborhood, whom he believed were the best-looking. According to Ralph, Jewishness represented a warmth, closeness, and a better way of life that he didn't have in his chaotic childhood.

After Ralph met his Jewish wife-to-be, he was told that in order to marry her, he needed to become Jewish. Ralph was subsequently converted to Judaism in 1965 by a Reform rabbi, after conversion classes that "lasted a couple of months." Ralph loved the idea of converting to Judaism, feeling that "another piece of the puzzle fell into place." Despite Messianic Jewish ideology that states "Once a Gentile, always a Gentile," he considers himself a Jew today because of that conversion.

Despite his delight in becoming Jewish, Ralph never felt comfortable in synagogue. He didn't have a nice home or car, and couldn't give money at fund-raising events. "Being Jewish takes money. It does!" While no synagogue member insulted him openly, he always felt inferior in a synagogue setting. Ralph's job in the Navy, with frequent moves, also prevented him from joining a synagogue. He was in Vietnam, which also still affects him deeply. When I asked, "When were you there?" he replied, "I'm still there," and began to cry. His family, especially his children, were also experiencing problems.

Starting in 1973, Ralph and his wife began an intense spiritual search. They moved to a house that was haunted, in which nothing worked correctly, weird acid rock music played at night, and doors opened for no reason. Both Ralph and his wife were completely frightened. A psychic neighbor, sprinkling holy water in the name of Jesus, cleansed the house. After this, not attending church or synagogue, they began to study with all kinds of occultists and read theosophy. This period lasted until the early 1980s, when the couple noticed they were being told contradictory things. "It's not the same occult as it was. The adversary [Satan] had gotten in and started to change things. This New Age stuff is totally wacko. If I chose to, I could still go back to my occult powers, but I've submitted that to God."

Salvation occurred several years ago. While Ralph had a decent job in a restaurant, the couple was still plagued by problems with their children. He also was estranged from his family over a piece of real estate. Family pressures and unresolved feelings of survivor guilt after Vietnam began to affect his work performance, and his boss also began to pressure him. He decided to commit suicide.

The night he was going to kill himself, he asked God to help him. Sure enough, a black minister who often came into the restaurant came in, and Ralph asked to speak to him in the back room. There Ralph burst into tears. "There's nothing as pathetic, as heartwrenching, as hearing a man sob. It just breaks your heart. I know because it's me." The minister prayed for him. "He prayed to the Creator in the name of Jesus, and all that weight was lifted off of me, it was refreshing. . . . Hey, I was Jewish, I didn't believe in this Jesus, but I saw what happened, and I felt the difference in me." After some time, and a meeting with a member at the local supermarket that he believes was orchestrated by God, he and his wife joined the church of the minister who had helped him as the only white members. His wife thought that if she couldn't get him to synagogue, at least he was doing something positive for God. At this point, Ralph was soured on the Jewish community, because when the family contacted Jewish agencies for a loan they were turned down. Subsequently he had lost interest in Jewish institutions.

After four to five months at this black Baptist church, both Ralph and his wife got saved. They stayed at the church for a year and a half, and then because of personal differences moved to a New Covenant Fellowship, a church that "loves Israel. The whole time we were going to the New Covenant Fellowship we were taught that the Bible was a Jewish book, written by Jews, for Jews, we were shown where Yeshua was talking to Jews about the Jewish people, and how the adversary doesn't want this fact to be known. . . . We learned from the New Covenant Fellowship that this is a Jewish God." When a Messianic Jewish musical group did a concert for the Fellowship, they became more interested, and joined the home study group that developed into the Messianic synagogue. "As I got involved here more and more I began to feel a kinship, a root, a bond with Judaism, even though officially I am a Jew. Through a formal conversion I am officially a Jew by choice. And I started wearing a prayer shawl and this congregation has been such a blessing." Although Ralph and his wife continue to have problems with their sons and their business, they feel supported and nurtured in the Messianic synagogue.

Deborah

Deborah is a Messianic Gentile in her late thirties, living about an hour away from B'nai Mashiach. Deborah is highly intelligent and a voluble speaker. Her bookshelves are filled with Messianic materials and Jewish resources (cookbooks, scholarly material), and her piano is covered with Messianic sheet music. I was strongly impressed with her erudition; she and I once had an hour-long discussion on the dispute between the Pharisees and Sadducees on the timing of Shavuot.

One of four children, she was baptized as an infant, but there was little religious content in their house. Her mother used to attend church with Deborah when Deborah was very young, but stopped attending to spend Sundays with her husband. Deborah then attended a Unitarian church at age eleven and twelve with her cousin, but her parents stopped her visits because of the "nice political things I was learning." Finally she attended an Episcopalian church for a year, but stopped going since she had no family or friends there. Despite these intermittent connections with religion, she likes to tell her friends that she was "raised heathen," thinking of the life and death of Jesus as merely a "historical fact." Her family environment, unlike Joan's warm and supportive family, appears to Deborah as cold and distant, with interactions "like mental abuse."

While she never felt God's presence as a child, as a teenager she "sensed his absence." A rather gory high school driving safety film caused her to wonder how the innocent teenagers depicted in the film could die if there was a just God. However, also in high school, she met a believer and dated him a few times. He took her to a meeting of his Christian youth group, where she heard about God. "What I was thinking was, if God exists, then He would love me, because I was looking for love. I didn't feel love at home, and I didn't have a lot of friends, and I didn't feel loved, period." She also began to learn about the Great Tribulation, and how believers could escape the destruction expected before Jesus returns by being lifted out to Heaven. "I needed love, I was looking for love, and I definitely didn't want to be in that Tribulation." One night, at age seventeen, she accepted the Lord in her bedroom, as a kind of "insurance policy," feeling nothing during the experience. While at that time she wasn't a regular churchgoer, she read the Bible, and learned "just how wrong" her mother's behavior was from a Biblical perspective.

In college, she took a course on liberal theology, which made her uncomfortable since it seemed to be tearing down her beliefs. "One guy is saying this, and the other guy is saying this, so I'm getting confused; there's got to be something wrong somewhere." This experience piqued her curiosity to know what the Bible really meant, and in her sophomore year in college Deborah began to attend Christian Fellowship meetings and began to learn the Bible systematically. Her boyfriend at the time got involved with the Foursquare Gospel Church (Spirit-filled) and got baptized in the Holy Spirit; Deborah followed his example. As a music major, she was attracted to the music in the church, but also to the healing, the relationship between people, "like a family type of thing." She also liked the personal prayers for people's health and welfare, not like the Presbyterian church at her college where people would only pray in a general way for health and happiness.

She married her boyfriend, who was becoming more and more critical of religion, and both of them entered a "backsliding" period. She moved to California with her husband, and for three years (1974–1977) she remained isolated from church life. After they moved back East, she went on a trip in 1979 to visit a charismatic couple they knew from college.

"That whole trip was planned by the Lord." The man in the couple said that the Lord would send someone to her to help her spiritually, and soon after a girl from an evangelical church called her because she saw Deborah's card up in the grocery store (for a job) and just felt that she had to call Deborah about spiritual things. "This is one of those cases where the Lord is insistent enough and He kept doing it until He brought about the circumstances where we met."

She began attending church again, a charismatic fellowship. At a Full Gospel Businessman's meeting a B'nai Mashiach musical group sang and Jim Feinberg gave his testimony. She loved the music—"it was really bright and alive"—and decided to visit the Messianic synagogue. At the same time, her sense of connection between Judaism and Christianity was growing through her own Bible studies. "There was a sense of cohesion and continuity between the two. I didn't see a break so much. Like there was scar material between the two."

When she visited B'nai Mashiach a year later, she was struck again by the music and the dancing, which she had formerly seen only in the movie *Exodus*, and was far better than the "charismatic shuffle" of her home church. She was also impressed with the Bible exegesis, and realized just how "Jewish" the faith could be. "I felt like I was the one who was out of place because they were the ones who were right."

Attending more and more often, she began to feel more at home. She got counseling for marriage problems and began to identify her prayer language (a "tongue") as Hebrew. She also met Gentile couples who helped her "learn the ropes" and feel less foreign.

The real turning point was her first international "Messiah" conference (of the MJAA) in 1984. While Deborah describes this as a "culture shock" because of the concentrated "Jewishness," at the conference she met Messianic Gentiles who looked Jewish and lived that lifestyle. This experience encouraged her to take on *kashrut* and other Jewish practices.

Despite her weekly attendance, Deborah feels "on the fringe" because of her distance from B'nai Mashiach, her Gentileness, and her recent divorce. Still, she has begun reading intensively on Judaism (including several difficult books by Jacob Neusner) and keeps all the Jewish festivals; she even attends a regular Conservative synagogue on an occasional Sabbath and holiday morning.

THE INCOMPLETE JEW

Before salvation, most Messianic believers told me, life was empty and meaningless. Their religious upbringing failed to fill them with God. While some Messianic Gentiles, like Deborah, speak of such hollowness in their Protestant or Catholic upbringing, Messianic Jewish testimonies were often especially vivid in underscoring the lack of spirituality in American Jewish life. While other intriguing interpretations of this language may be worthy of exploration, the empty/full dichotomy speaks directly to the "Jewishness" of the Messianic Jewish self.[1] Although Messianics who call themselves Jews[2] are an eclectic group, ranging from those raised in religiously observant homes to those raised with nothing religious at all, empty and negative experiences as an "unsaved" Jew are almost always contrasted to their full new lives as believers. For those with no synagogue attendance or Jewish adherence, the category of being Jewish was a category devoid of meaning. Todd said, "I guess it was more of my own sense that I was Jewish, but I didn't know, it wasn't supported in any great sense." For those raised with some connection to the Jewish community, their testimonies often include a sense of disappointment.

One type of complaint centered around the perceived ignorance of parents and elders. When one man looked to his parents to explain the mystery of mortality, he found they had no answers. Another man, a member of another Messianic synagogue, said that it really hit him when his grandfather, the founder of the synagogue where his family attended, talked about God "if there was a God." Clearly parents and relatives were extremely powerful role models for these individuals, even in retrospect, and Judaism was often considered bankrupt solely because their parents were unaware of or unconcerned with important theological issues.

More often parents and community are scorned for being "hypo-critical." While grandparents who kept more observances were often a more positive source of "what was Jewish," parents were perceived by these adherents as neglecting or rejecting many of the religious tra-ditions, even though the parents still identified themselves as Jews.[3] This split between cultural and religious adherence struck their chil-dren as "hypocrisy."[4] For example, while one woman's family felt it was important to be Jewish, the father took off from work for the High Holidays and stayed at home watching the World Series with the shades drawn so that the Jewish neighbors wouldn't know.

This accusation extended further, to the Jewish community at large. The synagogue, although ostensibly a religious institution, had become a social center rather than a spiritual site. Thus, growing up, Messianic Jews didn't personally "feel" God in the synagogue:

> There was nothing personal there [in the synagogue]. When I started to go to church, I could see there was a big difference between people who went to church and had some kind of personal meaningful thing and people who went to synagogue. And I thought that when I went to church service that I was hearing what the pastor was saying and I could apply it to my life, while my experience in synagogue was that there was nothing for me except for that I liked being around Jewishness. . . . And that's what I was looking for, I was looking for practical applications of this stuff. If you're going to give me something, it had better apply to my life, otherwise, why am I here?

Another man, in an informal conversation, put the question in much the same way: "Why is it that in synagogues they never pray for per-sonal situations?"—a crucial shortcoming for that Messianic believer. As we saw, Deborah had the same reaction to the Presbyterian church as having liturgy that was "too general."

Personal experience, for these believers, becomes the arbiter of what is "really real." They are not unique. American interest in the "self" has risen dramatically in the last four decades. In a world where rapid cultural and technological changes weaken social ties, it is the self, rather than the community, that can be counted on for both con-tinuity and meaning (Neitz 1987, 228). Adopting in part the coun-terculture's rejection of bureaucracy and social rigidity in favor of spontaneous individuality, Charismatic Christianity now shares with contemporary American self-help culture the emphasis on the self as the source of change, insight, growth and goodness (Back 1972, 77–86; Neitz 1987, 229–231). Not surprisingly, one of the deepest attractions for the Messianic believer is that direct, personal experience of the love and the power of God. In contrast, synagogue liturgy and sermonic messages put little emphasis on individual experiences or spiritual quests. Rather, prayers and messages are often communally oriented, reflecting Judaism as a religion stressing societal salvation rather than self-transformation (Ochs 1991, 25; Ophir 1996, 202).

However, it was not just the de-emphasis on subjective experience that made the synagogue feel secular; the contemporary concerns of the American Jewish community have often been couched in social or political, rather than spiritual, language. From the earliest Jewish migrations, the United States was a bastion for the pragmatic Jew; all-encompassing Jewish religious life was often seen as antiquated or inconvenient. By the 1950s, when radical politics and Yiddish ceased to be active vehicles for Jewish secular identity, the synagogue itself became the locus for Jewishness as well as Judaism, and secular Jews poured their ethnic and social interests into this erstwhile religious container. These "shuls with a pool" thus became social and cultural centers for Jewishness first, with religious concerns running a very distant second (Herberg 1960, 191–198; Sklare and Greenblum 1972, 89–96). It is this type of synagogue, most often Reform or Conservative, in which many Messianic Jews were raised in the 1950s, 1960s, and 1970s.[5] "I grew up . . . in a Conservative Jewish congregation, a mindless, [laughing] . . . no. Like, we went to Hebrew School and like whoever read Hebrew the fastest won. I couldn't take the hypocrisy, it was too much for me. I read the fastest, and I was an atheist, OK? So I got A's."

Prayers said in a foreign language also prevented spirituality, according to Messianic Jewish testimonies. Most said that as children, they didn't pay attention to the service, or even if they did they couldn't understand it. Either it was said in Hebrew, or the English words didn't seem to penetrate. A persistent image among those who went to a more "traditional synagogue" was that of "old men mumbling in the back," and a feeling in synagogue of either boredom or inadequacy since they didn't know Hebrew. One leader of the congregation delights in saying, in public gatherings, "Even if you don't speak in Hebrew, God can understand you."

Not only are parents and synagogues foci of anger and disappointment, but rabbis also don't fare well in the reminiscences of some
Messianic Jews. Three of the members told of being "dragged" to
rabbis who tried shock tactics:

> Ruth: So I went up. They sit me in this room with this, he must have been
> a Hasidic rabbi, so I said, "OK, what do you have to say?" He starts
> screaming at me. . . . I said, "I don't have to take this. I mean, like, talk to
> me." He didn't, so I said, "Ok, bye." That was the end of that. . . . I mean
> really, . . . it wasn't like I was like a genius on Scriptures, so he could have
> said, "What about this, what about this?" But he didn't want to do that.
> All he wanted to do was scream at me.
>
> C. H.-S.: What was he yelling at you?
>
> Ruth: Ah, "You're a traitor, you're a *meshummad* [apostate]," the whole
> thing. It was the first time I ever heard the word *meshummad*, you know?
> I mean, give me a large break. It didn't even upset me because here was an-
> other, this was so stupid to me, this was ridiculous. You don't even know
> what I'm thinking, you don't even know anything, and here you are . . .
> [voice rising, vehemently]. Why don't you talk to the other Jewish people
> who don't even believe in *God*? And who are on drugs every night, taking
> Quaaludes or something over there . . . at least I believe in *God*. Anyway,
> [voice much softer, more conversational] we didn't get that far, because I
> left. I thought he was an idiot, to tell you the truth. . . . It was so ridicu-
> lous. *You* would have thought it was ridiculous.

Comparing herself to drug users, Ruth states, "At least I believe
in God." She appealed to the commonality that she and the rabbi were
supposed to share—a reverence for God—that drug-addicted Jews,
presumably, did not. If God is truly the focus of the rabbi's life, he
should respect her for her faith, and spend his time with those Jews
"worse off" than she. Thus, his furious response was that much
more upsetting.

While attitudes toward the Jewish home and synagogue could be
quite negative, the picture was far from bleak. Some enjoyed synagogue worship for its feeling of "at-homeness," or its social atmo-
sphere. Many had fond memories of family Seders, Sabbath candles,
even Hebrew school. Most testimonies from born Jews pointed out
how they fulfilled expectations of Jewish loyalty presented to them by
family and community. They spoke of working for Jewish communal

organizations, attending Hebrew school faithfully, observing the holidays their families followed, seeking out Jewish friends. Some spoke of further experimentation—an "Orthodox" Jewish phase of keeping kosher and wearing a *kippah* (skullcap), of privately lighting Sabbath candles, of helping the rabbi during services, of going to Israel. All made it clear that they did not set out to deviate from the Jewish norm presented to them as children and young adults.

This pattern enacted in testimonies demonstrates one common way born Jewish members of B'nai Mashiach coped with a core ambivalence—the basic conflict between the Jewish norm of loyalty to eschew Jesus at all costs versus the evangelical imperative to accept salvation through Jesus. These testimonial narratives are meant to persuade both the unsaved Jewish hearer and themselves that what is available in Jewish life is simply insufficient for a meaningful life with God (Charmé 1984, 151–153; McGuire 1982, 50; Polkinghorne 1988, 152). Whether the past Jewish experience was understood as negative and useless, or intriguing and positive, something more was needed. We *were* loyal Jews, they say, but given the hollowness of Jewish life, it wasn't enough.

For those born Jewish, Messianic Judaism thus provided a powerful space of resistance against a totalizing liberal American Jewish discourse that put the bourgeois ideals of family and success at the center[6] and that siphoned off significance from categories it claimed to honor—God and Judaism. The meaning parents found in ethnicity was too local and too limiting; it was only in God that the believer found a sense of power and purpose.

THE IDEAL MESSIANIC SELF

In answer to my question, "Who is an ideal Jew?" one member replied: "The Biblical patriarchs. I like looking at Biblical models and applying them to my own lifestyle, not how they acted per se, but *their* relationship with God as a model for *my* relationship with God. I want to live a lifestyle that's emulating that." In the realm of personal spiritual growth, evangelical Christian discourse clearly dominates. Individuals of Congregation B'nai Mashiach are expected to grow toward a personal spiritual ideal that is often indistinguishable from an evangelical Christian ideal.

In salvation,[7] one accepts that all have sinned and fallen short of the glory of God, and only faith in Yeshua Ha-Mashiach (Jesus Christ) can allow one to stand in the presence of God and attain eternal life. A saved person experiences release from the bondage of unworthiness, meaninglessness, and isolation and enjoys the freedom to be loved and accepted. Beyond self-acceptance, one hopes to experience the joy of the Lord. As one woman told me, "It's important to hear that you get your joy from the Lord. You know, there is a difference between joy and happiness. Happiness is fleeting, it doesn't last, but joy is a deep feeling, permanent, in here [pointing to the stomach region]. Other people can make you happy, but you get your joy from the Lord." One is filled with the Holy Spirit,[8] and, with time, one can positively influence family, neighbors, and community by cultivating prayer life and quiet time with the Lord.

Thus, believers consistently praised Biblical figures, even Yeshua (Jesus), for these behaviors. Biblical Jews are transmuted into ideal evangelical Christians, much as medieval painters dressed Biblical figures in typical period clothing. In this way, a "good Jew" or "ideal Jew" is identical to an "ideal Christian."

In the case of Yeshua, this metamorphosis seemed to me especially strong. Early in my study I noted what was to me curious; neither from the pulpit nor in the adult education classes was Jesus held up as a model for tolerance, charity, compassion, or healing, all of which can be found in the stories and parables of the New Testament. His famous sayings found in the Sermon on the Mount, "turn the other cheek" and "love your enemies," were introduced into sermons only to be grudgingly accepted ("We don't like that, do we?" in the cheek case) or outright rejected (when the speaker had been castigated by a Gentile Christian for not loving Saddam Hussein). Yeshua's roles for Messianic Jews seemed to be the avenue to salvation or the exemplar of the ideal Messianic relationship with God. What remains central about the human Yeshua is not his teachings concerning the poor or downtrodden, but how he exemplifies evangelical spirituality.[9]

These same characteristics of the ideal Jew—prayerfulness and love of God—are seen in the leadership as well. "Clearly, [Daniel] and his family. I mean, if there's anybody who professed that and lived that . . . and is consistent and unwavering. [Michael]—he was a very Godly man, and there's very few of them around. When you meet somebody who spends time with the Lord, you know it." Put very simply, one man answered my question, "What is an ideal Jew?" with "a Messianic Jew."

JEWISH IS "NATURAL"

Jewishness, however, has not been limited entirely to a Christian spiritual plane, but remains as a cultural repertoire expressing Jewish kinship, which differentiates Messianics from other believers. Some positive characteristics understood as "Jewish" by the congregation, such as love of learning, expressiveness, humor, and warmth are therefore celebrated by the congregation. However, one's Jewishness can also be part of the inherited personality of the "old man of the flesh" that must be overcome to find a full relationship with God. Paradoxically, the very natural ethnicity that Messianic Jews claim as their birthright can, according to their ideology, be used by Satan as an unredeemed weapon in a spiritual warfare against God and the soul.

Messianic Jews emphasize the trait of overachievement as a particularly objectionable one. A pattern in several of the salvation narratives was the perception of perfectionistic or overbearing parents, which carries over to unwarranted perfectionism in the children. In Messianic statements and sermons, this overachieving ethos is often identified as an undesirable part of the Jewish "natural man" that needs to be eliminated. Part of the ethos of American life (Kaufman and Raphael 1984; Lasch 1978, 154–186), the need for achievement has been especially strong among some American Jews who have transformed the passion for sacred study into a passion for secular achievement.

This is clearly the view of some of the people I interviewed, who perceived their parents' love as achievement-based. I asked one man what it was he wanted, exactly, in his relationship with God. He said that his mother used to tell him all the time that he had so many God-given talents. If he had those talents from God, he also wanted the instructions on how to use them. Another man told me when he accepted the Lord, his parents' first concern was not that he accepted the Lord, but that this might affect the lucrative job he had managed to obtain. Joan explained that she didn't like her own faults. I responded with the following question:

> C. H.-S.: Did you think that people expected you to be this perfect person or something?

Joan: I think I had perfectionism. I definitely think so. That's one thing I think God is helping deliver me from. I did. Let me tell you, it was terrible, I used to think I was judged like this [hand raised high] and everyone else used to be judged like this [hand lower]. It wasn't fair, and then I would get angry, and God really showed me that's what I was doing. And I said, Lord, OK, I'm really used to behaving like this, you're gonna have to help me stop myself, this is a behavioral pattern for me. It stopped a lot. I don't know if that's part of what was used to get me to see what the truth was, but whatever it was, that got me there . . . even getting so upset, being oversensitive. I hated being oversensitive! You take everything personally, you know. That's not good. I just hated that. God just brought me through different things to see that. I could see that before, but I just didn't have any hope to get over that.

Given this emphasis on lofty and sometimes unattainable goals, the Christian message of salvation seems especially appealing. "All we have sinned and fallen short of the glory of God" is a potent message to those people who did fall short, or were afraid to fall short, of perceived parental expectations.

Moreover, because this truth was simple and easily accessible, one "didn't have to have a Ph.D. to understand it," relieving the adherent of the need to prove one's intellectual worth. This burden to be learned originated in the traditional Jewish world, where in order to truly understand the tradition, one needed to have a command of classical Jewish texts and commentaries. Even today, most Jews are familiar with the Jewish ideal that a good Jew is a knowledgeable Jew. In contrast, a faith in God that required neither Hebrew, nor Aramaic, nor years of intensive study in Jewish schools spared Messianic Jews yet another difficult ladder to climb. As Messianic believers often repeat, it is heart-knowledge that is important, not head-knowledge. More than once, Daniel has prayed to "Bind up the spirit of intellectualism" (emanating from Satan!) that separates the Jew from the truth in Yeshua. Anti-intellectualism, an American, popular evangelical and countercultural value (Hofstadter 1970, 81–116; Neitz 1987, 230), seems far more persuasive than the value of intellectual achievement in Judaism.

Expectations of success need to be fundamentally altered. In a Bible study, the leader said, "God does have a plan for our lives. It's preordained that God will do his will in our lives. We're just told, especially in Jewish families and other minority groups, that 'You've got to get ahead,' be a doctor or whatever." A Bible study prayer stated, "Lord we want to do big exploits, not to be big *machers* (big shots), but to see your Kingdom expand." At a woman's fellowship meeting, this theme was repeated.

> Karla: A lot of us, we come from those Jewish households where we have to prove ourselves, to be a doctor, lawyer, accountant or superman. But God wants to deplete us of *our* resources, to fill us with *His* resources. We shouldn't beat ourselves up about these things.
>
> June: I don't know where I pick this up; if good things are happening to me, I must be a good person. If bad things are happening to me, I must be a bad person. Everything's fine as long as you're a good person. I've heard this all my life.
>
> Karla: That's a Jewish shtick, too.
>
> June: I don't like to be weak in anything.
>
> Betty: Until you experience it. Then it's wonderful.
>
> Shoshana: That's a script I grew up with. I need to be successful, need to be a good person. Now the Lord gave me His script, I learned that ambition didn't matter.

Perhaps the best expression of being released from perfectionistic expectations is in the song "A Jew Born Anew" by Marty Goetz, a Messianic Jewish entertainer very popular on the Messianic Jewish circuit.

> Well, I'll only say this real quickly. This song does not meet with a lot of approval from a lot of people, because it sounds like I'm making fun of where I come from. Well, I don't at all, I honor my heritage, and I know that many, many others do too. It's simply to show you that no matter how many medals you get, no matter how many races you win, no matter if you're from a nation that has the Law and has tried to follow it according to the best of their ability, and even a nation across the sea that has been brought to life from death, there is no goodness except for the Messiah, except for the One that came and was and is and is to come.

In the song that followed, Goetz's use of his bar mitzvah as a symbol of pressured expectation turns the need to release Jewish perfectionism into an enormously powerful tune in the Messianic Jewish world.

Besides overachievement, other inappropriate behaviors are connected to the Jewish natural man. In answer to my question, "Do you
think there are ways of behaving Jewishly?" one congregational
leader responded, "Yes, unfortunately." Surprised, I asked, "Why unfortunately?" He responded, "I don't know, maybe it's my prejudices
coming out. There is no way of behaving Jewishly, I hope. Some
people believe that to be more demonstrative is Jewish. I just think it's
an excuse for bad behavior and liberalism creeping in" (Personal interview, December 21, 1990). Over lunch, Stewart and Lisa explained
to me why they had to cope with the special needs of Jewish believers.
Lisa explained, "Some Jewish people have problems with guilt."
Stewart chimed in with, "So you started the Civil War. Are you
happy now? Are you happy?" At my look of puzzlement, he said, "Do
you remember the special on Jewish humor?" I did remember it then,
and began to laugh. Stewart had been imitating a comedian who was
making exaggerated fun of Jewish guilt. Lisa continued, "A lot of
Jewish people feel guilty over things that they shouldn't feel guilty for.
There's also a certain heaviness. They take on themselves more than
they need to take on."

Thus, the Messianic Jewish self is a site of ambivalence and continual "working out" of one's Jewish identity. The natural Jew is both
positive and ineradicable, a component of one's self, and at the same
time associated with "natural man" and the perfectionism of parents,
which needs to be eliminated to live up to the Messianic ideal.

Despite the repetition of these themes in congregational sermons,
songs, and stories, each believer would articulate this ambivalence
somewhat differently, based on different experiences in childhood
and adulthood. Some Messianic Jews I met have far fonder and more
positive Jewish childhood memories than others; some Messianic
Jews had relaxed, rather than obsessive, Jewish parents.

However, this love-hate relationship with Jewishness does seem
to appear and reappear as a pattern of discourse. The struggle to affirm
Jewishness and yet separate from Jewishness ranges over the whole life
experience of the Messianic Jew.

MEN AND WOMEN

I first began to understand that Messianic Judaism "gendered" differently than liberal Judaism during my first interview with Stewart. I
asked him if the congregation would accept gay members. Given the

new levels of acceptance gay and lesbian Jews were enjoying in liberal Jewish synagogues, I expected that, even though there might be a certain level of discomfort, the Messianic group would follow the general trend of valuing every Jew. With an emphatic shake of his head, Stewart corrected me. "We don't believe that homosexuality is a Godly lifestyle. We would work with them, try to help them, but if they didn't change, they would be asked to leave."[10] This was my first surprise.

My second surprise came as women members got to know me and felt more comfortable with me. They began to ask, "Does your husband let you do this study?" The first few times I was asked this question, I was perhaps most startled that the women asking were around my age; I associated this need for a husband's permission to come from a far more senior generation. What did they mean, *let* me?

Forbidden homosexuals and suppressed wives certainly didn't "feel" Jewish to me. In fact, Messianic gender roles seem to owe far more to evangelical models than to contemporary Jewish views. Indeed, conservative religion can provide a site to express and at least partly resolve gender role uncertainties inherent in American society since the early 1970s.[11] Yet, once again, Jewishness complicates evangelical gender ideology.

One ideal of Jewish masculinity has endured from Eastern Europe to the films of Woody Allen—the brilliant, learned, sensitive, physically weak, completely impractical Jewish male. The shadow haunting this image has been the anti-Semitic rhetoric accusing Jewish men of effeminacy and instilling shame for eluding the "normal" male expectations of physicality and aggressiveness (Boyarin 1997). Even today, Jewish men may seek their identity between the stereotypes of the "all-American boy" and "Mama's boy"; it can be a troubling process (Klein 1980, 39; Schneider 1992, 15–19).

The congregation establishes a different role for the male, one which is familiar even to non-evangelical Christians from the popularization of such movements as the Promise Keepers. The man is the head of the household, just as Yeshua is at the head of the believers; after prayer and due consideration, the husband's word should be the final one. Additionally, a real man should be a fighter—if not physically, then spiritually. Biblical men are frequently taken as role models of spiritual strength and tenacity.

The transformation of the Messianic male extends to the body as well as the spirit. There is a strong emphasis overall on male physical culture in the congregation; sports competition among the men, for example, is an important part of the "Messiah" conference experience. Even Yeshua was physically fit:

> In addition to His non-Jewish image, Yeshua has oftentimes been portrayed as someone soft, weak and effeminate. Once again, nothing could be further from the truth. Yeshua was the son of a carpenter, and a carpenter Himself. His body was strong and used to hard labor. Being the oldest child of a large family, the responsibility for helping to support the family would have fallen upon His shoulders. . . . Every indication we have about Yeshua historically is that He was a strong, healthy man. He worked with His hands, walked for miles each day, preached to thousands for hours, slept on the ground and fasted and prayed for days on end. (Chernoff 1989, 27)

Descriptions and drawings of male Biblical figures and male Messianic believers reflect this word picture. Yeshua, Peter, Paul, and Moses are portrayed with muscles, tans, and attractive, clearly Semitic features.

The image of the strong aggressive male takes on a more modern coloration in the identification with Israel, especially the Israeli army. Mirroring some in the American Jewish community, Messianic believers find in the *sabra* (native-born Israeli) a symbol of Jewish physical power largely absent from rabbinic Judaism (Breines 1990). A few Messianic Jewish men in the congregation like to wear Israeli military jackets, and the analogy of believers being like "the Israeli army" arises in sermons and conversations. At the 1991 "Messiah" conference, the teenagers performed a dance based on a military theme, even wearing characteristic Israeli military clothing. Caring so much about Israel, the community reinforces the evangelical image of the strong male with the ideal of the Israeli soldier.

In fact, Jewishness has been transformed to such an extent that Daniel, responding to an idea that one can't be a believer and Jewish at the same time, responded: "That almost makes us like we are stripped, neutered almost, of anything Jewish that we have. . . . We have never given up that Jewishness." Here, in rather powerful language, Daniel explicitly connects masculinity with Jewishness.

In Messianic Judaism, the evangelical model of men being the leaders of the house and of the community allows Messianic Jewish men to continue to prize gentleness and caring, while ridding themselves of their inner "wimp" (Rose 1990, 104–105). In the congregation, personal violence among men is abhorred; one should always show the love of God through patience and humility. Men seem unashamed of hugging one another, praying with one another, or sharing their personal problems. One man, relating his Orthodox teenage life before Yeshua, talked in wonder at his reaction to a comment over his *kippah*: "I remember I shoved him up against the wall, and I told him I'd kill him if he touched it. [In a sarcastic voice] This is how I showed the love of God, in those days." Clearly, this man felt he had come a long way.

Demonstrative men are only acceptable if their affection cannot be misconstrued; homosexuality is a favorite target in the congregation. When leadership wants to make a point about a group of people's immorality, homosexuality is often the example of the cardinal sin. When the waywardness of today's liberal Jews is mentioned, invariably the fact that the Reform and Reconstructionist movements ordain gay and lesbian rabbis is included. After one sermon, Daniel prayed for an indwelling of the Holy Spirit: "Lord, fill us with your Spirit, give us oil in our lamps. . . . Remove any emotional problems, marital problems, thought life problems, any sins of lying, criticism, slander, of any *effeminacy* [emphasis mine], too much time in TV, in worldliness, anger and bitterness."

Indeed, most conservative Christians express fear and loathing of homosexuality. Evangelical groups stress God's power, so a hypermasculine ethos helps to manifest the reality of a powerful and empowering God who is, after all, Father (Flake 1984, 91–113). However, there is a particularly Jewish dimension to the Messianic rejection of gay and lesbian behavior: the need to remake the Jewish male image along normative heterosexual lines. Thus, Daniel emphatically, categorizes an image of the Biblical Jacob as being cheap, a cheat, and effeminate (because he lived in tents with his mother) as an anti-Semitic slur. Dismissing homosexuality for Messianic believers means dismissing a false, externally imposed image of the Jewish male as weak and womanly.

In contrast, "womanly" hardly meant "weak" in the model of the Jewish woman brought over from Eastern Europe. Household manager, mother, and worker, the ideal Jewish woman was intelligent, practical, and aggressive in the financial support of her family. Running counter to the decorative, gentle model of the "weaker sex" that still shapes American discourse, the Jewish woman was, however, depicted as overbearing and emasculating by generations of anxious Jewish-American male writers in the stereotypes of "Jewish mother" and "Jewish American Princess" (Frankel 1990; Prell 1992). Comparing their inferior "Jewish noses," "Jewish hair," and "Jewish hips" to the anorexic beauties adorning magazine covers and television (Fishman 1992, 31; Kaye-Kantrowitz 1982, 28–44), Jewish women too are caught between pride in their power and competence and the shame of difference (Klein 1980).

The image of the ideal Messianic Jewish woman, modeled after the ideal evangelical woman, does much to alter the hurtful representations of the "Jewish woman." Women's focus should be on the family: their most valued roles are those of wife and mother. Women are in fact encouraged to stay home until their children are school-aged; I was told by Stewart's wife, "Househusbands aren't Biblical." Even unsaved husbands must be listened to; unless he asks you to do something that goes directly against God, it is better to do what he wants, even if you have to miss a few prayer meetings or services.

Within congregational life, women are "the backbones," strong and supportive, but rarely visible. They are encouraged to be more private, effecting change and exercising abilities either in women's networks or under the guidance of men. Instead of leadership, women are exhorted to cultivate an attitude of nurturance and service.[12] Women shouldn't be "prima donnas," but be willing to serve, even, as Jackie Chazan emphasized, by serving food rather than taking a leadership role, no matter how tempting the latter option is. Women are the safeguarders of morality; it remains the woman's responsibility to dress modestly, especially in congregational dance, so as not to entice men.

Gender issues extend beyond the family to friendship. While in a group men and women seem to interact freely, some more intense friendships between members of the opposite sex are frowned upon. One woman who was separated from her husband took great pains to discuss her close relationship with a single man in the congregation, explaining that their long-held friendship made it acceptable for them to spend time together, although I hadn't asked!

While women can fulfill certain tasks, such as evangelism, hospitality, and prayer, because the "Biblical norm" shows no clear-cut case of women in authority, women should not be leaders. Until very recently, women Messianic rabbis were unthinkable, and women teachers were usually confined to teaching other women. If there are men willing to engage in leadership, a woman shouldn't have to take up a role that she is unsuited for. Rachel Wolf, a Messianic *rebbetzin* (rabbi's wife), finds that even the physical makeup of women makes them less desirable leaders: "Part of that understanding is leadership naturally befits the father. His lower voice, stronger muscles, and greater height gains him the innate respect of his offspring. . . . God has so arranged things . . . to make us inherently predisposed to look to men as 'ultimate' leaders" (Wolf 1995, 6).

The physical depictions of the Messianic Jewish woman complement the role she is expected to play. Women are portrayed, in pictures and in dances, with long flowing hair and long dresses—a graceful, smooth portrayal of the ideal woman. Indeed, one can see at a Friday night service a larger-than-usual number of older women, in their forties, with long hair, puffed sleeves, and flowers in their hair, accoutrements that go against the conformities of fashion. This flowing image seems to represent not the "power" of the Spirit, which can aggressively energize, but rather the gentle infilling of the Spirit in a submissive believer. Messianic Jewish artwork portrays Biblical women as invariably dark Semitic beauties with luminous eyes and long, flowing hair, creating a positive balance to the image of the Jewish woman.

Through this evangelical ethos, specifically Jewish concerns are directly and indirectly addressed. The stereotype of the Jewish American Princess is consciously rejected, along with any hint of excessive materialism. The congregation puts the life of the Lord above material gain, as is evidenced by the number of families that make a real sacrifice of job or neighborhood to buy a house in the urban blocks surrounding B'nai Mashiach. At baby showers and gatherings, women not only bring homemade gifts, but talk about the curtains they are making or the clothing they are sewing. One does not find an ostentatious display of wealth on any woman in the congregation. Living for material goods, or displaying excessive material wealth, is rather the sign of the unsaved Jewish woman. One of the wealthier members of B'nai Mashiach said at a women's group meeting: "After

I married George, suddenly I had money, I could shop at Emporium Armani . . . It's easy to go into the JAP [Jewish American Princess] thing. I hang out with my in-laws [unsaved Jews] with the big Park Avenue names. I went to a children's second birthday party . . . there were children with designer clothes. People look at the rocks on each others' hands. This is yucky, this isn't for me, I don't need to keep up with the Schwartzes, and everything else." Some Messianic women thus both believe the stereotype and consciously reject it.[13] The evangelical ethos has healed them from the stigma of JAPness.

What happens to the assertive Jewish woman is somewhat more complicated. Theoretically, the loud, dynamic model of the Jewish woman is eschewed. For example, one woman said that "like Jewish women" she tended to be overemotional and jump to conclusions. This was perceived as a negative trait. Ralph praised his wife for learning to submit, learning how not to be the "typical Jewish wife" who takes control of their married life. The strong, supportive wife of the Christian world replaces the stereotypical image of the shrewish Jewish wife and mother.

However, as is evident in the daily life of the congregation, the women are not shy in voicing their opinion, to men as well as to other women. In prayer groups women speak up as often as the men and pray as long as the men. In study sessions women ask and answer questions, and one woman in particular had no problem arguing with the male teacher over a point of belief. Women with grown children or single women are free to pursue careers; one woman who serves as a professor of Middle Eastern studies was pointed out to me with pride by a number of male leaders in the congregation. Even the wife of a *shammash* and mother of a toddler worked part-time without condemnation. And during a fierce male-dominated volleyball game during a Labor Day picnic, women were allowed to play if they could hold their own, as did one strong forty-ish woman member who was cheered by members of her own team and respected by the opposing side.

This assertiveness was noted by one Messianic Jewish woman, a teacher, who joined the congregation mainly because women shared the same cultural presuppositions. In the Gentile evangelical church she and her husband used to belong to, women in the congregation actually talked about the most efficient way to remove stains. The best kind of woman to be in that church was unintelligent and helpless. In contrast to the church of the "Stepford Wives," Jewish men wanted women who were not "airheads"; it was acceptable for women to discuss politics and intellectual matters. She found herself happy in a congregation that presupposed the intelligence and competence of women.

Even the theological imagery of men and women seems similar. In my encounters and discussions with both men and women, women speak about their faith intellectually and abstractly as often as men; men speak about their faith in emotional terms of love and peace as often as women. While during a praise and worship session I saw a woman pursing her lips and kissing the air, something I never saw a man do, there are no great differences in the verbal articulation of their beliefs.

How can submission and assertiveness work at the same time? How can one follow the evangelical ideal of submission and the Jewish expectation of assertiveness and intelligence? Some women, of course, find great meaning in nurturing the family and providing quiet strength. Also, the restrictiveness of this lifestyle may also be more apparent than real. For example, even for the evangelical woman, submission can be a highly flexible term (Griffith 1997, 183–186; Rose 1990, 115). So too for Messianic believers. Messianic Jewish women made it clear to me that submission did not mean tyranny, but only operated in the case of an insoluble disagreement. After the couple has prayed about it, thought about it, and discussed it, "if push comes to shove," the woman should accept her husband's judgment. Thus, submission is re-interpreted and ringed with caveats, making it more acceptable to the women involved.

There are, however, those Messianic women who feel that there is surrender in submissiveness. For those who have relinquished their careers for that of wife and mother, these feelings can be especially strong. At a regional fellowship meeting, a leader's wife spoke of her change from career woman to being a wife and mother as coming at a price. "I had always been success-oriented and career-oriented. Then I made a choice to stay home with my family. It was hard to get used to it. I have friends who were vice-president of Xerox, doing all kinds of things. Now I love being a mother and a homemaker. Because I really love God and want my children to grow up healthy and whole, I made a decision. I gave up that materialism, rather than going for the boastful pride of life. God has blessed us all from time to time, but only if we are willing to sacrifice." In fellowship meetings and private discussions, it seems easier for Messianic believing women to change their attitudes about a problematic event than to change the situation. Often, the overburdened life of a wife and mother is seen as a given, a difficult "given" especially for those who gave up a career to take on that job.

During a congregational New Year's Eve comedy show, one woman presented in a skit "the day of an average housewife." Though it began with quiet time and being with the Lord, it progressed to a chaotic and frenetic day that culminated with a trip to the emergency room, with no husband or other adult in the skit. The tag line was: "Make sure you have your quiet time every day, because sometimes the day isn't that quiet." In a women's fellowship meeting, when one woman in the group was ill, exhausted with child care while her husband spent long hours at a new job, no one suggested to her that her husband change jobs, but instead offered Bible verses and personal experience on how to cope with a situation that seemed to be out of control. In an interview, one bright woman who seemed tired of child care said that for her, after her salvation, the spiritual realm became so important that things like dishwashing and laundry were now "like shadows."

In contrast, some women publicly demonstrate assertiveness. Sometimes they are successful, as the woman at a congregational marriage seminar who protested the leader's idea that women are more intuitive by pointing out her more hard-headed nature in relationship to her husband. The leader of the marriage seminar's reply, that in her case she must have had a bit of a chemical or genetic imbalance, was met with some skepticism by B'nai Mashiach members. The fact that the leader was an evangelical Christian imported for the occasion, rather than a Messianic believer, undoubtedly helped her to be more forthright without condemnation. At times, however, women who assert themselves too strongly are running a risk. Women can be chastised in public by their husbands when they make a comment that seems too assertive. In a Bible study, one leader publicly silenced his wife, who had suggested a way to look up Bible verses, with a sarcastic comment: "*This* is a helpmeet suitable for me?" Both the evangelical ideal and the Jewish real uneasily coexist.

Others seem to be following a path of quiet rebellion, trying to reshape the evangelical ideal to take into account a more assertive view of women's capabilities. When interviewing one woman, the wife of a leader of the congregation who had been in the Messianic Jewish movement for close to twenty years, we discussed the subject of women in the congregation. A person who had been attracted to feminism as a college student, she is a strong individual who is not afraid to assert her opinions. Yet when I asked her about how she felt about the dearth of women's leadership roles in the congregation, she asked me to turn my tape recorder off. Continuing "off the record," she explained that she and at least one other leader's wife would like to see women in greater leadership positions, even if only with other women, such as praying for those lining up for prayer after a service, taking a greater official role in counseling, and other leadership functions. (Interestingly, it was her husband who told me during a different conversation that he believed that sometime soon we would see women Messianic rabbis!) The need to shut off the tape recorder showed me just how "dangerous" a topic this can seem. While she and others were trying to effect change through private channels, this was too controversial a topic to challenge leadership with. She is not the only woman who expressed frustration with the status quo; several Messianic Gentile women, coming from churches where women could preach and pray for men, found the Messianic Jewish movement "conservative" at best, wrong-thinking at worst. In a "Theology Forum" in *The Messianic Times*, an organ for Messianic believers, the only dissenter of five contributors to the topic of "women in leadership" points frustratedly to the status quo. Although women are in fact taking leadership in the Messianic movement, according to Kay Silberling, including "teaching Scripture" and "proclaiming the Gospel," unfortunately "many women working effectively for the kingdom are unacknowledged. At our conferences, women traditionally haven't been encouraged to be strategic players. Instead, we've been treated to classes on decorating and family issues *to the exclusion of* leadership and spiritual training. . . . A female 'brain-drain' in Messianic ministry is created as young, intelligent and capable women turn to secular jobs where they see room for their gifts. They've received little encouragement to use their gifts in a Messianic environment" (Silberling 1995, 6).

In the past few years, it would seem that the avenue of quiet change is beginning to make its mark, with significant alterations in the attitude towards women leaders. In 1996, two IAMCS congregations were headed by women. At B'nai Mashiach women are now allowed to be part of prayer lines praying for men as well as women; the earlier fear that women praying for men might experience inappropriate emotions or that the encounter might be sexually charged now seems to have been overcome.

At this juncture, the congregation and the movement is shifting rapidly. It will take time before the full impact of women's leadership is felt within the Messianic movement, and both men and women fully integrate the challenges of women's leadership with the evangelical arrangement of responsibilities and authority between the genders. Indeed, even the liberal American Jewish community, supposedly "liberated," is still grappling mightily with the challenge that women rabbis present almost twenty-five years after the first woman's ordination.

JEW AND GENTILE

No other group in the congregation has to work harder at a Messianic Jewish self than Messianic Gentiles. The entire community celebrates Messianic Jewish, not Gentile, holidays; Jewish artifacts are found in homes; Jewish foods are preferred at gatherings; Jewish jokes and Yiddishisms pepper the conversations; key Hebrew words and phrases are repeated in sermons; Messianic praise and worship uses Jewish-sounding music and Israeli-style dancing; and rituals are liberally borrowed from the synagogue. Messianic Gentiles therefore experience, in the words of one adherent, "what it is like to be a minority," even in congregations where the majority of members are Gentile in origin. This feeling is sharper at B'nai Mashiach, with a noticeably smaller number of Messianic Gentiles, many of them married to Messianic Jews.[14] In order to fit into congregational life, Messianic Gentiles need to take on practices foreign to them, and in essence recreate themselves as cultural Jews, all the time recognizing that according to official congregational and movement ideology, they can never become real Jews. Thus, while leadership stresses that there is no difference spiritually between Jew and Gentile, a bifurcation remains. Once again, the evangelical context of being one in the Messiah runs against the Jewish imperative: "Stay separate!"

According to the leadership in the congregation, there is no way to convert to Judaism; one cannot go from being Gentile to Jew. Messianic Gentiles can be "spiritual Jews" through accepting the Lord, and can even celebrate Jewish holidays, but they do not participate in the promises to physical Israel to return to the land, nor are the children of two Messianic Gentiles "Jewish." Since a good portion of the congregation are Messianic Gentiles (most of whom are married to a Jewish spouse), how they internalize and accept this ideology forms a significant part of the "Messianic believer's experience." Messianic Gentiles express both less and more of a Jewish self than the official ideology would lead one to expect.

Less Jewish

In the structure of the congregation, Messianic Gentiles who join the congregation are not always welcomed, unless they come with a Jewish spouse. Many of the Gentile couples and singles have been told, either by leadership or overzealous congregational members, that "they don't belong there," especially in the beginning of their stay in the movement. In fact, one couple, partly in reaction to this response, tried to "find a home" in other churches before settling down permanently at B'nai Mashiach. Certainly, Gentiles with emotional and spiritual problems are sometimes ignored; it was explained to me that the leadership doesn't have time to deal with them, since its primary commitment is to Jewish believers. Gentiles who are made welcome are those who are stable, who have a strong commitment to the Jewish people, and who can make a contribution to the congregation.

Even solid Messianic Gentiles can be cut out of the social loop of the congregation—not regularly contacted by telephone, nor invited to take part in the congregational discipleship process. Since discipleship is an important way to meet members of the congregation, not being a part of the process can isolate Messianic Gentiles.

There is also a power component to keeping Gentiles officially separate. The MJAA only allows single Messianic Gentiles or Messianic Gentile couples "associate status" (not allowed to vote), because of the plethora of evangelical Gentile Christians interested in the movement. If Messianic Gentiles could vote, they could overwhelm the Jewish members and take the movement away from a "Jewish context."[15]

Because the Messianic Jews want to retain Jewish identity, inter-marriage is a problem. Those who enter the congregation as inter-married couples are usually fully accepted (after all, Jackie Chazan is Gentile). However, single Gentile women are looked at with deep suspicion by at least two of the leaders' wives as only joining to marry Jewish men, and are sometimes strongly discouraged or even prohib-ited from dating Jewish men. There is a less exclusionary attitude to-ward non-Jewish men, but generally only Jewish women who are sin-gle and "getting on in years" are permitted to marry non-Jewish men. Even in this rule there are exceptions. Gentile believers of both sexes, whom the Chazans have known for a very long time, are sometimes seen more as "honorary Jews" and are not discouraged from marrying Jewish men or women.

Thus, the fear of assimilation, the need to "stay separate" and "maintain Jewish identity," undercuts the value of the Messianic Gen-tile "spiritual Jewish self." The real Jewish context strongly affects the official evangelical context of unity in Christ.

More Jewish

In response, some Messianic Gentiles attempt to uncover or establish a Jewish self. Some go to great lengths to find a Jewish origin, looking back in their family tree, hoping that a mysterious past, a Jewish-sounding surname, or some other clue will lead them to find a Jewish ancestor. One family, a blond Gentile couple with nine children ("each girl prettier than the one before" sighed Jackie Chazan, who really disliked the idea of so many Gentile girls tempting away born-Jewish boys from marrying born-Jewish girls) underwent great difficulties being accepted. Seeking to become a true part of the com-munity, they tried to trace their last name back to a great-grandparent or great-great-grandparent who was Jewish, but this effort was met by skepticism from the leadership, who said delicately that the whole matter of their membership was "still under discussion."[16] Others take a different step. At least three Gentile women in the congregation have gone through Jewish conversion *after* they became involved with a Messianic Jewish synagogue.

When I discovered this the first time, I was shocked, and asked how they could go through a Jewish conversion when they already believed that Jesus was their savior. Moreover, how could they convert to Judaism when their beliefs say that they can't change their "status" from Gentile to Jewish? One woman who underwent this type of conversion said that she knew it didn't really make her Jewish. Rather, she undertook the class at the suggestion of the leadership, to show the Jewish parents of her future husband that she had solidarity with the Jewish people. She also wanted their children to be permitted in Israel under the Law of Return. The Reform conversion she underwent, moreover, was by her own estimation not a "spiritual" experience. Although she expressed some discomfort with her hidden identity, it was a discomfort at being caught. The rabbi never directly asked her if she believed in Yeshua, and so she didn't need to lie directly. Although someone at the Reform synagogue recognized her as a Messianic believer, because he didn't make the connection that she was taking a conversion class at the building, she was able to complete her course. Finally, she stated that this was what God wanted her to do, and ultimately this decision was between her and God. She seemed uncomfortable talking about it. The other women I knew about converted for the same reasons, and used the same justification for their actions: since they were not asked directly about their beliefs, they didn't feel bound to announce them.[17]

This "don't ask, don't tell" stratagem allows Messianic Gentiles not only to have increased access to sharing the faith—an important consideration—but also to fashion themselves as more authentically Jewish. While the "converted" Messianic Gentile woman gives intellectual assent to the Messianic Jewish stance of "once a Gentile, always a Gentile," her willingness to go through what must have been a rather awkward and difficult conversion points out something deeper than the words—the desire to be seen as really Jewish, to be a part of the Jewish people.

Intriguingly, despite the teaching that Jews stay Jewish and Gentiles stay Gentile, sometimes adherents have a different view. The husband of one of the women who converted said that he considered his wife Jewish—after all, she didn't celebrate Christmas and Easter. As mentioned above, both Ralph and his wife considered Ralph Jewish as well, although he was born a Gentile and underwent a conversion to Judaism. Gentile children adopted by a Jewish couple, according to one leader, could also be considered Jewish since they were raised Jewish, although, once again, that contradicts stated ideology.

Messianic Gentiles are also among the most enthusiastic propo-

nents of "Jewish behavior." At least one man, although not converting formally, adopted a Hebrew last name and adopted Yiddishisms in
his everyday speech. The only four people I met who were interested
in following rabbinic *kashrut* (including separation of milk and meat
and only eating meat that was ritually slaughtered) were Messianic
Gentiles, not Messianic Jews. To an outsider, then, many of the Messianic Gentiles are "hidden." The congregation can "look" more
Jewish than it actually is.

Thus, in practice, the dividing line between Messianic Jews and
Messianic Gentiles becomes highly blurred. Messianic Gentiles are
sometimes not accepted fully, and this double standard can create a
great deal of pain for those who experience being "second-class citizens." However, some can make their own claims to Jewish authenticity. Even Jackie said, "[Michael] waited a long time to marry somebody Jewish," then corrected herself and said, "not that I'm Jewish,
but I have a Jewish heart." Another woman, who had a pretty good
case that one of her great-grandfathers was Jewish, spoke of her dilemma in this way. "When I go to fill out the MJAA form, I know I
should put down 'Gentile.' But the Holy Spirit keeps telling me, 'No,
you're Jewish.'"

THE FAMILY
Unsaved Relatives
One's self-concept is intimately tied to one's parents and close relatives. Thus, one of the greatest areas of struggle with one's "Jewish
self" among Messianic Jews is coping with the possibility of the death
of unsaved parents and relatives. The Jewish context calls for continued loyalty to parents; it emphasizes the role of children remembering the deceased through the *Kaddish* (a prayer traditionally recited
daily after the death of an immediate family member) and *Yizkor* (a
memorial service for the deceased held several times a year in synagogue). However, according to the evangelical theology accepted by
Messianic Judaism, those who are not saved are damned for eternity,[18]
which makes such memories unbearably painful. This belief is perhaps the most difficult for Messianic Jews, because even if the parents
of Messianic Gentiles are only nominal Christians, they are light-
years closer to the beliefs that make for salvation than are most of the
parents and relatives of Messianic Jews.

Judging by the number of prayer requests brought on a typical worship morning for family salvation, and the intensified efforts of Messianic Jews around the bedside of a dying relative, this is a matter of great concern. Messianic believers and congregational members will surround the bedside of a dying unsaved mother or father, praying constantly and urging the acceptance of Yeshua. Some children have "brought their parents to the Lord"; for example, one man was brought to the Lord by his sons after twenty-two years. In prayer sessions, I have heard dramatic stories where, at family gatherings, the saved children will force the issue despite the parents' reluctance to discuss it, relating with great happiness conversations in which parents seemed "really open."

After asking numerous people, I realized I heard *no one* who was willing to say that an unsaved friend or relative burned in Hell. When I asked, "How do you deal with that?" the following response was typical.

> Lydia: I do struggle with that, about my grandmother. . . . My father's mother, here's somebody who walked from one end of the earth to another in a snowstorm to collect money for Israel and [was] very very active in all kinds of Jewish organizations. . . . Everybody who knew her loved her. She was a beautiful person, she really was. I don't know where she is. And the idea that she could possibly be in Hell, is, like, abhorrent to me, I just don't want to believe it, but I do know that there is a very different issue just because of the fact that she didn't accept the Messiah.
>
> I don't know, I struggle with it. I struggle with it because I believe in God's grace and love and I figure He would give everybody a chance . . . and that it would be up to them, so I don't know, I'd like to believe everybody went to heaven. . . . When you read the Scriptures about what Hell is like, I certainly wouldn't wish that on anybody. But it's something I struggle with when people die who don't know the Lord, not just my grandmother.

For Lydia, the knowledge that her grandmother was, according to the Jewish context, a good Jew and a good person (collecting money for Israel, active in Jewish organizations, lovable) was clearly in conflict with what she knew was theologically correct from the evangelical context. Her seesawing discourse wavers between validating her grandmother and recognizing the evangelical reality of Hell, between God's mercy and kindness and the horrors of eternal damnation, between what she would *like* to believe about her grandmother's fate and what she *does* believe. Still, nowhere does she say that her grandmother is definitely in Hell, but instead, "I don't know."[19]

Some members needed to stretch fairly far in order to construct a "saved" diagnosis for their nearest and dearest. Stewart's wife, Lisa, hearing a sermon which included the words, "And don't think your grandmother is burning in Hell!" took that as a divine message that her grandmother was saved. Another Messianic Jewish man at the 1990 "Messiah" conference told of how his father died without accepting Yeshua. On an airplane soon after the death, he met a Messianic Jewish woman whose father was saved on his deathbed. He "just felt" that because of that encounter, *his* parent was saved as well.

In order to feel comfortable with the deaths of their loved ones, some even reshape the theology of the Messianic Jewish movement. This fascinating exchange between a Messianic rabbi and his congregant (at an IAMCS congregation in the South) took place in response to my question, "Are you afraid of your mother dying before she is saved?":

> Kitty: There is a resting place where non-believing Jewish people are. And when Yeshua comes back, they are going to be able to be saved.

> Rabbi Steven: It's still wishful thinking.

> C. H.-S.: OK, you would disagree with [Rabbi Steven] on his understanding of salvation, in terms of that issue. Is that a problem? I know that there is a sense of spiritual authority that the rabbi has. Is that disagreement a difficulty? A real difficulty?

> Kitty: I don't discuss it with him, that's all [laughs].

> Steven: No, because we're dealing with Kitty. Kitty has given her life to the Lord, and so I'm dealing with her on one level. She understands, she knows that it's important for her to let her family know what she's doing and to talk to her family about Yeshua, so I don't have a problem with that. What is the ultimate future event thing that we differ on, I found it, sometimes, you know, it sounds good, so I say wishful thinking, because, listen, if I was wrong I'll be thrilled.

> Kitty: And my dad, see my dad has died, I just want to know that, I need to feel, that for my own peace of mind, maybe it's wishful thinking, whatever, that he will have a second chance, *or*, there's still that feeling

that right before he died, we don't know that the Lord doesn't come down to people, and right before they die, they become a believer.

Steven: That's true, and I understand that. But again, since she's doing what we are all doing, in other words, her attitude is not, "Oh, I'm not going to talk to anyone in my family about it, I'm not going to witness to any Jewish people, because they're going to be saved." I happen to say now since we're all here that that's not her attitude and so I have no problem with that at all.

Despite these attempts at self-reassurance, the imminent death of an unsaved close relative or friend is a time of great anxiety and fear. When I asked why one woman appeared particularly fragile during a prayer meeting, I was told that her brother was dying and that she had been at the hospital room in a bedside vigil night and day, trying to get him to accept the Lord. The congregation may lend support through prayer either distantly or in the same room as the dying individual. This is clearly serious business. In the case of a parent, such vigils may be complicated even further by personal histories; if the adherent's acceptance of Messianic Judaism left a bitter rift, it may be the last time to convince the parent that the child was correct in his or her beliefs. At a moment when the need to feel closeness to the parent and continuity with the parent's values is the greatest, the fact of the child's belief in Yeshua may be a formidable stumbling block. If the parent accepts Yeshua, however, any incipient guilt and estrangement can be retroactively erased. It is a time of strong and complicated feelings.

Children
One of the values that strike B'nai Mashiach members as particularly Jewish is the care and concern shown about children in the congregation. The coordinator of the Sunday school contrasted B'nai Mashiach's approach to those of Gentile churches, where one could enter and see the children just sitting quietly in the pews alongside the adults. "For Jews, children are at the center of our lives. We tend to give them too much material wealth, when in reality we need to give them love. Some of us grew up without it [love]. Some people give children material things and others give them spiritual things. We want to give them spiritual things first."

Just as American Jews sometimes see Jewish traditions as something done for the children, so too do B'nai Mashiach members. The traditions serve as teaching tools, especially for the children. "It touches all five senses—the smell of the fragrant wine, the sight of the candles, the sound of the blessings, the touch and taste of challah. It has been shown that children learn better when they experience things with their senses." Hanukkah and Purim, according to Jackie Chazan, are also holidays primarily celebrated for the children.

In their education at both Talmidim and the weekend Shabbat service and Sunday school, children receive a microcosm of what goes on "above stairs" (all classes are held in the basement area). Children are encouraged to talk about their personal relationship with God, to solve their problems with prayer, and to intercede for others in prayer. Being raised in the movement as a "natural thing," it would seem that some of the intensity of their parents' struggle between Jewishness and evangelical faith is diminished.

On Friday night, the children experience a mini–Sabbath service, including blessings over the wine and bread, some Messianic dancing, prayer, and then a Christian video or some other project. On Sunday morning,[20] the children receive a Bible curriculum. Both sessions last one hour each, during Daniel's sermon.

Noticing that the stated principles of the school address spirituality, serving God, and self-esteem, not Jewishness, I asked the coordinator about the activities the children do around Jewish holidays. Her answer was a mixture of the Jewish and evangelical. On Sukkot, they made items to hang in the congregational *sukkah* (the hut built to commemorate this "Feast of Booths"). They rehearse songs and dances that they perform in front of the congregation during holidays. "Of course," she cautioned, "we put a Messianic emphasis on this. Without Messianic emphasis, it's just a regular old ritualistic type of thing." The children learn the Messianic meaning imbued in each holiday, how it relates to Yeshua and the New Covenant. Thus, the "doubling" of the Messianic Jewish message is repeated for the children. On Passover, the children might see the film "Pesach at Bubbie's" (a standard Jewish film showing a traditional Seder at a grandmother's home) but also do crafts of lambs, reflecting the belief that Yeshua was the Lamb of God.

In Talmidim, the Messianic Jewish day school, such education is more intense. The "Fundamentals of Biblical Judaism" course

teaches children about Biblical promises of God and Biblical principles, in much the same way as adults are given the material in their
classes. One exchange on Isaiah 55:8–9, with sixth to eighth graders,
seems typical:

> Ruth: It's telling you that nobody is like God.

> Rachel: It's comparing our thoughts to His thoughts.

> Teacher: And so, what is the conclusion that you draw from that. How
> should we live our lives?

> Moses: God is smarter than we are.

> Wendy: You should put God first. He's more powerful and He knows
> what we are doing.

> Moses: We should trust in Him, He should guide us.

> Teacher: What is the negative way of saying this? What are we not sup-
> posed to do?

> Moses: Lean on our own understanding.

> Teacher: That's right! Man should be as smart as possible, but at the point
> that you think you know everything, you are in trouble with God.

As "above stairs," personalization is very much in evidence. The
teacher continues to explain the Biblical meanings in Isaiah, and
reaches Isaiah 58. "When we fast, we want to see the results of fasting.
To loosen the bonds of wickedness in our own beings. It's not talking
about wicked people now, but ourselves, for us not to be wicked, to
set ourselves free. One of the reasons we do fasting and praying in the
congregation is right here in Isaiah 58."

Education in Jewish identity is mostly confined to learning about
holidays and the Bible. Children at Talmidim also get elementary Hebrew language instruction. Very occasionally, they have guest speakers. According the principal, several years ago the head of the Jewish
Defense League of Liberty came to speak to his class. (I cannot believe he knew that this was a Messianic Jewish school, although the
principal assures me that he was informed). I served as another guest
speaker, as the "price" for my all-day visit to the school.

The small group of six young teenagers asked me questions that one might expect—"What is your belief about God? What is your belief about the Bible?" We discussed my view of Jesus, *kashrut*, and Jewish Law. In a rather funny moment, one girl raised her hand and asked, "Mr. —— [the teacher] wanted us to ask you why you take so many notes at services." The session became an information exchange both on theology and the process of my study. Apparently the teacher was rather surprised at my theistic understandings of God; he expected a Reconstructionist to be, in his words, "more of a secular humanist," and told the class that this expectation he had was clearly false.

The students were an interesting group. There were three Messianic Jewish boys, one of whom was clearly a young zealot, debating with me to show how rabbinic kosher laws were human inventions, rather than Biblically based interpretations. The others in the class were three Messianic Gentile girls, who seemed a bit lost; one of them began a question to me, "In your synagogue or church or whatever . . ." All were unfailingly polite, and very bright.

My feelings about this coerced participation on my part were, not surprisingly, mixed. On the one hand, I enjoyed the interaction, and I felt comfortable that I could give something back to the group for my months of intrusion, questions, visits, and note-taking presence. It was only right to provide something of value to them after they had provided me with the substance of my study. However, I was equally uncomfortable about providing something of value to the group. Would my discussion of Judaism be something enlightening and helpful to the children, or would it be used by the teacher as an example for more effective evangelizing? Would I be giving ammunition as well as information to this Messianic Jewish congregation? This same problem cropped up in a number of different contexts. I had to purchase books and tapes from the congregation, pay to be part of their Passover Seder, and subscribe to a Messianic Jewish newspaper where the subscription money is said to go directly to evangelizing the Jews. In each case I knew that I was financially supporting something that as a rabbi I opposed; in each case I knew as a scholar that the information I received was invaluable and inaccessible in any other way. In each case, I had to compromise with my conscience, which added to the tension that was continually mixed with the exhilaration of the study. It remains an unsolved moral dilemma.

Along with the factual instruction of which I was a part, children are expected to develop spiritually. Besides their daily time of prayer, students are taught about Yeshua, and are encouraged to make professions of faith. Generally, according to one teacher, children make professions at the age of five. However, between the ages of ten and thirteen, they begin to question their salvation and often reduce it to mere intellectual assent. So the school has started a rededication ceremony, where children sign a rededication form. In comparison with the simple professions of five-year-olds, there is more discussion of behavioral changes that are expected to accompany salvation, "that Yeshua needs to be the Lord of your life."

Besides reflecting the congregational emphases on prayer, Bible readings, and faith, as well as those aspects of Jewish culture important to the adults, Talmidim children are taught that they need to share with unsaved Jewish children. I heard of some examples in an interview with the principal.

C. H.-S.: Do the [Talmidim] kids witness to other children?

Principal: Absolutely. The students are encouraged to witness to unsaved students. For example, one girl comes on the bus with [Orthodox Jewish] students. . . . Their discussions come into what we discuss in "Fundamentals of Biblical Judaism." . . .

One particular girl has been witnessing to two [Orthodox Jewish school] girls on the bus. The girls haven't been willing to bring a Bible on the bus. We gave her some tracts to give to them. I'm sure they ended up in [the Orthodox Jewish school] somewhere, in the trash can. Then the parents told their kids not to talk to our students.

This is where our education between fact and opinion comes in. We tell our students if they come up with an opinion, to ask them where they got things from. They do things because their rabbis tell them to, or because of rabbinical teaching, which is the antithesis, well, not quite the opposite of Biblical teaching. There are sharp disagreements.

The students got upset because the Bible our student used had an Old Covenant and a New Covenant, so we gave her a JPS Old Covenant, but they just didn't want to discuss it. So now, it's gotten to where they start playing music for each other.

Despite being part of a small school (forty to sixty students) in a small congregation, with its intensive social scrutiny, the children seem fairly well behaved and as healthily obnoxious as any children that age. Some of the children are very much involved in secular culture, watching cartoons on Saturday mornings and playing Teenage Mutant Ninja Turtles.

Still, it is clear that in this congregation, in some respects, there is less of a line between childhood and adulthood than in other child-rearing environments. The pressure of public confession, the expectation of "sharing," the practice, as adults do, of prayer and Bible reading, quickly place children in the same realm of discourse as the adult members of the community. One Messianic Jewish children's songwriter even includes songs affirming the children's Jewish identity and portrays sad, unsaved Jewish relatives. Children are expected to have to take up the issue of contested Jewishness as well.

It does seem, however, that for some members of the second generation, the obsession with identity is getting a bit boring. They are still very much aware of some of the struggles; they especially understand the distinction between Jewish and Gentile believers. One young Messianic believer put his views this way:

> Paul: Jews believe in Yeshua. . . . I think that it's talked about in that sense—You're OK. What I would like to see is that to be more internalized and natural. Of course we're Jewish. But it's not, so that's why it's talked about so much.

> C. H.-S.: Do you feel that you have it completely internalized?

> Paul: Not with me completely, because I'm constantly challenged on my Jewishness. I've been thinking about it lately. I know more about Jews and Judaism than most Jews. . . . But what if I didn't? It shouldn't be based on how much I know, even, that I'm Jewish. . . . It's not normal for someone to come up to a traditional Jew and ask, "How are you Jewish?" It's unheard of. . . . Instead of just a negative definition, I want us to bear fruit, to prosper, instead of asking "Are we Jewish?" all the time.

When one begins to examine the ideas of Messianic believers in B'nai Mashiac about "the Messianic Jewish self," the complexity of the formulations belie the concept that this is an easy hybridization of two religions. While on the surface the equation "we are Jewish by ethnicity, believers by religion" would seem an adequate explanation of Messianic believers, in fact it is far more complex. The Messianic understanding of the Godly self is taken almost entirely from evangelical sources, but through enacting this definition ambivalences about Jewishness surface in a continual negotiation of identity. Facets of the "Jew within" are celebrated, sanctified, modified, and discarded; the "completed" Jew of Messianic discourse is never quite complete, but always a work in progress. Evangelical roles both heal Jewish gender woundedness and clash with Jewish expectations. Basic loyalty to deceased family and friends cause Messianic Jews to practically negate a central tenet of evangelical theology. The pull toward Jewish authenticity even causes Messianic Gentiles to seek Jewish roots and ties in ways contradictory to the evangelical emphasis on spirituality. In the following chapter, we will see this struggle reactivated in the conception of "community."

CHAPTER 4

Community

Moishe Rosen at the "Messiah" 1991 conference:

> The next impediment to evangelism is a misunderstanding of ourselves.
> I'm gonna talk to you like you'd be my own family. I want to be candid.
> What is it that binds us together? Is it our Jewishness or our Jesusness? Let
> me put it to you this way. A simple test. Think with me. Suppose the rab-
> bis are right and you can't be Jewish if you believe in Him, that He died
> for your sins and rose again from the dead. Suppose they're right when
> they say that these are two mutually contradictory positions. We know
> they're not right but will you assume that they're right, and that each of
> us has to choose and the choice is, either to believe in Him or trust in Him
> for our salvation, or to be Jewish? That's the choice. How many here are
> going to choose to believe in Him? [Here Rosen raises his hand mean-
> ingfully—several hundred people, almost every other hand in the audi-
> torium, follow suit. Some of those who have their hands raised are not
> Jewish.] How many here are going to choose to be Jewish if that means
> rejecting Him? . . . [only two hands are raised, both by elderly individ-
> uals].
>
> We are believers in Him *and* Jewish, *and* Jewish. But in order to un-
> derstand ourselves, let's get our priorities straight. He is first of all, above
> all, and most of all, and the fact that we are Jews, is incidental.

A conversation at the snack bar at the same conference:

> Man: I am not a *Christian*. I don't consider myself a *Christian*. I am a *Messi-*
> *anic Jew*, not a *Christian*. Christianity is a religion, they celebrate all these
> pagan customs, like Christmas.
>
> Woman: You need to be careful about that. I used to say that, but you have
> to be careful not to go overboard. People who are Gentile use the word

"Christian" to mean born-again. You can really offend them or confuse them by saying that you aren't a Christian. We always need to remember that all believers are one body.

Man: That's true. We have to teach them though. If it's pagan, it's wrong.

When I embarked on this study, an evangelical friend said to me: "I know that for Jews, the primary distinction is between Jews and non-Jews. For evangelicals, the primary difference is between the saved and unsaved. How do Messianic Jews deal with this?"

How does the "Body of Messiah" stand up against "The People of Israel"? Which communal identity is foregrounded? There remains an inherent contradiction, a struggle, between American Jewish languages of community and evangelical Christian discourses of community. Both call for a primordial and exclusive identification. Being Jewish *or* being saved should be one's primary affiliation, certainly not both.

M. H. Kuhn suggested that one's "orientational other" consists of four elements: the others to whom the person is most emotionally connected, the others from whom the person gets vocabulary and key concepts, the others who have provided the person with meaningful roles, and the others who sustain or change the person's self-concept on an ongoing basis (Kuhn 1964). As we have seen, and will continue to see, *both* the Spirit-filled Christians and the American Jews are the orientational others for Messianic Jews, with all the complications that involves.

I attended a "post-Hanukkah" party held at the home of a Messianic Jewish couple on Christmas Eve. As I walked up the front steps, I noticed a *mezuzah* on the doorpost of the modest brick Colonial. Inside, greeting the crowd of adults and children, blinked strings of Christmas lights winding up the stairs. The decor was equally eclectic. On the wall of the living room hung a graphics poster of the Jerusalem skyline, while on a small table stood two small cloth dolls, an old man and woman dressed as Eastern European shtetl Jews. On the wall of the dining room hung a picture of an old Jewish man with a long white beard and traditional clothes peering with an expression of puzzlement and sadness at a Hebrew scroll; the black, white, and gray painting was entitled "Isaiah 53." On the mantelpiece stood Shabbat candlesticks almost covered with old wax drippings, *kiddush* cups, and a display of holiday cards—some Hanukkah cards, some Christmas cards, some season's greetings. A Messianic card showed a lamb's head (representing Yeshua) inside a Star of David, celebrating the "Messiah day of Yeshua ha–Mashiach." Upstairs, removing my coat in the spare bedroom, I noticed a small wooden bookshelf containing the works *Basic Judaism* and *The Living Talmud* next to evangelical Christian books such as *How to Change History through Fasting and Prayer*. On the floor were two gift boxes wrapped in green paper, with "Season's Greetings" written on them. During the party, a small gift exchange took place, and a couple came in bearing a gingerbread house—most conspicuous for the Jewish star painted in icing on its front door.

Whom do Messianic believers belong to?

WE ARE THE BODY OF MESSIAH

To examine this question further, I borrowed an excellent question from Roy Mittelman's research on Moroccan Jews. He asked people to fill in the blank in the following statement: "We are Jewish, they are _____" (Mittelman 1987, 202). Knowing full well the added complication of the question, I presented the statement as, "We are Messianic Jews, they are _____." I was curious to see if members could "oppose" their identity to others. Generally, people were puzzled and somewhat upset by the question.

> Tina: I just have so many thoughts that cross my mind . . .
>
> C. H.-S.: What were some of the candidates, then?
>
> Tina: I don't know, the way you're saying it sounds sort of like "Well, we're Messianic Jews and the rest of the world really stinks."
>
> C. H.-S.: It doesn't have to be that way.
>
> Tina: Well, I guess I don't like to see myself as, like, superior because I'm a Messianic Jew.
>
> C. H.-S.: OK, that's an answer.
>
> Tina: I don't see it as something to stick in somebody's face.
>
> C. H.-S.: OK.

Tina: There's so many other people that aren't . . . there's people who are
Catholic, and there's people who are Jewish who don't believe in the
Messiah and there's people who are Protestant. . . .

C. H.-S.: There's so many "they's" and just one little "we" . . .

Tina: I guess you could say that, but anybody who's a believer, I mean he
might not be a Messianic Jew, but we're brothers and sisters in the Lord.
It's not like we're better or worse or similar or different.

The answer above (which was fairly typical) showed a clear reluctance to set off Messianic Jews in opposition to others, but also somewhat of a confusion as to communal identity in general. This answer
assumes saved Gentiles as an implied opposite, and expresses a concern to remain connected to "brothers and sisters in the Lord." While
a few respondents contrasted Messianic Judaism with traditional or
"regular" Judaism, none explicitly opposed Messianic Judaism to
Gentile Christianity. More common was the preservation of the
saved/unsaved dichotomy: " 'They' are all those who don't know the
Lord." This inability to separate Messianic Judaism from Gentile
Christianity is all the more notable because of the fundamental Jewish
distinction between Jew and non-Jew, a distinction which Messianic
Judaism retains to a strong degree.

Of course, Christian theology makes the unity of all believers in
Christ a central tenet of its belief system. Messianic Jewish congregations, as mentioned above, can be 70 to 80 percent "Messianic Gentile." If for no other reason, these numbers would blunt any desire to
"rebuild the wall of partition."

Those Jewish believers saved by non-Jews also have a good reason
to see these individuals as brothers and sisters in the Lord. Indeed, it
was the very ability to get beyond the strong categorizing of parents
and community that attracted two of the women to the belief in
Jesus. These women were impressed that Gentiles, the traditional
"Other," showed such love and concern for Israel and the Jewish
people.

The adherence to the standard theology of Protestant Christianity and the personal experience of individual believers is reinforced
through the power of institutional evangelical Christianity. As we
have seen, ties with Gentile Christianity are fairly evident. Beyond

providing the origins and the funding for Messianic Jewish congregations, Gentile Christianity is present in a number of other interactions. Daniel was a key speaker at a huge conference on the Holy
Spirit, and many of the good "believing books" talked about in the
congregation come from Gentile Christianity. For example, it was
suggested to one man, receiving vocational counseling from a congregational leader, that he read a book by Kenneth Copeland. Because
of the structural, financial, and ideological connections with Gentile
Christianity and Gentile Christians, it is no wonder that they want to
keep open lines of communication with "our brothers and sisters in
the Lord."

Despite these ties, few members of B'nai Mashiach would identify with institutional Christianity as strongly as David Stern, author
of the *Messianic Jewish Manifesto*:

> But when I call myself both Jewish and Messianic, I am thereby identi-
> fying with both the Jewish community and the Church. . . .
> • As a victim I feel negatively toward the persecutor—as a Jew I
> feel bitter about what the Church has done over the centuries to my
> people.
> • As a Messianic I have gratitude toward the Church, despite its be-
> ing a persecutor, because the Church, either directly or indirectly,
> has made the Messiah known to me. . . .
> • But I am also the persecutor, for identity with the Church as per-
> secutor is inevitably part of the baggage that comes with joining the
> Messianic Community. To whatever extent I may represent the
> Church I can be repentant on its behalf and seek the forgiveness of
> the Jews. But I cannot expect them, as unsaved people, to be willing
> to forgive me. (Stern 1991, 25)

At B'nai Mashiach, members seem reluctant to accept the role of per-
secutor. Certainly, one reason is that they do not wish to be seen by
the Jewish community as a "church outreach," since that would im-
pair their evangelization efforts. However, they also have a more
complex reason to distance themselves from the Christian milieu.

Part of the self-definition of Jewishness centers on the feeling of
marginality, of being a minority in a sea of potentially hostile others.
The awareness of anti-Semitism energizes alienated Jews and informs
the politics of the largely liberal American Jewish constituency;
seeing themselves as underdogs helps them to feel solidarity with oth-

ers who are disenfranchised. To be Jewish in America is to carry a consciousness of victimization past and victimization present (Lieb-man and Cohen 1990, 31, 43–45, 49, 105). It explains the high per-centage of Jews who feel that anti-Semitism is still prevalent in the United States, despite statistics that show extremely low levels of anti-Semitic sentiment among Americans (Kosmin et al. 1991, 29).

Thus, for Messianic believers to be identified as Jewish, this en-trenched American Jewish worldview must be acknowledged in some way. In Messianic hands, this marker of loyalty to a people is activated in a different context, that of the evangelical subculture. Unlike lib-eral Jews, who sometimes judge evangelical/fundamentalist Chris-tians as irredeemably anti-Semitic by virtue of their religious beliefs, Messianic believers attempt to educate evangelical Christians much as liberal Jews attempt to do with their liberal Christian counterparts. Messianic believers are quick to note anti-Semitism in the evangelical subculture. Messianic believers give talks about Messianic Judaism to the believing churches, to show that Jewish practice is good, not evil. As Stewart told me, "We are good Jews! We combat anti-Semitism!"

This sense of the doubtful trustworthiness of one's spiritual brothers and sisters adds a certain tension to the relationship between church and Messianic synagogue, a tension that allows the Messianic movement to remain separate from the larger evangelical commu-nity. "False doctrines" that evangelical churches adopt that take away the promises from physical Israel are often spoken about in sermons and at conferences. This creates a sense of division between Gen-tile churches and Messianic Jewish congregations. As Jackie Chazan stated at a teaching at the "Messiah" 1989 conference, when church doctrine arises that calls into question the central role of Israel and the Jewish people in the story of salvation, even those Jews assimilated in the churches are not safe.

Perhaps the most important obstacle to feeling part of the Gentile church is the importance of being Jewish as ineradicable, highlighted in the nomenclature "Messianic Judaism." The choice of this name was originally a declaration of independence from Protestant de-nominational control; now it continues to point out difference.

In order to handle the tension between being both a part of and apart from evangelical Christianity, B'nai Mashiach members do seek to dissociate themselves from "the church" in a number of ways. The primary method of managing this dissonance is to see the cultural manifestations of Gentile Christianity as separate from the true theology of Gentile Christianity. It is the "pagan trappings" of Gentile Christianity to which members have the most objection, trappings which can distort the message of Christianity itself. At the most extreme, Gentile Christianity is seen as the impure or inferior expression of the "true Judaism" that Jesus intended.

For example, a man who once served as a Messianic rabbi of a university group, a great majority of whom were not Jewish, felt he had to train them in Messianic Judaism:

> Brian: I remember I was very strong to these people. I said that we have to use the word "Yeshua," we can't use any non-Jewish terminology and so forth. And I had to train them, because I was convinced it was the only way. I remember a Scripture that was in Isaiah that says that "Remove, remove the stumbling block from my people," and I knew that the stumbling block was Gentile Jesus Christ, because it was a stumbling block for me. I didn't want to be in the church. I related to this tremendously and I knew that I had to instil this in the people. . . .

> C. H.-S.: What was the difference in your mind between Jesus Christ and Yeshua the Messiah?

> Brian: He was . . . I have no concept of Jesus Christ, if that makes sense to you . . . I don't believe in Jesus Christ. Does that make sense?

> C. H.-S.: I'm not sure.

> Brian: I understand what Christianity is. I understand who Jesus is to Christians, but that's not how he is to me at all.

> C. H.-S.: Well, what's Jesus to Christians?

> Brian: Like, I think there's a tremendous amount of ignorance. Like when people pray to Jesus I just . . . [here he makes a face of irritation] it grates at me tremendously. They just don't understand at all the whole concept of prayer in Judaism and as Yeshua understood it. You don't pray to Jesus, you pray to God.

> C. H.-S.: But wasn't Jesus God?

> Brian: [slowly] He is, was, yes of course, but you don't pray to him, you pray to God, and Yeshua, by nature of his being God and the Messiah, is

what enables you to come into God's presence, you pray in the name of Him. And the reason that you pray in the name of the Messiah is because He is in that position, he is that mediator, OK. The majority of Christians, the Christian world, doesn't really understand the concept of their own faith. Does that make sense? So you see, I don't have a concept of Jesus Christ, I understand it, but I don't believe it. I don't identify with these other things.

Even Messianic Gentiles in the congregation regret the pagan origins of Christmas and Easter:

Joe: Well, Easter—Estre—a pagan name attached to a religious feast, and the evidence shows that it's celebrated as a spring festival.

C. H.-S.: Yeah, bunnies with eggs.

Joe: Which really infuriates me beyond all measure. I have problems with what the church has done in terms of accommodating pagan culture. . . . Easter is not commanded by God, nor is Christmas, nor is the feast of the Immaculate Conception. . . .

Diane: Every celebration that has been set up by man himself has been corrupted by man, like Christmas. There's nothing wrong with celebrating the birth of the Messiah, but we've corrupted it. The same thing with Easter. Man has set it up, and it has become corrupted. . . . Well, it's just like when they ask people not to wear crosses, visitors, they ask them to tuck them inside of their clothing. Well, I understand that and I think they should abide by that. One of the things that is encouraged here is to . . . bring out unsaved Jewish friends and relatives, especially on Friday nights. If they see someone with a great big cross around their necks, they would say, "Where are you bringing me to?"

As with the resistance against sterile liberal Judaism, Messianics clearly contest the ubiquitous homogenization that Christianity represents. Once again, Messianic Judaism establishes a place of opposition, this time to the hegemony of Gentilism that seems to expect that acceptance of Jesus as Lord and Savior must also come with ham, churches, crosses, organs, and robes.

The visual symbols of Gentile Christianity do seem to be a problem for many of the believers. People raised in strongly Jewish environments often talked about the cross, the organ, and the choir robes as particular "taboo" symbols: the choir robes reminding people variously of Roman Catholicism or the KKK, the organ reminding people of stereotypical Protestantism, and the cross reminding Jewish people of violent episodes when individuals wearing the cross massacred Jews in the name of Christ. By disallowing the use of such symbols in the worship and architecture of Messianic Jewish synagogues, and by calling those symbols "pagan," the "disloyalty" issue—the idea that a Jew who has converted to Christianity has gone over to the "enemy"—is muted. The ambivalence created by being both Jewish and Christian is quelled, because the most obvious symbols of Christian belonging, which resonate as symbols of persecution for Jews, are simply removed. The struggle between the two worlds is repressed.

Or is it? At certain times such terminology becomes unavoidable, despite the careful "Judaizing" of Christian language. During a teaching on Matthew 16:24, "Take up your cross and follow me," an elder was forced to explain:

> We don't talk about the cross too much at [B'nai Mashiach]. That's understandable, since people burn them into other people's lawns, people wear them and aren't believers, and as Jewish believers, many have been persecuted in the name of the cross. But we can't get away from the term—we can't say "Take up your tree and walk with it," it sounds like we're dragging a tree across the front yard. . . . The cross symbolizes many things. It symbolizes the cruelty of the world, and the scorn for the things of the Lord, the people of the Lord and the Lord Himself. . . . But it also symbolizes loss. It also symbolizes the love that Yeshua has and that God has for us, that he doesn't want us to be lost.

While in this Sunday morning session the teacher tried to make the cross an acceptable symbol for Messianic Jews, others take different approaches. During a B'nai Mashiach Yom Kippur service, another prayer leader using the same verse in his talk felt the need to distance their worship from this potent symbol. "I want to conclude with 'take up your cross.' It doesn't sound very Jewish. It's not, don't worry. It's Roman!" In yet another evocation of this verse during Sunday morning services, the assistant Messianic rabbi used humor to defuse the anxiety this symbol creates, substituting the word "Magen David" (Star of David) for the word "cross," evoking some laughter. Each method—careful explanation, redirection, and humor—points to the dissonant feelings created by the cross, for Jews an uncomfortable symbol of a violent Christian world, for Christians the proud representation of a faith and community. While the Jewish community believes that such muffling of Christian terminology is merely a proselytization technique of Messianic Jews, the discomfort shown at its mention even among a group of solely B'nai Mashiach members points out its deeper significance—as an indicator that Messianic Jews have crossed over to become "other." The rhetorical devices mentioned above help to ease the contradiction between the Christian usage of the cross as a symbol of hope and the Jewish recognition of the same symbol as a symbol of danger, between being part of the Christian world and being part of the Jewish world.

However, despite these strains, the sheer numbers of Messianic Gentiles in the movement and the interlinkages with the wider evangelical community determine a strong sense of connection with the saved. In a community that has established itself as challenging the status quo, matters of belief often take primacy over the external divisions supported by society (Douglas 1970, 160–161). Sharing a common faith language, believers from all backgrounds can share experiences using special spiritual language barely comprehended by non-believers, the language of "anointing," "condemnation," and "spiritual warfare."

In the congregation, people who assumed I was saved would speak to me warmly and openly about their lives and faith; it was only after they asked, "How long have you been a believer?" and I answered, "I'm not," that their attitude would notably change. Some would go into "testimonial mode," sharing their experience in the hopes that it would strike a chord. Others would shy away from me suspiciously, questioning me closely on my motivations. Clearly, as an unsaved person I was seen either as a potential saved person, or "open," who should be witnessed to in an appropriate fashion, or as a dangerous element who should be shunned. While many members had the grace to interact with me in a more natural and unself-conscious way, especially as they got to know me, not all were able to manage it. I clearly was in "another category."

Perhaps the clearest example of this was a friendship I struck up with a woman at one of the "Messiah" conferences. A Messianic Gentile from the congregation, a smart, funny woman approximately the same age as I (late twenties to early thirties), got to chatting with me at an MJAA conference. I simply assumed that she knew who I was, since this was toward the end of my study with the congregation and I had made no effort to hide my identity from anyone. However, as we talked, I became less and less convinced that she knew who I was. She was completely natural with me, not constrained, feeling free to critique sessions and individuals in a way I had rarely encountered to that point. I decided not to lie, but simply to continue being her friend. Besides, I reasoned, what was the harm? I did tell her I was doing research on the group. Sooner or later, I felt, she would put two and two together.

It wasn't until later in the conference that she finally caught on. We were sitting together in the huge gym of Messiah College, made over into the central gathering place for the conference, for the evening entertainment/inspiration. The bleachers were filled with two thousand people, eagerly talking and waiting for the music to begin. As the musicians came on and started to play their catchy brand of Messianic Jewish music, to thunderous applause and cheers, my buddy was bouncing up and down like a kid, singing along, with a big grin on her face. She looked at me, puzzled, as I sat there quietly. Several times she asked, "Aren't you excited? Why aren't you happy?" I explained that I was enjoying the music. Finally, she got up to dance and wanted to know if I wanted to come, also. When I declined, one thing led to another, and finally she said, "You *are* saved, aren't you?" I had to say no. She was really shaken, and I felt rather guilty. I asked if it would make a difference, and she said, "Yes, because with someone who is saved I can talk about certain things, and we understand each other right away. With someone who isn't saved . . ." It was clear that the close friendship she had hoped for was torpedoed by my admission.

The next afternoon she came up to me with a certain resolution in her eyes. "I prayed about it," she told me, "and God gave me an answer this morning. How do you picture God?" "Why?" "I know God like a daddy. I can be a small child and just climb up into His lap." I explained to her that I could see God as a partner, even as a Master, but hardly a Big Daddy. I felt that religious maturity involved accepting oneself and one's actions as an adult. She looked at me with some pity. "Then you can't be close to God the way we are." Apparently, God told her I was lacking in the kind of experience that would enable me to be saved, and so I might be an object of compassion, but not of fear or anger. She decided (also with God's help) that I was a germ, a harmless microbe passing through the Body of the Messiah, rather than a deadly virus that would infect that Body. We resolved, after the discussion, to remain friends.

Nonetheless, because the very existence of Messianic Judaism is predicated on an ongoing loyalty to the Jewish people, this "saved-unsaved" dichotomy is far from sufficient. The Body of Messiah is a valued metaphor, describing a society in which Messianic Judaism seeks to locate itself. At the same time, Jewish believers' bodies and blood are "naturally" connected to the Jewish community and to Jewish families of origin. Thus, it is not surprising to see attempts to pull the two together. As one person said, referring to the audience at the "Messiah" 1991 conference: "We are *mishpocha* (Yiddish for family), the Body of Messiah."

THE COMMUNITY OF ISRAEL

When one enters B'nai Mashiach and listens to a sermon or discussion, the phrase "our people" is never far from the speaker's lips. When I asked about the import of this oft-repeated statement, I received two answers: first, to make it clear that although the American Jewish community says it isn't so, Messianic Jews claim membership in the Jewish people and, second, that Jews are "our people" in the sense of "our responsibility" to bring to the Lord. The constant use of the phrase "our people," in B'nai Mashiach sermons, classes, and discussions is perhaps their most frequent declaration of that loyalty. However, for American Jews, these uses of "our people" are mutually exclusive. You can't consider yourself part of *our* people, proclaims the Jewish community, if you are actively working to eradicate us spiritually.

Given this suspicion on the part of the American Jewish community, when Messianic Jews share their beliefs with unsaved Jews, they receive a variety of reactions—from mostly outright hostility to occasional open interest. By openly proclaiming their belief in Yeshua, Messianic Jews can be removed from Jewish organizations, or at the very least told that they are no longer Jewish. Because every connection with the Jewish community outside Messianic Judaism is made with those unsaved Jews (relatives, friends, strangers) whom Messianic Jews have a mandate to save, it is no wonder that Messianic attitudes toward the Jewish community in general are colored by their experiences on the mission field.

What makes this relationship especially difficult is that the congregation's ingroup is also the outgroup. The Messianic Jews have the task of proclaiming their Jewishness and their love and loyalty to the Jewish people, while at the same time assessing their own spiritual superiority by continually comparing themselves to unsaved Jews.

It is not surprising, then, that positive images and verbiage about traditional or secular Jews co-exist with some highly problematic understandings of the Jewish community. Messianic believers have the difficult task of identifying most strongly with their "greatest enemies."[1]

Traditional Judaism

At the 1990 "Messiah" conference exhibition hall, in a show of artwork created by Messianic believers, one painting depicted an old man praying, hunched over, by the Western Wall. Coming out of the Wall in an "apparition" was Yeshua, one hand placed comfortingly on the man, his other hand holding the man's prayer request. To me, the man looked sad and downtrodden; however, one woman, a Messianic Gentile, found it "wonderful" and "sensitive." This portrait of a despairing traditional Jew, clearly not seeing the almost invisible Yeshua, was hung next to paintings of old rabbis portrayed in a positive light, teaching young children or blowing the *shofar*.

Clearly for some Messianic Jews, despite the blindness to truth that the first painting displayed, the mystique of the Orthodox as "real Jews" has not dissipated. The Orthodox are recognized by B'nai Mashiach members as the only other Jewish group that believes the Bible was given as direct revelation by God, the only other Jewish group that believes in the power of prayer and the possibility of miracles. This perceived kinship cannot be duplicated with liberal or secular Jews. As Daniel remembers, "I went to the University of Cincinnati, and in the early 1970s when I went there, there was a large Orthodox Jewish enclave, and I went over these scriptures with the students verse by verse, line by line. I didn't know Hebrew then, and it was a real blessing for me to learn this method of careful Scripture study." The Orthodox are respected for their learning:

> I remember when we were, when I was in the service and we were stationed up in Saratoga Springs which has got a fair Jewish community, in

fact it's got a very Ortho, or *had* a very Orthodox synagogue up there.
There was a kosher butcher in town and my wife and I wanted to make
London broil, we had read the recipe, we were into all these new recipes
and stuff and I walked in there and I say, "I'd like a flank steak, please!" and
he looked at me like I had just come in there with a swastika or something
[laughter]. And he proceeded to explain to me that they don't sell flank
steak and he gave me a Biblical lesson before I even became a believer. (Eisenberg 1988)

The impatient Orthodox Jew was not tolerant of error. However, the
butcher gave the speaker a "Biblical lesson before he became a believer," which shows how this Messianic Jew admired his erudition.

The swastika statement is very important. As a Messianic Jew, being seen as a traitor by the traditional Jewish community, the speaker
felt marked by a swastika. Here is a clear awareness of exclusion. He is
well aware that despite his admiration for the butcher's learning, he,
as a Messianic Jew, will be seen as the enemy. Thus, this is a story both
of attachment and of resentment.

Because of the reverence many liberal American Jews and some
American Christians accord the image of the "Jewish sage," witnessing to traditional Jews does not always come easily to Messianic
believers. In a 1991 B'nai Mashiach adult education class, someone
noted,

As I started last week's class, I just want to refresh that, and remind everybody and myself as well that we're dealing with this from the standpoint
not of wanting to ridicule contemporary Judaism. . . . The whole focus
that got me into this kind of study was that Paul bore witness of our
people, many of them, and said that they have a zeal for God, but not in
accordance with knowledge.

One way to avoid vilifying traditional Jews is to demystify them;
they do not have a better understanding of the Bible than Messianic
believers. Perhaps the nicest depictions of traditional Jews came in
stories in which Messianic believers witnessed to puzzled Orthodox
men and women. These potential believers were seen as sincere, but
misled by the Talmud-centeredness of Orthodox Judaism. "I want to
take the mystery and fear out of this—that what a rabbinic Jew knows
'up here' shouldn't frighten you off to share with him. The Talmud is
just the teaching of man about the Scripture. If it's wrong, you or I or
anyone else has the opportunity to challenge it."

However, Messianic Jews do experience opposition from the observant Jewish community; many of those who actively work in anti-missionary organizations are Orthodox, as is the Israeli rabbinate that is keeping Messianic Jews from entering under the Law of Return. After a tour of Israel in 1990, "Nate," a Messianic musician, described a TV show there talking about Messianic Jews, which had on as guest an Orthodox politician warning against numbers of believers coming over, much to the incredulity of the secular host: "You mean that you wouldn't let Jews in just because they believed in Yeshua?" According to Nate, this is evidence that "Most Jews want to let us in, no matter what. But Orthodox Jews want to keep us out."

Nate's discomfort with Orthodox Jews was clearly far more personal. He and his Messianic Jewish logistics man for the tour went to the Holy Land Hotel to see the model of the Second Temple. There they met an Orthodox Jewish man, who offered to give them a guided tour of the place. "Instead, he gave us a guided tour of all of Judaism—Talmud, Mishnah, he wanted to take us on a tour of all those books. It was a real trial for us, because he said things we didn't believe in. . . . We didn't even talk to him about the Messiah—we didn't want to. . . . This guy wasn't angry in the sense of being nasty. But he was troubled—very troubled. Orthodox Jews are very confused. They did not have answers as to what God is doing in Israel. 'Oy, it's getting worse.' We, Messianic Jews, do have answers, answers from the scriptures, they really don't and so are literally frightened." For Nate and his entourage, then, the Orthodox Jews they met in Israel were obstructions to Messianic immigration, symbols of religious confusion, and sources of danger.

Given these attitudes when discussing traditional Jews, Messianic rhetoric sometimes goes beyond the "Jew as lost" and edges into "Jew as evil." What is keeping unsaved Jews sad, benighted, and "veiled" is primarily Satan himself. As a Messianic rabbi stated at the 1990 "Messiah" conference, "When we set our sights to conquer little men in little black hats and black beards and *pais* (earlocks), they're not the enemy; the enemy is the one behind them, causing their blindness."

Here, the distinction between "saved" and "unsaved," the evangelical context, really begins to cut and shape the Jewish context of peoplehood loyalty. In a casual conversation, a Jewish believer told a story of a girlfriend who had accepted Messiah, and who was placed in an Orthodox yeshivah to "straighten her out." In the yeshivah Bible study, Isaiah 53 was "deliberately skipped over" in an act of outright deception.

Rabbis were not the only ones who were seen as deceptive or Satanically influenced. One woman told me about the Lubavitch Hasidim speaking to "spirits" and fortune-telling, all of which, as she was happy to point out, were against Scripture. While at best traditional Jews are respected, or affectionately seen as misguided, at the worst they are seen as a spiritual threat.

Secular and Liberal Jews

In a memorable sermon, Stewart stated that although he was not raised in a "rabbinical Jewish home," he was raised in "bagels and lox" Judaism, in which "most of our people" were raised. Some of the elements on the list were very familiar to me: going to a specific bagel shop every Sunday morning; going to synagogue on High Holidays, but at no other time, and women attending only if they had new dresses; giving money to the Federation of Jewish Agencies; planting a tree in Israel; having a bar mitzvah; eating Chinese food once a week, even though it wasn't kosher; being a doctor, lawyer, or accountant, but better yet if you finagled your way into a "good deal"; hanging out at a Jewish section of the beach; upsetting your grandmother if you intermarried, but it was still OK; having a grandparent living in Miami Beach; buying suits from certain men's stores popular with the Jewish community; getting the Jewish paper every week; putting your wedding announcement in the Jewish paper; and if you're an elderly Jew, regularly taking the bus to gamble. "But that's OK! That's Judaism!" Stewart repeated, with fine sarcastic emphasis. "These things are considered Jewish. But if you accept Yeshua, you are no longer Jewish."

Unlike this form of Jewishness, "Messianic Judaism has emerged once again, like a garden in a desert." While most Jews don't care about God, and are more interested in preserving culture, tradition, and "the Jewish race," God isn't interested in outward trappings but in the inward heart of man. "This is Biblical Judaism—not the rote traditions of man, but the vibrant and indwelling presence of God in our hearts!"

As in so many other places, the Jewish community is made a backdrop against which Messianic Judaism stands. In this case, ethnic Jewish characteristics predominant among liberal Jews, which for the most part are portrayed accurately, are somewhat satirized and juxtaposed against the sincerity and Godliness of Messianic Jews. The predominant critique in this sermon was on the materialism of secular or liberal Jews, from the relatively neutral purchase of bagels and Chinese food to the more ominous "finagling" into a good deal.

It is not surprising that materialism is targeted, because it is often seen as the major obstacle to effective witnessing among unsaved Jews. Overabundance distracts and financial comfort muffles the ultimate questions one needs to ask in order to engage in a spiritual quest. A commonly voiced frustration is the complacent reaction some Messianic believers receive from friends and relatives: "If it makes you happy, I'm glad. But I don't need that God stuff."

Liberal rabbis, as leaders of this community, are dismissed as hopeless causes: "Some people ask, 'Why don't we see rabbis being saved?'" Daniel asked in a sermon. "The rabbis today, the few who read and believe in the Bible, are in the Talmud, not His word. God can't speak to the others, they are only philosophically connected to Judaism. In the end of days, rabbis will come to the Lord, but I'm not looking for it." They spend too much time on social work and Jewish history, rather than on the Word of God.

At the most extreme, liberal rabbis, as traditional Jews, can be seen as deceptive and dangerous. Kitty was outraged that the Conservative and Reform rabbis of her past "kept information" from her. "Then I *read* Isaiah, and then I got *angry*, because I thought, 'Well, why weren't we ever *shown* this?' Here we're such good Jewish people, and we go to Temple, and we read the prayerbooks. . . . I mean, this is *our history*. Why don't we really know it?" According to Messianic believers, therefore, liberal rabbis mislead, rather than lead, their congregations.

Nature and Culture

As shown in the last chapter, Messianic believers assert that "Jewishness" is natural. Unsaved Jews are thus sometimes seen as more "natural" in the sense of being unrefined or raw material. Because of this, the connection of unsaved Jew with "earthiness" and nature sometimes takes a less than flattering form. Occasionally people refer to the "carnal" behavior of secular Jews and Orthodox Jews. In fact, one man in his testimony referred to Orthodox Judaism as "carnal Judaism," referring specifically to *kashrut* laws to point out an Orthodox Jewish preoccupation with the physical, rather than the spiritual, universe. Another woman laughed at what she saw as the immoral and "disgusting" behavior of Lubavitch Hasidim that she knew, who sat "with their legs apart" in skirts. Paradoxically, however, Jews are also seen as the bearers of artificial culture over against the "natural" spirituality of Messianic Jews. The "man-made" rules of what is Jewish, whether the Talmud in the case of rabbinic Judaism or the "cultural rules" in the case of liberal/secular Jewry, add unnecessary complications to what should be a simple relationship to the Almighty.

This paradoxical symbolization of "Jew" as representing both bestial nature and artificial culture has had a long history in anti-Semitism. Indeed, the view of Jew as the carnal, violent rapist has co-existed with the Jew as perverter of culture in many societies, notably recently in Nazi Germany (Rubin 1990, 29–30). I emphatically do not mean to imply that Messianic Jews hold to Nazi beliefs! Still, some of the old classifications are alive and well.

When Jews encounter Messianic Jews, they are often shocked at the Christian theology espoused by these Jewish-looking people. How can someone who looks like my mother, my brother, my daughter, who wears a *kippah*, be seriously talking about the atonement by the blood of Yeshua, God's word in the New Testament, and the need for salvation from sin? For me, the theology was not alienating. I knew that Messianic believers held evangelical views, and I had been around enough evangelical Christians to be comfortable with these expressions of faith, to respect their depth, and even to admire their sense of a universe charged with Godly meaning. What gave *me* an uncomfortable chill was the enmity expressed toward other Jews. Somehow, these sporadic denigrations of Jews seemed to temporarily snap the sense of connection I felt toward Messianic Jews as Jews; while I could possibly understand the motivations of Christian Jews, I couldn't understand Jews echoing anti-Semitic sentiments.

It was not that I hadn't ever heard harsh words being bandied about between Jewish organizations and Jewish individuals. Jews are a self-critical people, and with quarrels lately between Orthodox and liberal Judaism, the rhetoric has gotten quite fierce. However, this disagreement was qualitatively different. The tales of plotting rabbis, satanically blinded traditional Jews, and carnally obsessed liberal/

secular Jews reminded me too much of persecutions past and present. Despite my sense of friendship, and at times even a feeling of kinship with the believers I met, remarks such as these would catch me up short and remind me of an essential "otherness" to the Messianic community.

How did these particular stereotypes enter into Messianic Judaism, a movement which purports to present Judaism and Jewishness in a positive light? This paradox can be traced back to the fundamentalist churches and individuals who supported missions to the Jews. David Rausch notes that despite the staunch support of Israel by Christian Zionists and their abhorrence of the overt anti-Semitism that could be found in places like Nazi Germany, these affirmative attitudes dwelt side by side with beliefs in Jewish conspiracy theories, the coming of a Jewish Antichrist, and the marking of Jews as Christ-killers (Rausch 1993, 205–210). Rabbinic Judaism was frequently referred to as lifeless and empty; Reform Judaism as overrational. Jews then sought spiritual satisfaction in all the wrong places: radical politics, Christian Science, theosophy, even moral corruption (Ariel 1991, 112–117; Evearitt 1989, 189–190, 202; Marsden 1980, 210). Sobel, tracing the history of Hebrew Christianity, rightly notes that these anti-Jewish suspicions become part of the Hebrew Christian church itself (Sobel 1974, 251), and thus, one can conclude, part of Messianic Judaism. While such language would provide an interpretive lens to members' experiences with the liberal Jewish community, it would even more thoroughly shape their opinions of Orthodox Jewry, which few encountered in any depth before they became believers. In the latter case, members have come to their knowledge more from Christian discourse than their own experiences.

However, intersecting with and congruent to the inherited rhetoric of Messianic Jews are the experiences of Messianic Jews as members of the counterculture. As seen in the discussion of testimonies, the protests that Messianic Jewish young people in the counterculture made against "establishment" Judaism were in many ways identical to the accusations that the countercultural movement made in general to the ethos of the parents: that they were bureaucratic, rule-bound, unnatural, formal, and forced. Not so coincidentally, these accusations mirror classic anti-Semitic stereotypes of Jews. The accusation that the Jewish "parent generation" is materialistic, "unnatural," and overly cultured is the same accusation anti-Semites make about the dangerous, cosmopolitan, modernistic, and corrupt Jews. The claim of the counterculture of returning to an effortless natural life mirrors the claim of Messianic Jews of returning to effortless, natural religion, removing the unnatural accretions of rabbinism. This "personal experience" of these now-grown countercultural children, which rejects the ethos of their parents, makes real the old anti-Jewish stereotypes. The materialism of the Jews, that anti-Semitic canard, takes on "flesh," becomes alive, because of the clash of values teenage Messianic Jews had with their "establishment parents."

The notion that Jews are dangerous is also supported by the experience of those who personally endured the intensive Jewish communal protests against B'nai Mashiach. For example, on the back of pictures of well-known anti-missionaries in Jackie's scrapbook were scrawled very unflattering inscriptions: "Violent, dangerous, a violent front man," "Devious con-man," and of the "Lie, cheat, steal, murder philosophy." There seems to remain an anger, sometimes directed against "Jewish leadership," for the systematic exclusion of Messianic Jews from Jewish institutional life.

In part, Messianic Jews try to be philosophical about their disenfranchisement, telling themselves that truth is not a popularity contest. A guest speaker at B'nai Mashiach, a Messianic rabbi, proclaimed that sentiment flatly; "You think the Jewish community will approve your beliefs? Don't kid yourself. One of the errors that we have had in the past is trying to prove ourselves to the Jewish community all the time. If I can only prove myself to the Lord, I don't care what others believe."

In an interview, one person put it quite clearly:

> I think that as Messianic Jews we feel isolation from the very community that we feel a part of. So you're right, it's difficult. You feel one with Messianic Jews. You feel a kinship to the Jewish nation and Jewish people, yet you realize that you're not part of it, but you want to be part of it, but you're not.
>
> I'm talking about that paradox. . . . We take the scriptures about the remnant, the remnant is the perfect role model for a Messianic Jew, because the remnant was so different from the majority, even though they were part of it. . . . So we feel that we're a remnant people. We feel that we're distinct, yet we're a part of the whole, and yet we're not part of the whole.

The "saving remnant" is a helpful mediating category between sustaining an ideological loyalty to the Jewish people and the reality of rejection. It allows the anger that Messianic Jews project onto the Jewish community to co-exist with their self-definition as Jews, indeed as the truest Jews. Still, as seen above, this does not eliminate the disturbing contradiction of having "your people" be "your enemy."

Many Messianic Jews, despite their frustration with the American Jewish community, remain eager to be recognized. An oft-told narrative (repeated at the 1991 "Messiah" conference) was the encounter in Israel of a B'nai Mashiach singing group with Shlomo Carlebach, the famous Jewish folksinger from whom they had taken their signature song. One of the members of the group recognized Shlomo Carlebach in their hotel. Immensely excited, she ran up to the rest of the group and started to tell them about it. "Shlomo Carlebach!" they exclaimed. They approached him and asked to perform for him. After they performed his song, the story continues, he was so delighted that he invited them back to a two-hour teaching session he was giving so that they could perform their songs. After the performance, they proceeded to "witness" to the room of Orthodox Jewish men until the wee hours of the morning. The awe they displayed with the repetition of his name ("Shlomo CARLEBACH!!!") and their undisguised pleasure at his acceptance of them (reportedly, when he was told about their beliefs he responded with: "Some like fish, others like chicken") show the strong desire of some Messianic Jews to be accepted by the mainstream Jewish community.[2]

When such inclusion is not forthcoming, a feeling of unjust isolation arises. At a regional prayer meeting, the couple hosting the meeting (Mike and Sue) asked for prayer on their behalf. Both Messianic Jews, theirs was the second marriage for both of them, with children from their previous marriages with Jews. Sue's ex-husband was having their son's bar mitzvah in a local synagogue, and the rabbi, knowing Sue and Mike were Messianic Jews, wouldn't allow them to participate. They were meeting with the rabbi that evening, and hoping for a change of heart. Individuals at the meeting prayed that the rabbi's heart would be softened, that he would become more tolerant, and that he should see that this was part of Mike and Sue's heritage, since they were still part of the covenant with the Jewish people. One woman emphasized in her prayers that Mike and Sue were entering into it in the right spirit, not seeing it as a showcase for Sue's son or a party and that Mike and Sue weren't "planning to burn a cross at the synagogue" and "hold a tent revival meeting." Even though the liberal Jewish synagogue is held up to scorn as shallow and wrong-thinking, here it becomes a desired space, part of the legitimate Jewish community that Sue and Mike long to belong to. Just attending the service wasn't enough; Jewish parents should be part of the ceremony, and so Sue and Mike sought that same privilege.

In this case, prayer helped the Messianic Jewish parents to cope with the situation. However, reactions to this kind of treatment differ. After seeing a film on how Israel is portrayed in a biased, negative way in American media, the leader of a Bible study group opened it up for discussion:

> Steve: How should we respond to this as Messianic Jews? Should we join major Jewish organizations? Also, does what Israel is going through right now remind us of our own experiences as Messianic Jews?

> Jane: I don't agree that Israel's problems are like our problems as Messianic Jews. Israel's problems are much worse than Messianic Jews. As far as action is concerned, I think we should do what it said in the film, we should talk to people about Israel. For example, my co-workers think of me as Jewish, so with them I could defend Israel. Even if they didn't consider me Jewish, being a non-Jew who supports Israel is an even greater testimony. We should also call in to talk shows, since they won't ask us if we're Messianic Jews.

> Lisa: To belong to any of the major Jewish organizations, you have to hide your faith, hide that you are a Messianic Jew.

> Steve: The Jewish community calls us traitors. How can we support Israel in them?

> Richard: Even Jewish organizations are not doing much about this problem.

> Jackie: That's right! When more of the members were teenagers, and were going to the two universities, Hillel told Messianic Jews to be quiet about the Palestinians on campus, not to make waves, because it would be more anti-Semitic for them. But Messianic Jewish students demonstrated

against Palestinians, when they got out of hand on Land Day, and we published pamphlets about it and everything.

Steve: Well, in those days there was something with the second generation, the post-Holocaust generation, "don't make waves." But . . .

Christine: I don't know, maybe I don't have the same kinds of problems because I'm a Gentile. I had no problems with being Messianic or associating with a Messianic movement. I was doing a paper on anti-Semitism for school and I contacted the director of ADL [Anti-Defamation League], and he let me interview him and he wanted to read the paper when I was done. He even wanted me to join the organization and participate in marches against the KKK. There wasn't a sense of exclusion.

Steve: It's not the same. The feeling of betrayal isn't there. For Gentiles, sometimes it's a problem, sometimes it isn't. In Jewish organizations, there are certain lines. You can't talk about your religious beliefs or convictions. Once you begin to do that, you've crossed the line.

Christine: Well, can't my being part of this organization serve as a testimony to my faith, that my faith would lead me to do this? I don't have to evangelize. . . .

Steve: Of course, there are all kinds of testimonies. But after you've been involved with a group for a while, you want to express your faith and to share it. They don't allow that.

May: I feel uncomfortable even in purely secular organizations, because after the lecture there is socializing and everyone wants to know where you are from and everything. . . .

In this interchange the dilemma is nicely put. Jewish believers feel like they want to do something for Israel, but know they are not welcome. (Indeed, the puzzlement of the Messianic Gentile woman is also instructive. While Messianic Gentiles want Messianic Jews to be accepted by the Jewish community, their experience of exclusion can be much milder, and thus they may not feel outrage or urgency concerning such exclusion). The ongoing sense of injustice is important as well. The leader of the group clearly wanted to make a link between the way Israel was being "bad-mouthed" by the American media and the way Messianic Jews were being "bad-mouthed" by mainstream Jewish organizations. The film itself was so strong that it aroused real feelings of anger against the media for their bias. By making this parallel the leader allowed that anger to be actively projected onto the mainstream Jewish community.

This projection of anger takes unexpected metaphorical twists. One man, responding to my question about how people in the congregation handle insults from the Jewish community, answered, "I don't think people are constantly wounded. We have a pretty tight community. It's not like we are insulted every day. It's not like we have this yellow patch on our coat or anything." Here, the Messianic Jewish experience is compared to that of the ghetto Jew, and the mainstream Jewish community plays the role of Christian/Nazi. If to be a Jew is to be persecuted, the Messianic Jews are "the Jews" of the Jewish community itself! At its most extreme, although this is not common, this anger can be transformed into a complete negation of unsaved Jews: "Pray for [Liberty], make those who say they are Jewish and are not[3] to come and bow down and accept you and enter into true Judaism which is Messianic Judaism."

A third response, beyond eagerness for belonging or bitterness, is to withdraw into the Messianic Jewish world as the believers' only community. The larger the movement grows, with the Gentiles in it somewhat accepted as "honorary Jews," the more its members can do in-house and the less they have to interact with the Jewish and Christian communities that disconfirm their self-definition.

This last understanding has been raised from a matter of sociological fact to political platform. At the 1991 "Messiah" conference, the suggestion was raised of developing a "*meshummad*'s [apostate's] ghetto," which would allow "distinctive action as a cohesive unit," establishing political strength so that the Jewish community would have to listen to their claims of self-definition.

These three approaches are not serial; Messianic Judaism employs all three simultaneously. An excellent example of this can be found on the subject of *tzedakah*, giving money to Jewish causes, a popular way in which Jews measure their own commitment to the Jewish community. Jews who may not belong to synagogues or other Jewish religious organizations find their sense of community in contributing to the welfare of Israel, local Jews, or Jews worldwide. The practice of *tzedakah* binds the Jewish individual more firmly to Jewish history and Jewish destiny. In the Florida Messianic congregation that I visited, children contributed faithfully to the Jewish National Fund, well-known for its program of planting trees in Israel. In 1995, Congregation Rosh Pina in Baltimore gave five thousand dollars for a new reservoir (Hardie 1995, 2). Another purchase of trees, this time by the MJAA for fifty thousand dollars (Henry 1996, 8), was eventually scuttled by the Jewish community when the gift became widely known.

However, when such outreach is thwarted, members can turn inward. Tom (see chapter 1) offered a unique perspective:

C. H.-S.: Do you feel any kind of solidarity with the Jewish people?

Tom: Yes I do. I think I feel more solidarity with the Jewish people, well I can't say that, than some people at [B'nai Mashiach]. . . . We're no better than the Orthodox or the Conservatives because we do to them what they do to us. And that's wrong, and I don't think they realize that they're doing it. They ostracize them just as much as you, as all the other denominations do.

C. H.-S.: That's true. You only hear one side of the story at [B'nai Mashiach], that's for sure.

Tom: Right. And I think that as Jews, no matter what we believe, I think we should all stand together. And I understand where the Orthodox are coming from because they're very, very religious. They don't want to do anything wrong as far as the word of God goes, but you still have to love your race just for that reason, because they're your own nationality, you know what I'm saying? You can't just, be Oh well, I'm a Messianic Jew, I don't want to have anything to do with you guys. Or I'm an Orthodox Jew, I don't want to have anything to do with . . . I think we should put aside all our differences and just unite and at least stand for one cause, for Israel, at least keep the state of Israel going and then worry about our differences later.

C. H.-S.: The reason I'm asking is that there's a lot of things that go on in the Jewish community. There's a lot of fund-raising.

Tom: Exactly.

C. H.-S.: You can't do it without money, and I don't see a lot of connections with [B'nai Mashiach].

Tom: Right. I think they don't do it because they're afraid of condemnation or something. I think the reason they don't is that they think they are labeled as Messianic Jews and that nobody likes them, which I don't think is true. I think if they would start outreaching and start doing things, they would be accepted. I'm sure the secular Jews have no problem with them. The only ones that might are maybe the Orthodox and maybe the Conservative, but I really don't think, but if they really started reaching out and showing, "Hey we're Jewish just as much as you guys are, except we believe the Messiah's come and you guys don't, but someday we're all going to believe the same thing, no matter what," I don't know. I think they're intimidated by their beliefs. I think they feel they let the Jewish people down, 'cause the way they talk, don't you get that impression?

C. H.-S.: That they let the Jewish people down.

Tom: That they're apologizing for their beliefs or something. If that's what they believe, stand up, be strong. Don't let your beliefs intimidate you [so] that you're not going to outreach to the Jewish communities, you know what I'm saying? Not outreaches to evangelize, but . . .

C. H.-S.: Right, to do what I just said, to give money and support in the physical sense. Would you feel it is a personal responsibility to give money to support Israel?

Tom: Oh, I do, I give money to plant the trees in Israel, I give money for sports for Israel, I don't give money to the Jewish religious organizations, but to the secular organizations, I'll give. I mean, I see nothing wrong with that.

C. H.-S.: And you don't give to Jewish religious organizations for the same reason that I wouldn't give to . . .

Tom: Messianic Jewish organizations, right.

C. H.-S.: Because you don't believe what they believe.

Tom: Right. But I would give if . . . If what we're doing is by God, then there's nothing anybody can do to destroy it. If I give money to anti-missionaries, that money isn't going to do them any good, really.

Although Tom's views about the openness of the Jewish community perhaps are overly optimistic, he contrasts his willingness to support the Jewish community with the fear and even guilt of the rest of the Messianic community, which prevents them from making such a connection. Thus, as one woman told me when I asked about giving money to the American Jewish community: "I give my tithe to the congregation. The Messianic Jewish community is my community." In parallel to the Jewish community, which has scores of organizations to raise and send money to Israel, an organization has been developed through the MJAA to give money to Israel—the Messianic Jewish Israel Fund (MJIF), which funds Messianic ministries in Israel both on an individual and congregational level and fights for *aliyah* rights for Messianic Jews.

However, seeing themselves as that separate from the Jewish community could lead to an unexpected consequence. By the time such strength is developed, Messianic Jews could weaken the remaining elements of their affective tie to the mainstream Jewish community. The greater the cohesive identity as "Messianic Jews," separate from "Jews," the more such a risk is run.

Yet, the alternative is that ever-present struggle of "which people are we," which can be exhausting at the very least. This is evident in the answer of one woman to "We are Messianic Jews, they are _____."

> Ruth: I don't know, it depends upon who I'm talking to. Well, let's say that you go to this conference in Argentina, and they're deciding to change the name of it from the Hebrew Christian Alliance to the Messianic Jewish Alliance, then they would say, "We are Messianic Jews, they are Hebrew Christians." OK. So let's say that you are in a synagogue and you're talking with people who are screaming at you, then I'd probably say "I'm a Messianic Jew, you're just a regular Jew," not *just* a regular Jew, but you don't want to say that "I'm a Messianic Jew, you're unsaved," you know. . . . Let's say I go and I sing in a church . . . how do I talk to them?

> Brian: As a Jew.

> Ruth: That's right. But then what do you say when they say, "You're a Messianic Jew, you're not a Christian," because they will, some of them, and then you have to go into the whole explanation, and if I'm tired I'll just say, "I'm born again, OK?" I just don't want to go into the whole thing.

CHAPTER 5

History, Prophecy, and Memory

> We . . . humbly request, as fellow Jews, and as fervent followers of the
> Hebrew Scriptures, that we be accorded the same respect, recognition,
> and rights as the rest of the nation whose heritage, history and destiny
> we share. . . . We are Jews. We were born Jews, and we will die Jews.
>
> *An Open Letter to the Supreme Court of Israel*, 1990:4

To gauge the affective depth of Messianic identification, we must examine not only the horizontal, communal dimension of belonging,
but the vertical as well. Connection to a people consists not only of
contemporaneous community, but also of selected attachment to the
words and deeds of former generations as well as a shared vision for
the future. Both Jews and evangelicals have strong views on the meaning of history and the direction of destiny, and the way that Messianic
Judaism appropriates its past and its future is largely determined by
their discourses.

History has always been important in Jewish life; the imperative
to "remember" is repeated throughout the Bible. While Jewish his-
toriography from Biblical times through the medieval period can be
seen as a vehicle for remembering crucial Divine-Jewish encounters
(Yerushalmi 1982, 11–24), the purpose of history began to change in
the nineteenth century. "The modern effort to reconstruct the Jewish
past begins at a time that witnesses a sharp break in the continuity of
Jewish living and hence also an ever-growing decay of Jewish group
memory. In this sense, if for no other, history becomes what it had
never been before—the faith of fallen Jews. For the first time history,
not a sacred text, becomes the arbiter of Judaism" (Yerushalmi 1982,
86). The very survival of the Jews through the depredations of the
Middle Ages and the horrors of the Holocaust points to a destiny beyond themselves and serves as a secular substitute for Divine cho-
senness. Emotionally merged with the painful and glorious history of

the Jewish people, Jews could find transcendent meaning for their lives in their commitment to that people.

Despite the importance of Jewish historical memory for modern Jews, memory as such can be difficult to sustain in American culture. As Robert Bellah points out, one of the enduring characteristics of American culture is the ability to start anew, to leave memory behind (Bellah et al. 1985, 55–62). In the 1960s and 1970s this element was accentuated as young adults, accustomed to rapidly changing technology and a TV culture communicating visual immediacy, favored the "now" of intense experience (Ellwood 1973, 8). Although the history of Jewish immigration to America and the events of the Holocaust and the founding of Israel have provided American Jews with powerful narratives (Neusner 1981, 1–11; Sklare 1974, 19–27), Messianic believers don't see Jewish history as the crux of Jewish identification.

This explains the bifurcation of the Messianic believers' attitudes toward history in general. On the one hand, factual history is perceived as utilitarian, a "science of events" that can prove the veracity of Biblical claims. Many of them spoke of how the historical accuracy of the Bible, both in describing events of the past and predicting events of the future, particularly the founding of the State of Israel, convinced them that the Bible was authoritative and could be trusted. On the other hand, history for its own sake is not enough. As one Messianic Jew stated, "I majored in Jewish studies. . . . I learned history, traditions, and that was only the tip of the iceberg. But no one really seemed to know God, or talk about Scripture. Our people are reading a lot of books and traditions, but only by reading the Scriptures can we know what God wants for us in our lives. Jewish history and tradition are exciting. I loved that stuff, history and traditions, I still do, but without the Scriptures, it's just history." As Daniel asserted in a sermon: "But if the Bible is just poetry, or just history, or just culture, it means nothing! I love the Bible because it is the WORD OF GOD!" The text, and the history it describes, is valued because it is "ontologically-charged language" (Soleau 1997, 818); it brings God's voice across the millennia directly to a believer's situation. While individuals in the congregation can and certainly do have a strong historical sense (several are quite learned, in fact), history is not emphasized in the public discourse of the congregation.

At a Bible study I attended early in my study, two Messianic Jews, Samuel and Sheina, learning I was not a believer, began to ask me questions intensively to determine my distance from salvation. Had I studied the Bible? Yes, I replied, but more from an intellectual perspective. Samuel started saying that the Bible was simple, that Abraham, Isaac, and Moses weren't seminary students. I answered, lightly, that knowing the truth would be easier if God was as discernible to us as he was to Abraham. "Oh, but he is, he is!" Samuel and Sheina reassured me. As Messianic believers, they could have the same kind of relationship with God as did Abraham. Biblical figures become important precisely because the gap of history can be eradicated; they can be made immediately present in the life of the believer. They are people "just like us." The historical patina that in other times and places suffused Biblical figures and events with a larger-than-life glow is absent.

In fact, critical historical consciousness comes into play not to bring aspects of the past near, but to relativize and distance them; for example, responding to Paul's admonition that men pray bareheaded (1 Corinthians 11:4–7), *kippah*-clad Messianic Jews sometimes say, "That was only for that period of time, but not now." To place something "in its context" often means to diminish or deny its relevance to the modern day.

However, the history of experience, meaningful events in one's own lifetime, is valued. This is borne out by a piece of an interview I conducted with the principal of Talmidim. I was asking about his claim that students are given freedom of opinion.

> C. H.-S.: But there are hard and fast ideas like 1967 and the outpouring of God's spirit? [that God's hand was definitely in the refounding of the State of Israel and the reunification of Jerusalem, and that they were both events on the end-time continuum.] Suppose a student said, "I don't believe this 1948 and 1967 stuff?" Wouldn't you be upset?

> Principal: No, I'd be happy that he cared so deeply about it.

> C. H.-S.: But what would you do?

> Principal: We'd go into God's Word and see which interpretation it supported.

C. H.-S.: But you do have an opinion, right?

Principal: Yes, because people in the congregation are products of that. We've seen it. We can be practical about it.

This last statement partially explains why the history of the State of Israel is strongly emphasized, since it has been experienced in the lifetime of these believers.

Although history and narrative are not as important to the congregation as in other religious groups, members do need to negotiate two areas of highly charged history. Both the protracted experience of Christian anti-Judaism and the contemporary catastrophe of the Holocaust threaten to put a wedge between Yeshua and Yiddishkeit.

THE HISTORICAL MIDDLE

For many American Jews, the long history of Christian persecution of the Jews creates a powerful identity structure. As it is recounted, Jews are victims—innocent, inherently peaceful, morally superior— in contrast to their violent and irrational persecutors. More than theological differences, this history seems to set Jews and Christians distinctly and irrevocably apart. Messianic believers thus have a peculiar loyalty issue. Whom do they identify with, the Christians who slandered, oppressed, and massacred Jews, or the unsaved Jews who suffered under Christian rule?

One way Messianic believers overcome this difficulty is by interpreting the historical division between the Jewish and Christian communities as a regrettable wound that their Messianic synagogues seek to heal; they see themselves reconstituting the time before the "enemy" became the "enemy," when Christianity was still Jewish. By locating their historical authenticity at a point before the Jewish-Christian rupture, Messianic believers hope to transcend the wishbone effect of being pulled into two different histories. By identifying with the first Yeshua believers, Messianic believers today assert that they are the true heirs of the original Gospel message, a claim shared by most Christian groups (Wacker 1988, 196–219). At the same time, they believe they are rediscovering the true spiritual Judaism that mistakenly became the "road not taken" with the advent of the Talmudic era that needlessly obfuscated the timeless truths found both in the "Old and New Covenants." Messianic Jewish history shows, in Daniel Chazan's words, "how Jewish it is to believe in Yeshua the Messiah."

This claim to *Jewish* historical authenticity is emphasized in an emphatic discourse. For example, a common evangelical outreach method is to point out perceived Messianic prophecies in the Hebrew Bible that were fulfilled by Jesus. Messianic believers share the standard evangelical list of Hebrew Bible sites for such prophecies: Isaiah 53, Isaiah 7:14, Isaiah 9:6–7, and Micah 5:2, among many others. This method, however, can have a far greater impact on Jews than other "non-believers," because if *Jewish* prophets actually foretold the Messiah, and Yeshua fulfilled those prophecies, than he must be the *Jewish* messiah, or so the reasoning goes. Thus Jesus receives a unique Jewish stamp of approval—"It's OK to believe in Yeshua! [Belief in] Yeshua is Jewish!" It is common, in the middle of a sermon, for Daniel to assert, "Sin is a Jewish concept!" "Satan is a Jewish concept!" "Sacrifice for sin is a Jewish concept!" "A relationship with God is a Jewish concept!" Looking at Romans 9–11, which pictures Gentile Christians as having been grafted onto the Jewish olive tree, Daniel interprets, "This is one fold—this is a Jewish fold and a Jewish faith, He's the Jewish messiah! We open up the fold to enter Gentiles into the Jewish fold!"

In one Sunday service in 1990 Daniel said that in order to find this Jewishness he had to put aside two thousand years of history, even persecutions that happened in the name of Yeshua, because this was a man-made dichotomy. In another B'nai Mashiach teaching session:

> There's no real conflict between the belief in the Jewish Messiah and maintaining one's identity as a Jew, but there is a conflict that has come up across . . . about 1800 years or 1700 years, of "church history" . . . that it is not the natural condition for a Jew to believe in Yeshua, that the natural thing is that the Gentiles, who by far outnumber the Jewish people, are naturally believers in Yeshua and that the Jewish people are naturally not. And this is not the case. The faith in the Messiah is a Jewish faith. The Messiah is Jewish, the Scriptures which prophecy His coming are Jewish, all the men who originally served Him were Jewish, the New Covenant Scriptures were written by Jewish men, and it is only across the span of this 1700 plus years that this attitude has crept in simply because the Gentile believers have outnumbered the Jewish people. (Cohen 1985a)

Beside the need to prove the Jewishness of the faith, a strong Pentecostal influence, coming to Messianic Judaism through the Jesus people movement, also reduces the pertinence of the bifurcated history of Judaism and Christianity. For Pentecostals, "virtually everything that had happened since the Day of Pentecost was pernicious at worst, irrelevant at best. . . . For most Pentecostals . . . the long history of the church was not so much evil as simply irrelevant" (Wacker 1988, 200–201). The Pentecost experience, described in the book of Acts as disciples of Jesus aflame with the Spirit of God and manifesting this experience through speaking in tongues, serves both as a model of Divine inspiration and a hope for a God-filled future. In 1985, one member of the congregation, speaking about a huge anti–B'nai Mashiach rally drawing angry Jewish protestors, praised the congregation's response of prayer and singing as a remarkably moving experience of the Spirit of the Lord. "I just consider that we were just a few moments away from an Acts 2 experience. . . . It could have been the Book of Acts all over again, and I fully believe that one day that is exactly what we will see." The mutually supporting influences that would call for the diminution of post–New Testament history—the Pentecostal indifference to that history and the American and countercultural trend toward immediacy—are enhanced by the inherent difficulty of the Messianic task to straddle the fence between Jewish and Christian allegiance.

Given all these reasons to let the historical middle drop out, it is not surprising that the Middle Ages are not a special topic of Jewish historical education at Talmidim. Most of the mentions of this history, in fact, are negative; from the pulpit, it is declared that Jewish and Christian history after the first few centuries created an artificial and unnecessary division between Jews and Christians. From a Messianic Gentile, "You had the rabbis going off this way, the Greek-speaking church going off this way, and what Messianic Judaism is, to my mind, is the repudiation of the medieval period, just forget the medieval period and get the people back to the Word of God." Even in adult education sessions (February 1991), which covered the Middle Ages in teaching about traditional Judaism, rabbinic writings of the Middle Ages were referred to as "the chain of distancing" [from God] and "All Man's commentary." God's hand in literature, according to Messianic Judaism, ended with the New Testament.

Although the historical middle in the congregation is mostly avoidable, examples of the cognitive and emotional labor involved in finding a middle ground can be found. Sometimes, it is the Christian side of the division that needs to be supported. During a session at the "Messiah" 1990 conference, the topic of Christian anti-Semitism was raised, and the audience began to shout out names of particular Christians known for anti-Jewish writings: "John Chrysostom!" "Augustine!" The speaker, a bit surprised, recovered and joked, "Yeah, let's get 'em!" He then followed with, "Let's keep it in perspective. I came to love the Lord through godly Gentile people." In this case, Christian anti-Judaism, even from those Church Fathers whose theology Messianic believers mainly ignore, could not be stated as a bald fact. It had to be tempered, reconciled, with the ties that bind Messianic believers to evangelical Christianity.

At other times, like the Protestant evangelicals with whom they are closely associated, Messianic Jews lay blame on the Roman Catholic Church for distortions in faith and practice. Messianic Jews can condemn Catholics for Christian persecution of Jews, the usual "villain" of Protestant theology, and still be part of the general "believer's discourse." For example, during the Yom Kippur service at B'nai Mashiach, I was puzzled by the recitation of *Kol Nidre*, a prayer which is commonly associated in the Jewish mind with the tragedies of forced conversions to Christianity, especially during the Spanish Inquisition. Why would Messianic Jews mourn over conversions to the correct faith? One woman I asked about this said, "I wouldn't want to become Catholic, either!" Here, once again, Jewish and Protestant contexts are highly congruent. The negativity towards Catholicism is not constant, but it serves in those moments when the Messianic Jew seeks to distinguish him or herself from Gentile Christianity without "rebuilding the wall of partition." It is easier to say that those Christians who persecuted Jews were not *really* Christian.

The historic relationship with Protestant history, however, brings in a greater sense of dissonance. While it is easy to reject the Catholic church, how is a Messianic believer to respond to Martin Luther, whose writings in later life, such as *Concerning the Jews and Their Lies* (1543) demonized Jews and Judaism (Oberman 1984, 113–124)? Most Messianic believers who treat this question accept Luther's anti-Semitism as an aberration, even the work of Satan blinding him to the truth, while they profess to love Luther for his role in the Reformation (Rosenberg 1995). Perhaps this ambivalent stance is made somewhat easier because Luther's hatred of Jews was effected with paper and ink, rather than with physical blows. Still, the complex reaction a figure like Luther can evoke is a good reason to ignore that part of the past altogether, as I found in an interview:

C. H.-S.: I ask you this because you said that you studied Jewish history in Hebrew School. How can you reconcile the history of persecutions when a lot of people did it in the name of Jesus?

W.: The one thing I learned is that just because someone says they are something, it doesn't mean they are. Even today they can say they are Christian, but are they really bearing fruit in that way? . . . If that's how they're going to behave, kill and all that, would God do that, would a loving God do that? No.

C. H.-S.: So none of these people who persecuted Jews were real Christians.

W.: No, not as far as born-again, I mean I don't know, God only knows, but I don't think so. I don't know if they were born-again, but think about people who hid Jews that weren't Jewish and risked their lives, in areas of France or wherever, so I guess the thing is that just because it's a bad salesman selling the product doesn't mean the product is bad.

. . . I think there can be born-again believers who are, I guess they can be anti-Semitic. Like there are certain things that cause division. They're wrong, obviously, because it's a Jewish Bible, it's a Jewish Messiah, but there were some people who didn't see that, like Luther. . . . We still sin. . . . Look at the Corinthians, look at the things that they were doing, but they were still saved. They still did immoral things, but they were still saved.

C. H.-S.: So who is a born-again believer is a gray area.

W.: Sometimes. But the truth is the truth, men are still men, and they still sin. The bottom line is the truth is the truth. Like if you talk to Orthodox people they bring up all these other things. They bring up all the other issues. They lose the issue. Is Yeshua who he says he is or not?

The last line of this interview segment is instructive. One can see in this question an allegiance to a transcendent Divine truth, compared to which peoplehood loyalty pales. Another interview expanded this idea.

C. H.-S.: Which are your people, the believing killers of Jews or the unsaved Jews who were being killed?

Y.: These are things that I've totally been thinking about, even like the past week. I've always related to the Jewish people because, for a lot of reasons. Because they're my people, my family came from Russia on both sides. I never could relate to Gentile Christian mobs doing things, I guess partly because I never could relate what they were doing as particularly Christian, in the sense of what the Messiah said and what is written in the New Covenant. I don't believe that the New Covenant is intrinsically anti-Semitic and I think that it was a feudal society. Everything was bound up in religion. The church and the state were completely intertwined. They might be angry and express it in a religious way. Take things out.

I don't know if they were doing it consciously as an excuse, but these things were completely bound up in their language. I don't see it as a Christian thing. I don't know, maybe these people did have a real relationship with God, but how do you define that, that's really hard. It's hard to do today, and it's hard to go back in history to see that. But I think it's really clear that there are things that just wouldn't be done by people that really loved God. They should love the Jewish people, I think that's in the Bible, so I don't really look at them as Christians.

C. H.-S.: Let's face it. There would be several centuries where you would be hard-pressed to find any Christians, according to your definition.

Y.: I don't know, it's a problem. I mean, when I think about the masses, a lot of them were really ignorant, I think a lot of them were taught, I think Catholicism was really far from what the Messiah was really teaching. I guess you have to call it Christianity, because what else are you going to call it? But it's not what I believe, it's not a Messianism that I can relate to. It's not a tradition that I feel that I draw from.

There was a confusion when these two members were pushed to articulate their loyalties. Both conceded that the dichotomy between being born-again and being anti-Semitic was not as clear-cut as the public rhetoric would indicate. While the first interviewee sought to move the argument to different grounds, the second tried to contextualize the response of the mobs. Although the second respondent did express an alienation from that form of Christianity, neither one could absolutely repudiate anti-Semitic Gentile Christians as "unsaved."

This dichotomy may be eased with the creation of a specifically Messianic Jewish history. During "Messiah" 1995, one Messianic speaker attempted to trace a Messianic Jewish lineage through the Middle Ages, citing the Pasaginians, a medieval heretical sect that believed in Christianity while following Jewish practices, as well as mentioning the possible crypto-Jew Columbus. In this way, the conflicted historical middle may yet play its part in the consciousness of the Messianic movement (Chamberlain 1995).

THE HOLOCAUST

B'nai Mashiach makes no public commemoration of the Holocaust. Significantly, while the congregation celebrates Israeli Independence Day, the day set aside in the Jewish community for Holocaust observance goes by without notice. Like medieval history, the Holocaust is not emphasized in Talmidim (it is taught as part of world history) or in Sunday school, nor was it covered in the Sunday adult education courses (although, again significantly, Zionism was taught for several weeks). While there is some awareness of it in the congregation, and an occasional activity concerning it, the Holocaust is more peripheral than central in the group's self-expression. For an American Jew raised in a synagogue and cultural milieu where Holocaust memories and metaphors were constantly evoked, the almost complete absence of such language in the congregation was noticeable. However, as we will see, the congregation has a kind of subtext about the Holocaust, an awareness that runs under the public absence.

The Holocaust presents an even more difficult issue than medieval anti-Judaism. "The Holocaust has become the primary historical event around which the American Jewish community unites. In media events such as the television series 'Holocaust,' in the proliferation of books published on the subject, and in the disproportionate popularity of college courses, Jewish identity in America has been tied to the Holocaust, perhaps to a greater degree than the State of Israel" (Biale 1986, 201). Painful memories of the Holocaust are shared, not only on Yom Hashoa, the day set aside to mourn the genocide, but also on Yom Kippur, the holiest day in the Jewish holiday cycle.

Part of the problem of the Holocaust is putting it in a theological framework. In Messianic Judaism, there are two extremes. Some see that Nazism itself comes directly from Christian anti-Judaism (Gordet 1989), and the other pole understands Israel's own sins, most specifically the rejection of Jesus, as the ultimate cause of the Holocaust

(Leventhal 1988, 106–107). Most Messianic believers find a position in between.

At the 1990 "Messiah" conference, I became involved in a long conversation that points out some of the theological dilemmas of working with the Holocaust. The first person I spoke to was a twenty-year-old Messianic Gentile, who said that the Holocaust was Satan's doing, not God's. I replied, "If God controls everything, and God controls Satan, then God must have caused the Holocaust." She said again that she didn't know, but the State of Israel came out of it. I replied, "That's a heck of a price to pay, especially because according to your theology, many of the Holocaust dead would be in hell." She said that the six million weren't damned, because "maybe they got an image of Yeshua right before they died."

At this point she graciously fobbed me off onto a Messianic rabbi. I asked the question again: "Why did God allow the Holocaust to happen?" In an annoyed voice, he responded, "How should I know?" Then, somewhat apologetically, he provided two explanations. The first was that God was inscrutable, the second that human beings had free will and the Holocaust was a result of the evil of mankind. At this juncture, I repeated my earlier question. I asked, "Doesn't God control everything?" He responded, "The harsh answer would be that they were sinful and were being punished." He compared this to a father who, when a child crosses a street without permission, beats him with a belt so that he will never do it again. "Of course, if you just see the father hitting the kid, you would think it was brutality." I answered, "This is different. You couldn't control your son from making the wrong choices. God is with us every minute. If He could save us, why didn't He? He doesn't need to kill us off. Would you kill your son in such a cruel way to prevent him from crossing the street?"

His answer then switched to "emphasizing the positive": "I do know that God's prophecies are being fulfilled." He talked about the regathering of the Jews in the land of Israel. He continued talking about the many miraculous things that God has done. I said, "Wait, but God has done some terrible things, also. When it's good we only ascribe it to God but when its bad it's our fault?" Suddenly, he looked at me, surprised by the question. "You are a believer, aren't you?" When I said "no," we moved to a whole other area of discussion.

In this conversation, a number of theodicies were attempted: Satan caused the Holocaust, the people in the Holocaust got their just reward in Heaven, Israel is the reward for the Holocaust, God is inscrutable, evil is the fault of human beings, Daddy God did it for our own good, and God is faithful because the State of Israel was founded. The sheer amount of "switching," especially on the part of the Messianic believer, shows how difficult it would be to present the Holocaust in any public way. Which theodicy would be chosen? This conversation also points out certain weaknesses in theology; trying to hold onto the "good Daddy God" imagery can lead to metaphorical absurdity, or at least triviality, in the face of such an event. Without the secular cushion of enshrining the victims without mentioning God, with the Messianic need for clear theological direction, this topic presents difficulties.

The response that "maybe they were saved in the end" was repeated to me by others in the Messianic movement. In only one interview was a person willing to de-sanctify Holocaust victims, and be willing to admit that they were damned. Significantly, this person is a second-generation Messianic Jew. "The Holocaust—any words I use are going to be insufficient to describe it. . . . But these people were going to die of something anyway. And I know that is sounding really hard-hearted, but I think that each person is held accountable for the way they lived, and they did live for a time. I look at people who live today, if a friend of mine would die today, it would be the same thing."

The struggles between seeing Holocaust victims as martyrs or damned might explain why Messianic Jews are led away from a more public presentation of the Holocaust. However, since many in the congregation were raised in the American Jewish culture of venerating Holocaust history, glimpses of "Holocaust loyalty" emerge in different places.

For example, I asked Stewart why the congregation showed a Holocaust movie in 1989. He replied at first, "We just wanted to show something of Jewish interest." Not satisfied with this answer, I probed, "A lot of people show things about the Holocaust and have an agenda of things they want people to learn from it. What do you want people to take away from it?" Speaking carefully, he said that he thought it was important for the congregation to learn about what happened, to learn about Jewish history, "to get it in their minds and in their hearts," that "our people have suffered, and we should know about that" so that it would "never happen again." He related the congregation's work in combating anti-Semitism in the churches as helping to accomplish that goal.

In that conversation, it was clear that Stewart knew the right "buzzwords" of the American Jewish community. The centrality of Jewish suffering and the necessity of ensuring Jewish survival was clear in his second answer. Despite this, his initial response did not include those buzzwords, which he gave to me only after prompting on my part. Rather, he began simply by saying that it was something "of Jewish interest" as if one was talking about an Israeli dance or a blintzes bake sale. He knew the American Jewish Holocaust litany, but its articulation had to be evoked.

The "evil" of the Holocaust, part of the general American vocabulary as well, is more easily found in Messianic Jewish statements. Hitler is still seen as the epitome of evil; during the Gulf War, Messianic leadership constantly compared Hussein to Hitler (as did American leadership!). Ironically, Hitler is also used as a measuring stick of Messianic Jewish identity. Since "Satan knows who is Jewish" by trying especially hard to kill Jews, and Hebrew Christians were also put in concentration camps, this validates the Messianic Jewish identity. If Hitler would have considered them Jews, so the argument goes, then they should be considered Jews by the mainstream Jewish community. I have already mentioned in chapter 4 the evocation of Holocaust symbols (the "swastika" and the "yellow patch") to indicate distance from and tension with the established Jewish community. These symbols of persecution are a part of the vocabulary of some Messianic believers.

As in the American Jewish community, Messianic Jewish Holocaust survivors and children of survivors have their own mystique. Survivors who are believers are especially important to counter claims from the mainstream Jewish community that the Messianic Jews are "finishing Hitler's job." Messianic Jewish survivors are their link to "true Jewish peoplehood"; Messianic Jews "suffered for their Jewishness too."[1] In line with this, a public claim to be a child of survivors is sometimes used as an implicit claim of Jewish identity by the speaker, a pedigree of authenticity. Thus, while the Holocaust is not often publicly commemorated, and hardly mentioned in sermons, there is a kind of subterranean connection to some of the "sanctified" elements of the Holocaust from the Jewish context.

However, it is unclear how long such attachments will continue. One Messianic Gentile, a relative newcomer to the congregation, to whom I spoke about my theory of the "absence of the Holocaust," gave a rather matter-of-fact answer to the lack of the importance of the Holocaust. "It's just history," she stated, surprised that I thought its absence was significant. As the years go on, the inability of this congregation to actively incorporate the Holocaust may lead to this evaluation being predominant.

ELLIS ISLAND: THE NEUTRAL ZONE

Unlike the Middle Ages and the Holocaust, Messianic believers can more easily appropriate the immigrant experience as part of their history. While the damnation dilemma still exists, immigrants are not sanctified victims, as in the Holocaust. And, unlike the Holocaust, films like *Fiddler on the Roof* and *Yentl* have romanticized the immigrant life, removing much of the hostility that actually existed between Jews and Gentiles in Eastern Europe. Thus, congregation members, in various ways, feel comfortable in plumbing this relatively unproblematic area of Jewish history.

One can see some symbolic ethnic expressions which connect to the shtetl–Ellis Island nexus. Messianic Jewish singing groups sometimes dress in costumes vaguely reminiscent of immigrant/shtetl wear (the men's vests, for example). One man, when talking about the problem with the zoning board when the congregation tried to buy its first building, said, "May God keep the zoning board far away from us!"[2] As mentioned above, some Messianic believers display in their homes American Jewish shtetl kitsch, including lachrymose rabbis and apple-cheeked *bubbes*, to demonstrate continuity with the Old World, "authentic" Judaism of their grandparents and great-grandparents.

Because the immigrant generation is commonly viewed by American Jews as more religious than present-day Jews, this neutral area of history is tailor-made for legitimation narratives. At least two Messianic Jews used the religious experiences of their grandparents to convey that what they were doing was authentic Judaism.

The first story was told to me by a lovely woman at a local Bible study, whom I will refer to as Nancy. She seemed to bring it up out of the blue, and when I wrote it down later I couldn't imagine why she had told me this story. Nothing I had said seemed to prompt it, and it seemed to be self-encased (after the narrative was done, our conversation of the moment also ended).

She began to talk about her Orthodox grandmother, saying she had just learned that this woman, whom she always thought was Orthodox, was not. Her grandmother started out as a radical, a revolutionary against the Czar. She was going to marry another revolutionary, but the pressure in her small town was enormous to marry someone "normal." Meanwhile, the man who later became her grandfather loved her grandmother, but she didn't love him. He had gone to America, and after her young revolutionary died, the disapproval of her was so strong in her hometown that she wrote him and said, "I don't love you, but I'll make a good wife." He agreed, and she took the boat to Ellis Island. Meanwhile, he had an accident and lost one of his legs, and was standing waiting for her, thinking that when she saw him she'd turn right around on the boat and go home. However, Nancy's grandmother said that when she saw him standing there, her heart just filled with love for him.

The couple had three boys, all of whom served in World War II. The grandmother prayed that if they all came back safely she would devote her life to serving God. They did all come back safely, and she became Orthodox, serving God "in the only way she knew how," by joining a burial society. Nancy said, "I just found out about this months ago; I thought she was always like this."

Now this is a fascinating story in any light. I certainly enjoyed hearing it, and I'm glad Nancy shared it with me. Still, I was puzzled. Why this story? And why tell it to me? While she and I had engaged in some small talk, much of our conversation up to that point had been colored by an "evangelistic" slant. The questions she asked and the topics she discussed seemed more thoughtful, more designed to get me to think about God and life in certain ways, than simply to engage me in aimless chatter. Besides, this story was told with particular intensity and verve. What was going on?

Then I realized that her grandmother's experiences paralleled in some way her own salvation experience, as well as the salvation experience of other Messianic Jews. One does not have to be born a traditionally religious person; her grandmother wasn't always that way.

In some ways, she was seeing her own experience validated by her grandmother's. The experience of a spiritual journey, far from being limited to Christianity, is also Jewish.

In another example, a Messianic rabbi was searching for an authentication of a Messianic lifestyle that included strong faith in God and some observance of Jewish traditions. Remembering with great emotion how his old Yiddish-speaking grandfather would stand all night and all day praying during Yom Kippur with hardly a break for rest, he said with fervor, "My *father* was there because he had to be there. My *grandfather* was there because he wanted to be there. . . . And he really believed that he was coming into the presence of God and to walk after Him." In this narrative, the Americanized father was the wrong model, while the grandfather, untainted by American ways, was showing true spirituality (Yellin 1988).

Clearly, in both the Messianic rabbi's and Nancy's narratives there is a deep affection and admiration for their roots. Nancy's narrative of someone who became God-fearing as an adult is a mirror of her own "salvation" narrative. However, note a key sentence in each narrative: Nancy's statement, "She served God in the only way she knew how" and the rabbi's sentence "And he really believed that he was coming into the presence of God . . ." serve to remind the listener, and the narrators, that neither the grandmother nor the grandfather were doing anything that truly brought them closer to God, according to evangelical beliefs.

Thus, these role models are never comfortably absolute. They are forever just a bit tainted. Included in the most positive affirmation of the Jewish past is a question, an underlying discomfort, a struggle for first-generation Messianic Jews.

ISRAEL

Israel plays center stage in Messianic life both in history and in prophecy. Evangelical and Jewish contexts are congruent here to a large degree; while Jerry Falwell and Menachem Begin may have disagreed about the spiritual meaning of the State of Israel, both supported Israel with the same conservative political vision. Messianic believers can strongly support Israel and feel comfortable, not torn.

Sobel provides another, very persuasive answer for the unwavering Zionist support of both Hebrew Christianity and, later, Messianic Judaism:

First, to be sure, it was important to stake a claim to being Jewish that could not be set aside by any deviation—be it to Christianity, communism, or agnosticism. If one who was born a Jew identified himself as a Jew (and what firmer affirmation of one's Jewishness than a desire to see the people reconstituted a whole nation in their own land?) then he *was* a Jew. . . . [H]ow could the Jews continue to stigmatize the believer as apostate, traitor, assimilationist, or worse? (Sobel 1974, 224–225)

Israel also reminds Messianic Jews of God's faithfulness and power. Every event in Israeli history, from its founding to the 1967 war to the Gulf War is framed as God's action in the world. Leaders of the congregation and the MJAA teach that Messianic Judaism is "spiritual Zionism," paralleling the development of "physical Zionism"; both manifest the Divine Presence in the flowering of the Land and the flowering of a spiritual revival among the Jewish people. Israel and the Jews are also the key to the end time, confirming the importance of Messianic Judaism.

Finally, Israeli history brings the Bible to life. A number of Messianic believers have visited Israel, either in their teenage pre-believer days or in their post-conversion days. According to Messianic testimonies, seeing the ancient Land where events in the Bible really happened started quite a few young Jews on their spiritual quests—if the Bible is suddenly made real, what about God? For those who were already believers, walking where Yeshua walked, visiting the Temple site, hearing modern Hebrew spoken, all confirm the authenticity of Bible-based faith.

This connection to Israel I understand well. Despite my less-than-successful encounter with Middle Eastern culture during my first trip to Israel at eighteen, I felt that my Jewishness was tangible for the first time. I could touch and see Jewish history—the synagogue at Masada, the archaeological treasures of Jerusalem, the mountain where Saul fought. There was something powerful in the rocky soil, in the rushing waters of Ein Gedi, in the wind that stirred the trees of our moshav at sunset. For the first time, I felt that there was something substantial in Judaism, something more real than holiday meals and the boredom of archaic English read responsively from thick black prayerbooks in a relentlessly suburban sanctuary. I can only imagine the emotional impact Israel would have for Messianic believers. Not only would the ancient stones and byways confirm the truth of the

Bible, but the revival of the modern State of Israel would serve as concrete evidence of God's hand in human affairs today, the same hand that, according to the Messianic movement, established and nurtures the spiritual revival of Messianic Judaism.

The unique outlook of Messianic believers intertwines their very existence more closely with Israel's destiny than even the average evangelical believer or normative Jew. For most American Jews, Israel represents a safe haven, Jewish survival after the Holocaust, and an ongoing Jewish future—as long as there is an Israel, there will be Jews.[3] For evangelicals, the restoration of Israel represents the fulfillment of prophecy and the beginning of the end time. For Messianic believers, all of these are true, but there is an even more intense bond to the Land—they see Zionism and Messianic Judaism as two sides of the same coin of revival. If Israel is weakened or destroyed, if the physical side of the revival fails, the spiritual side, Messianic Judaism, could become vulnerable. Thus, more so than evangelicals, even more so than many American Jews, Messianic believers need a strong, healthy Israel to sustain their identity.

During "Messiah" 1990, in a darkened gymnasium with over two thousand people, these connections to Israel were performed publicly. As the crowd sat in noisy anticipation, the theme music from the movie *Exodus* began to swell, and people in costume entered the auditorium. A historical panorama was enacted, beginning with Moses parting the Sea of Reeds through the tragedy of Exile. Suddenly, a light shone on an Israeli flag, and the room burst into applause. The physical regathering of the twelve tribes of Israel was dramatized. Then a new banner, with the word "Mashiach" written in gold letters, inaugurated a spiritual ingathering, symbolized by girls holding white candles running to the flag. This pageant makes clear that for the Messianic movement, Jewish physical and spiritual liberation are one.

The theme of how "Zionism and Yeshua go hand in hand" continued throughout the evening. Michael Chazan was compared to the Zionist Vladimir Jabotinsky; Zionist conferences of the nineteenth century were paralleled to Messianic Jewish conferences. The attempt of Messianic Jews to enter Israel under the Law of Return was likened to Jews unsuccessfully attempting to flee the Holocaust by going to Palestine. Finally, 1967, the year of the recapture of Jerusalem, was explained as the beginning of the outpouring of God for Jewish salvation, the beginning of significant numbers of young Jews accepting Yeshua as Messiah. Like physical Zionism, Messianic Judaism (spiritual Zionism) pioneered a return of the people to their roots—in their case, a return to their spiritual roots through a relationship with God. While a vast majority of the Jewish people didn't accept Zionism one hundred years ago, or Messianic Judaism today, through perseverance and hard work, declared the speakers, Messianic Judaism will succeed as spectacularly as the Zionist movement.

In the congregation, this parallel of Messianic Judaism as "spiritual Zionism" is taught in the Talmidim curriculum. The very Hebrew name of the school points to this self-conscious historical construction. One student said, "The way I grew up in [Talmidim] is the way I kind of fixed it in my mind and accepted it. That there was a physical Zionism, a physical revival of the Jewish people. Messianic Judaism is a spiritual revival of the Jewish people." In June 1991, the "Jewish history" month in the Sunday morning adult education classes was limited to a two-week teaching on Middle Eastern politics and a two-week teaching on political and spiritual Zionism.

It would appear from the link that Messianic Jews have forged between Israel and the Messianic Jewish movement that many Messianic believers would seek to live in Israel. Ironically, Messianic Judaism seems to have inherited the paradoxical form of American Zionism that infuriates Israelis, a Zionism that requires support of the State of Israel emotionally and financially, but discourages *aliyah* (immigration to Israel). As Daniel stated, "I don't believe all Jewish believers should make *aliyah* to Israel. I have seen some people who were called, and they do very well. I have seen some believers who were not called, and have misread the vision, and don't do very well at all. If you think that all Jewish believers are called to Israel, you're wrong." Unlike American Jewish Zionists, who have difficulty justifying their decisions to remain in comfort in the United States rather than move to Israel, Messianic believers can explain their reluctance as God-ordained, rather than a matter of individual choice. Ambivalence is curbed by reliance on God's guidance.

For those who feel called to live in Israel, their religious affiliation presents a real obstacle. Unlike others who are born Jewish, and can automatically become Israeli citizens under the Law of Return, Messianic Jews are understood to be Christians, giving up their Jewish identity with their spiritual choice. Like Father Daniel in 1962, any Jew who accepts Jesus has been understood by the Israeli government as eschewing membership in the Jewish people (Tec 1990, 230; see also chapter 7). As long as their faith was known to the Israeli government, Messianic Jews could still become citizens, but not *Jewish* citizens, and not automatically. Given their strong identification with Zionism, their desire to evangelize as many Israeli Jews as possible, and the ever-present need to authenticate their Jewishness, the MJAA and the congregation were involved in an effort for Messianic Jews to be allowed into Israel under the Law of Return. Instead of coping with their outsider status, Messianic Jews sought to change it.

In a letter written under the auspices of the newly reconstituted International Relations Committee (IRC), the Messianic Jewish Alliance of America explains Operation Joshua, the campaign to get Messianic Jews into Israel under the Law of Return, which began in late August 1990. On December 25, 1989, the Supreme Court of Israel turned down the appeal of Gary and Shirley Beresford, Messianic Jews, to change the Minister of the Interior's decision denying them the right to make *aliyah* under Israel's Law of Return. Living quietly in Israel, they were apparently "turned in" by their son, an observant Jew. Their case became a rallying point for Messianic Judaism and its Gentile Christian supporters.

The fight to be permitted *aliyah* isn't just a political maneuver, but a very emotional issue. One afternoon, after services, I was asked by Samuel to sign the Operation Joshua petition. Samuel was one member who always felt very alien to me, despite our numerous conversations at regional prayer meetings and congregational events. A bright man with a strong Jewish background—post–bar mitzvah study, rabbi's assistant—he joined Messianic Judaism in his twenties after military service and intensive Bible study. If anyone could be described as a zealot, Samuel would fit the bill. His side of our conversations usually included calculated, harsh, and sometimes unwarranted statements against present-day Judaism; he needled me about the abysmal state of Jewish Biblical knowledge and lack of faith, and, devoid of warmth and humor, answered my questions defensively.

I explained I couldn't sign the petition, because I couldn't agree that Messianic Jews should be given the automatic right of citizenship in Israel. Surprisingly, in his first display of spontaneous emotion, Samuel became visibly angry and upset at my refusal. "So, if a Saddam Hussein or Hitler comes to America, you would say that we couldn't go to Israel?" he said furiously. After exchanging heated words, we apologized to one another, but I remained surprised at the sensitive nerve I had touched. For him, this was a matter of personal safety; Israel was to him, as to other born Jews, the safety net from persecution. To have this security denied was the ultimate blow. No longer interested in managing their identity through internal reassurances of authenticity, in this instance they sought to change the facts on the ground—the very definition of "Jew."

Attempting to publicize its case and sway opinion, the Alliance published a full-page advertisement (Open letter 1990, 4). The advertisement spelled out the Messianic Jewish claims for continued Jewish identity. A partial paraphrase follows:

> 1. Born Jews who are secular, Hindus, Bahais and Buddhists can be Israelis, but Messianic Jews cannot.
> 2. In the Bible (1 Kings 18:20), Ba'al worshippers were still considered to be Jewish.
> 3. No, Messianic Jews don't accept the Oral Law, but neither do Ethiopian Jews.
> 4. Akiva followed a false Messiah, and was still considered Jewish.
> 5. Hitler would have counted Messianic Jews as Jewish.
> 6. If Messianic Jews are excluded from Israel because of their faith, who will be next?

More concretely, the IRC started a petition drive to get a minimum of one hundred thousand names both of Messianic Jews and evangelical Christians to pressure the Israeli government. In the Operation Joshua handbook of the MJAA, this is seen not just as a political effort, but also as part of spiritual warfare. "We know that eventually we will be granted our God-given rights in the land of Israel, but until then, we must be persistent in our efforts to bring pressure upon the earthly authorities in Israel. In the spiritual realm, we recognize that 'we war not against flesh and blood, but against powers and principalities'" (Messianic Jewish Alliance of America [MJAA] 1990). Thus, in this decision, the Israeli Supreme Court carried out Satan's wishes. In even stronger language, the handbook compared the fight for *aliyah* to other fights of the MJAA against the disseminations of *The Protocols of the Learned Elders of Zion* and against European anti-Semitism (MJAA

1990, 3). To liken this fight to battles against incipient Nazism again places the established Jewish community as an opponent. Thus, while Sobel was right that proving Jewish loyalty through Zionism appears safe, this fight for rights may lead to the unintended consequences of further emotional distancing from the Jewish community.

The struggle continues. While in 1993 the Beresfords were warned that their time in Israel would soon be up, the influence of evangelical Christians allowed them to stay in the country, but only on tourist visas. Two other Messianic Jews were contacted about possible revocation of their citizenship in 1995, but no action has been taken (Beiser 1995). Messianic Jews continue to attempt to enter the country secretly. At "Messiah" 1990, I was forbidden to attend a meeting of those Messianic Jews contemplating a move to Israel, lest I tell the Israeli government their identities; it was suggested in a main session at the conference that at a time when an overloaded Interior Ministry had to cope with an influx of Russian and Ethiopian Jews, now was the time for Messianic Jews to make *aliyah*. Authorities would be unable to check on the religious identities of the immigrants. Today, Messianic Jews continue to enter Israel covertly, while working toward a change in the law.

THE END OF DAYS

Everything that happens to Jews today bears a significance beyond the political, according to Messianic Judaism. All events, past and present, point to a physical and spiritual fulfillment that is just around the corner—the return of Yeshua. In B'nai Mashiach's dispensational timetable, in 1967, when Jerusalem was back in Jewish hands and large numbers of young Jews were being saved, the "time of the Gentiles" had ended. God seemed once more to be pouring out physical and spiritual revival to the Jewish people. The entrance of Jews to Israel from the former Soviet Union and Ethiopia is the fulfillment of the promise of the regathering of the Jewish people made in the Hebrew Bible. The existence of Messianic Judaism itself is the repentance sought by Isaiah and Micah that will bring the people of Israel closer to their God. Each of these developments is but the harbinger of the Great Tribulation of the Book of Revelation, a seven-and-a-half-year period of trial under the Antichrist that will culminate in the return of Yeshua. Jews and Israel now play a key role in these end-time events.

However, there are those in evangelical circles who would deny Jews their importance. Both in the congregation and at conferences, the prophetic movement alternatively called "Kingdom Now" and "Dominion Theology" was discussed with alarm. This "wrong" prophetic interpretation not only questions the Messianic Jewish view of the future but fundamentally challenges the Messianic Jewish movement's reason for being.

The most famous supporter of "Kingdom Now" is Earl Paulk, pastor of a large charismatic church. He espouses a postmillennial doctrine: Christ will return only to a vastly improved world created by a perfected church. Any mention of the end time in Scriptures was fulfilled in 70 CE when the Second Temple was destroyed and the church became the new people of Israel. The promises in the Bible relating to Israel therefore apply to the church—one should not expect a literal renewal of the Land of Israel or regathering of the Jewish people to precede Christ's Second Coming (Barron 1992, 69–71). This ideology has swept through charismatic churches from its introduction in 1984, attracting pastors with its upbeat message of empowerment to change the world for the better (Lindsey 1989, 36). However, for Messianic Jews, the adoption of "Kingdom Now" by those congregations with whom most Messianic Jews share not only evangelical theology but particular beliefs in faith healing, speaking in tongues, and other works of the Holy Spirit is dangerous. Interpret Biblical passages symbolically or allegorically, as do "Kingdom Now" followers, and the people of Israel lose their importance. Messianic Judaism's mission, to usher in the great Jewish revival before the End of Days, dissolves into a parochial attempt to convert a limited ethnic group for no apparent reason. The Messianic Jewish movement seeks support for its work among fellow evangelicals and charismatics; this theology denies them relevance and thus undercuts their very survival.

Even end-time blueprints that accord Jews a central place may be subject to modification. Although B'nai Mashiach shares with the Messianic Jewish movement in general a premillennial outlook, that Yeshua needs to return before the perfect millennium of peace and justice can be established (in contrast to the postmillennial, perfectible-world theology of "Kingdom Now"), Daniel strongly questions the idea of premillennial rapture.

Rapture is perhaps the best known of the elements of evangelical end-time events. Before the period of the Great Tribulation, many evangelicals believe they will be raptured, transported to Heaven, where the sufferings of the unbelievers under the Antichrist won't touch them. In the evangelical imagination, cars will suddenly be left without drivers, houses without occupants. "Particularly as Jewish believers, as we take a look at this rapture theory, we are redefining it, in the light that the Lord has given to us as far as Messianic Judaism is concerned. . . . With the pre-tribulation rapture theory, I believe there are certain subtle and not so subtle prejudices against Jewish people and against even Jewish believers. Some intend it, some don't."

This theory is problematic for two reasons. The most obvious is that it negates the very self-defined mission of the congregation and the Messianic movement in general. The large majority of unsaved Jews are expected to come to the Lord only during the Great Tribulation. However, if Messianic Jews are raptured up, no one will be around to fulfill the "Messianic vision" of "harvesting" new believers, and one of the main reasons for having separate Messianic Jewish synagogues in the first place is fundamentally challenged. This *cannot* be true in Messianic Jewish eyes.

The second problem is the lumping of that handful of Jewish believers with "the church" in the Rapture, which once again threatens the congregational claim that they are truly Jews.

> But what about us as Jewish believers right now? . . . Well, they'll say, "Well, you're a part of the Church. You're not really Jewish anymore. There are Jews and Gentiles and now the Church. . . ." It isn't true. We are a part of the Body of Messiah in that sense, but we have never given up that Jewishness. . . . They fail to understand the foundation of this very faith in the Jewish Messiah which is Jewish, one hundred percent through.

In a last, more altruistic emphasis, there was also expressed a concern about unsaved Jews going through the nastiness of the Tribulation. One woman told me it would be like an abandonment if they left the unsaved Jews alone to endure those difficult times. For all these reasons, Daniel reminds his congregation unceasingly, "We are going through it!"

CHAPTER 6

Practices, Rituals, and Life Cycles

There are a lot of pitfalls in Messianic Judaism. On the one hand, I've seen people go off into a Yeshua-flavored Orthodox Judaism, you might say. And let me tell you, Orthodox Judaism, I'm not interested in. Some liturgy of our people is fine, I think, that's good and we do it at [B'nai Mashiach], and I think it's important to maintain that. But I'm not interested in Yeshua-flavored Orthodox Judaism, are you? And our people aren't! That's why only a tiny percentage are in it! Nor am I going the other way, in which today there even seems to be a lot of Messianic Jews who are going away from their Jewishness and identity. The Lord impresses on me twenty years later, "Get more Jewish!"

Daniel Chazan

I think that's the exciting thing about Messianic Judaism, is that we're not afraid to walk down paths that have never been walked down before. We have the complete freedom to go by Jewish traditions, Christian traditions, or neither, because they generally are not the bottom line on really how we apply the Scripture. I think that's very important. We can be the trend setters, so to speak, in some of these areas.

B'nai Mashiach adult education class, January 13, 1991

THE FRIDAY NIGHT SERVICE

A typical Friday night service at B'nai Mashiach begins at eight o'clock. As you walk up to the low-slung white building from the adjacent parking lot, people are purposefully walking toward the building, almost all with Bible and notebook in hand. Most appear to be in their thirties and forties, some with children in tow, many greeting friends and acquaintances. Several teenagers outside are having a conversation, and at the front door a man greets and directs newcomers. Inside, in a foyer area where the gift shop is located, there are materials to pick up, including a list of weekly synagogue activities, brochures in English and Russian explaining Messianic Judaism, and a flyer for a special concert at B'nai Mashiach.

Walking into the sanctuary, you are hit by a wall of sound. The sanctuary, roughly hexagonal in shape, is fairly crowded with at least two hundred people in attendance, all seemingly talking at once. While many are dressed nicely, there are also people in torn jeans and long hair, providing an air of informality. Many of the more casually dressed, as well as some teenagers and some first-time visitors, sit in a section at the very back of the room. In the front is a raised platform on which are chairs as well as a podium with a microphone. At the back of the platform is what looks like the Ark, a raised "closet" that usually holds the Torah during Jewish services. At the side of the pulpit, at floor level, a group of six musicians are tuning up. The carpet is a rich red, the walls white, broken by windows and a few pictures, with a very clean, spare feel.

A young-looking, well-dressed man calls for attention, announces the beginning of the service, and prays to God extemporaneously that God's presence be felt in the service. Then the ushers in the back close the doors, and the congregation rises and the man leads the singing for the Shema. Both lines of the Shema are sung in unison to a traditional Jewish Friday night melody. Then, the man asks people to "turn around and greet one another." This greeting time lasts about five minutes. Some people are content to shake hands and exchange names, others will ask you more questions, especially if they have never seen you before. If you ask, you will learn that the "young man" is the Messianic rabbi, who is really in his forties.

There is an announcement of praise and worship. A middle-aged man is now at the podium, naming a song. Suddenly you hear loud, lively music, with a lot of percussion, the kind of music that makes you want to dance. And indeed, several people move up the aisles, look at one another, and begin to dance, forming a circle at floor level in front of the platform. Some songs draw in almost a hundred dancers in concentric circles; others are danced by a few women only, involving complex and flowing movements. The people dancing seem to know the dance steps well, and are smiling and happy.

In the congregation, some people sit and sing, others stand while singing, raising their arms up in the air, eyes closed, brows wrinkled intently. Some are smiling, others are laughing. You might notice someone behind you quietly murmuring in tongues, syllables that sound like a made-up language. You see first-time visitors nudge one another in delight at the praise and worship, or look on with a puzzled expression.

After a set of songs, the song leader calls up a singing group, accompanied with instrumental music, who will perform one or two Hebrew songs of impressive professional quality. You also see a performance of the resident dance troupe, in Israeli costume, dancing to Israeli music. The song leader will finish up with one or two songs, and then praise and worship is complete.

During the next hour, the service continues. After an exhortation that tithing will bring financial and spiritual blessings, ushers pass around baskets for the offering. The Messianic rabbi makes announcements from the podium. Congregation members pass out cards to be filled out by first-time visitors desiring further contact.

The room is then darkened. A married couple is called up to the platform. The woman, with a lace covering on her head, lights two candles set on a low table at the side of the podium. The woman circles her hands around the candles three times, and, covering her eyes, recites the following blessing: "Baruch atah adonai, eloheinu melech ha-olam, asher kidshanu bidvaro ve-natan lanu Yeshua meshicheinu, ve-tzivanu le-hi-ot or le-olam." Then she raises her hands toward the sky and recites the same blessing in English: "Blessed are you, Lord our God, King of the Universe, who sanctified us by your Word, given us Yeshua our Messiah, and commanded us to be a light to the world." After an extemporaneous prayer, she steps down from the platform.

The man in the couple then continues, reciting from John 7:37–38. "Yeshua stood and cried out, saying 'If any man is thirsty, let him come to me and drink. He who believes in Me,' as the Scripture says, 'from his innermost being shall flow rivers of living water.'" He then sings the full traditional Jewish *Kiddush*, sanctifying the Sabbath over a glass of grape juice. You notice that, as in a traditional synagogue, people join in singing "Ki vanu vacharta . . ." at the end of the recitation. You also notice that the *Kiddush* is not translated.

Then the man takes a tiny piece from the covered challah at the table, and says, "Yeshua said to them 'I am the bread of life; he who comes to Me shall not hunger, and he who believes in me shall never thirst'" (John 6:35). After reciting the traditional Jewish blessing for bread in Hebrew with the addition "be-shem Yeshua meshicheinu" (in the name of Jesus our Messiah), he eats the small piece of challah.

Following this you hear the announcement, "Now we will pray for Israel." This section includes prayer for the safety of the nation of Israel and the salvation of the Jewish people.

The lights are raised, children are dismissed to the "children's synagogue service," and for the next hour the message is given. You will notice there is a lot of humor and personal examples, and that verses from all over the Bible are woven together to form the "text" of the message. You probably will note the presence of B'nai Mashiach themes: revival is coming soon, the importance of prayer life, the need to share with unsaved Jews. You will also note some congregational members assiduously underlining in Bibles and taking notes in separate notebooks. At the end of the message, Daniel prays that those who are unsaved accept salvation, a prayer that recaps many of the themes of the message. At this point, you will hear the musicians beginning to play again. After this prayer, with "your heads bowed and eyes closed," Daniel asks those who accepted the Lord that night to raise their hands; each "thank you, Lord" indicates another hand that he counts. He then invites everyone to stand for the Priestly Benediction, sung in Hebrew and then repeated in English. The congregation is then dismissed.

If you decide to stay and chat, you may note knots of people discussing mundane matters, or praying together. If you are new to the congregation, and openly unsaved, a person from the congregation will probably ask you some questions—"Have you ever read the Bible?"—and show you some key passages, especially if you are Jewish. If you wander out into the foyer, you will see people eagerly buying materials at the gift shop. The last person might leave as late as an hour after services are over, at eleven o'clock.

ELECTIVE JUDAISM AND THE LAW

It is actually the ethnic definition and flexible parameters of American Judaism that allow Messianic Judaism to incorporate Jewish ritual practice at all.[1] Given Christian interpretation, combining Messianic belief with Jewish law would seem completely contradictory, and bound to fail.

The evangelical traditions shaping Messianic Judaism make the distinction between works and faith evident from the time of Paul. The rigorous demands of the Law, which no one can follow perfectly and which thus create unrighteousness and failure, are contrasted to the unmerited grace bestowed on a believer that makes one whole with God. Thus, anyone who follows Jewish law is suspected of not being a true believer, of being a "Judaizer," of trying to win God's favor rather than accepting His love through the salvific act of Jesus. Because of this concern, early Hebrew Christianity had decided not to highlight Jewish practices, and even up to the late 1960s such "Jewish practices" were carried out haphazardly, if at all. As Jackie Chazan said, in those early days "you could teach about Jewish Law, you could teach about Jewish tradition, you could teach about Jewish background, but don't observe anything."

At B'nai Mashiach, in a 1991 class on Romans, this subject is raised:

> If you use that [following the Law] as your measure of justification and of righteousness, when you hear about Yeshua, you don't need it. Isn't that right? You don't need justification by faith in Yeshua, because you already have justification by the doing of the Law. . . .
>
> The doing of the Law can never produce righteousness in any human being because the Law cannot be done, and the Law is designed to point up sin, so that we understand our need for a relationship with God. That's what he's saying here I believe, but you can't turn your back on that relationship using your efforts. They are actually mutually exclusive. . . .
>
> If you're doing the Law you're trusting in your own efforts, you're not trusting in God. And he's maintaining that the only way to become righteous is to trust in God. The doing of the Law cannot produce that trust in us.

However, once that relationship and trust are achieved by accepting Yeshua as savior, ask present-day Messianic believers, why *not* do those aspects of Jewish ritual and lifestyle that deepen one's faith and enrich one's Jewish identity? If one understands that one's salvation is not bound up in observance of the Law, one ought to be free to enjoy the positive aspects of Torah which, after all, was God-given. In contrast to an evangelical context that views with suspicion any "Judaizing" trends, "you pray about it and you choose."

This was not an isolated innovation in the evangelical movement. The patterns of Jewish practice instituted by B'nai Mashiach, and in general by congregations in the Messianic movement, follow what

Charles Liebman has called "folk Judaism," Jonathan Woocher has labeled "civil Judaism," and what Marshall Sklare observed in the worship and beliefs of Lakeville Jews (Liebman 1973; Sklare and Greenblum 1972; Woocher 1986). Alongside the more formal and authoritative understandings of Judaism emanating from American rabbinic leadership, there is a more informal understanding of how Judaism ought to be practiced that binds much of liberal Jewry together in reordering rabbinic priorities[2] and selectively observing ritual. Support of Israel and of democratic values can take precedence over prayer and study (Woocher 1986, 63–91). "Kosher-style" and "kosher-sensitive" replace *kashrut*; lighting Sabbath candles can be followed by a night of entertainment. "Symbolic ethnicity" (Gans 1979) enables American Jews to hold onto peoplehood and tradition without taking on overly burdensome requirements (Waters 1990, 147). One can pick and choose those elements of Judaism that most satisfactorily convey Jewish identity without accepting an entire official "package" of practices.

Messianic believers have developed explanations defending this "pick-and-choose" behavior as the *correct* religious response to the fact of salvation. One should not do too much; in fact, saved Jews who assiduously follow *mitzvot* even at the cost of cutting themselves off from the Gentile community show themselves to be not in a true relationship with God. The unity of all believers must not be riven by ritual. Still, it is God's will that a believer's Jewish identity be maintained; thus, the Holy Spirit is personally involved in guiding each believer to the appropriate level of Jewish ritual. The belief in God's special care and concern for each believer provides a surety of purpose that helps Messianic Jew and Gentile weather the confusions and tensions of identity negotiation, and helps them see any difficulties not as dispiriting confusion but as birthpangs before a glorious future.[3]

Ritual not only expresses the Jewishness of Messianic believers, but also fashions the identity of those believers. Performing Messianic identity through ritual creates a fact on the ground, an unarguable reality of men and women seamlessly celebrating Jewishness/Yeshuaness, an experiential bulwark against all external negation and inner doubts. In singing, dancing, prayers, and ceremonies, Messianic believers mirror to one another the strength of community, the authenticity of their identity, and their surety in the "Messianic Vision." Nowhere is this more clear than in their praise and worship.

PRAISE AND WORSHIP

As in the Jesus movement, the Messianic synagogue movement began to adopt contemporary musical forms to worship, with a "Jewish twist" of a strong rhythm and minor key. As early as the 1960s Jackie Chazan began to experiment with putting "Messianic words" to Yiddish tunes; one of those songs, "He Put Laughter into My Soul" is still used. Today, the congregation has a repertoire of over one hundred songs, out of which a clear twenty or thirty are the "favorites." Many of the tunes are written by congregants, some by other writers in the Messianic movement, and a few by Charismatic Christians. Music is used not only in praise and worship but also "plays under" prayers, setting the mood. Sizeable singing groups perform for the congregation as well as doing concerts in churches and at public gatherings.

The heavy reliance on music, the strong part it plays in congregational life, is significant. Despite fears of electrocution, a band played poolside at the "Messiah" 1990 *mikveh* (baptism). A running joke is that almost everyone in the congregation was once a member of one of the singing groups.

This emphasis has as much to do with the quality of musical experience as with the considerable musical talents of the congregation. The content of music is not discursive, but emotional (Merrell 1985, 73–74). Music, rather than linear thought, can make a worldview more vivid, more true, and more convincing (Schmid and Kess 1986, 12). In Messianic Judaism, Jewish-Christian consolidation is most powerfully expressed and experienced through their music. Melodies reminiscent of Eastern European and Israeli Jewish music evoke a strong positive connection to Jewishness while "praising the Lord."

Not only the music itself but the words of the songs powerfully pull together evangelical and Jewish themes. Although some songs are taken directly from Psalms, others have a meaning that is more significant to Messianic Jews. For example, a popular B'nai Mashiach song entitled "Sh'ma" sandwiches in between the first and second lines of that Jewish monotheistic credo another line in Hebrew: "the Lord is our salvation." However, the word that is used for "salvation" is "Yeshua," the same word that Messianic Jews use to indicate Jesus. Thus the translated line could actually read, "the Lord is our Jesus." This "double entendre" allows the congregation to affirm high Christology within a central symbolic affirmation of Jewishness, the Shema.

Many other songs weld "Jewish" and "Yeshua" themes together, often at the last line of a stanza or the last stanza of a song. A very subtle blending of such themes is in the very popular congregational song, written by Elisheva Shomron: "Holy, Holy, Holy is the Lord of Hosts, who was and is and who will come." Sung in Hebrew, the first three words of the song, "Kadosh, Kadosh, Kadosh" are also found in a section of Jewish liturgy called the *Kedusha*, where the congregation sanctifies God's name. A Jewish congregation will stand and customarily rise on tiptoe for each mention of "Kadosh." Thus, this song "feels" Jewish. However, unlike the *Kedusha*, which is based on Isaiah 6:3, the Messianic line is actually Hebraized from the New Testament, Revelation 4:8. The second half of the line in Shomron's song refers to Yeshua.

These songs, "Sh'ma" and "Kadosh," appear to express a holism between the Jewish and Christian worlds; they evoke something familiar in the Jewish context—the Hebrew language, the "Shema" and the "Kadosh, Kadosh, Kadosh" so familiar in a Shabbat morning service in particular—and reinterpret it into an evangelical context so that both meanings are affirmed simultaneously. In both songs, Jewish tradition can be seen as inadequate, for the words need to be changed to reflect the new realities of salvation. At the same time, the tradition is honored as the vehicle of these realities, in using both Hebrew and Jewish-sounding music. After all, it is only in Hebrew that the double meaning of Yeshua (referring to Jesus the man and salvation the concept) can be conveyed in one word. Jewishness is thus both transcended and privileged, a conundrum that leads to tension in other areas of Messianic life; here, communicated through melody and rhythm, it appears undivided (Bakhtin 1981, 298). Even for those who are simply aware that this is a Jewish-sounding song about Yeshua, the coalescence of Jewishness and salvation is convincingly conveyed.

Other songs convey a sense of structure, necessary distinctions between Messianic believers and others. "Fall upon Us Now" is a song that asks God for His Spirit to fall on the singers immediately and "with power," and was often sung in connection with exhortations for greater witnessing efforts among unsaved Jews. "He is my defense, I shall not be moved" is a song sung quite frequently at the conferences and in the congregation as a vehemently sung answer to perceived persecution of Messianic believers by unsaved Jews. Each expresses a division: the first, from the Gentile church, the second, from unsaved Jews. They reinforce the hierarchy that places the saved Jew above both the saved Gentile and the unsaved Jew.

DANCE

The other key part of praise and worship, the dance, also offers the possibility of structuring Jewishness and embodying identity (Hanna 1979, 104). Dance is part of congregational life not only in praise and worship (about six to eight "dance songs" per service), but also in the "special performance dances" in the congregation, which also fill each Messiah conference. Dance also is continually depicted in Messianic artwork and brochures. Children are continually performing dances at conferences or at congregational special events.

Messianic dance developed in concert with Messianic music. Some young Jewish believers entering Hebrew Christianity in the 1960s and 1970s had exposure to Israeli dancing through Hebrew school, camps, and the burgeoning folk dancing movement of that era. Israeli dancing was a symbol of Jewish pride and connection with the Jewish state. Thus, the young founders of Messianic Judaism actively enrolled in Israeli dance classes to learn the steps and transposed them into original Messianic Jewish dances.

Certainly, congregational dance can evoke many other associations besides Jewish ones, as both laity and leadership expressed them to me. Dance, in its flowing grace and movement, can parallel the flow of the Holy Spirit in the life of the believer. The kinds of people who dance together—old and young, men and women, Jew and Gentile—were noted by one congregant as a demonstration of the breaking down of man-made divisions in the Messiah, both now among believers and at the end of days.

Despite this, many of the social and hierarchical divisions present in the group are also reinforced in the dance. Because dance evokes bodily power and self-mastery it often reflects political power as well. Dance can serve to create a number of we-they markings (Hanna 1979, 128). This occurs in the praise and worship dances of B'nai Mashiach.

Because many of the songs have specific choreography, they cannot be danced by first-time visitors to B'nai Mashiach, but only by those who attended dance workshops and learned the steps. This separation has the effect of dividing the long-time members from the novices, allowing the more experienced group members to be the ones to express their salvific joy in dance.

However, while some long-time members have made dance a central activity, dancing most if not all of the tunes, these members often have a more marginal place in the power relationship than do the established leadership of the congregation. Active dancers include teenagers raised in the movement, the mother of a core member, a Gentile man finding difficulty gaining acceptance in the congregation. Perhaps in some ways dancing "proves their worth," demonstrates to the congregation and themselves their rightful place of importance in Messianic Jewish life. Dancing thus becomes a site of power, a place to express a belonging that some have yet to achieve.

The dance circles, taking place in the front space between the congregational seating and the leadership on the platform, reinforce the literally "exalted position" of leadership by focusing the congregation's eyes on that height differential. This division is both reinforced and undermined, however, by the ideological stance of both the congregation and the song leader which asserts that he is led in his choice of songs and style of leadership by the Holy Spirit; ideally, he is not powerful in and of himself but is merely a conduit for God's inspiration. It is not his power, but God's anointing.

Besides illuminating the leadership/laity differential, dance also is a site where gender relationships are mirrored. The men in the congregation occasionally dance in a men's group, putting their hands around each other's shoulders in a male friendship gesture. Once women pick up cues that this is a men's circle, no women venture in to dance with the men. When there are two concentric circles, it is more often the man's circle that goes in the middle. Even if a woman wanted to dance with the men, it might be difficult. The circle whirls twice as fast as usual, while the men seem to exert a tremendous amount of effort. This aggressive male dancing style has cross-cultural similarities (Hanna 1988, 29, 96, 161). In these circles, little flowing grace is shown; if God is felt to be present, it is God's power that is emphasized. The occasional separation of men and women in the dance and the aggressive/exclusionary style of the male dancing reinforces proper family structure within a generally more fluid gender interaction (Cucchiari 1990, 8). In the dance, then, members can fashion themselves as Messianic women and Messianic men, Messianic congregants and Messianic leaders.

It is also clear that dance is strongly connected with Jewishness. The leadership connects the presence of God evoked in praise and worship with the dances of the State of Israel, which embodies the historical mythos linking the spiritual Zionism of Messianic Judaism with physical Zionism. The dancing and music together resemble nothing so much as a Jewish wedding, a similarity that congregants themselves recognize, thus joining Jewish ethnic celebration with the spiritual "joy in the Lord." Because "[d]ance may often be a vehicle of self-assertion symbolically establishing identity as a counter to . . . a competitively heterogeneous situation" (Hanna 1979, 142), doing Jewish dance proves one's Jewish authenticity. Most important, because Messianic dance adds a spiritual spontaneity missing from "formal" and "dead" Jewish and Gentile services, it once again proclaims the superiority of the Messianic Jewish vision over and against the unsaved Jew and godly Gentile.

What is Jewish is admirable, fun, something ethnic and cultural to be proud of. Yet, what is danced at the front of the congregation is not simply the hora to the words of Jewish folk songs. The Israeli dance steps must be changed to evoke grace as well as liveliness, the emotion must be deepened by dancing for the Lord, not dancing in mere human celebration. It is Messianic Jewish dance that King David danced before the Ark, not, as one adherent put it, the artistic dance by the "nunny bunnies" of post–Vatican II Catholicism. It is Messianic Jewish dance that will lead the joyful parade into Jerusalem at the end of days, not the Gentile charismatic shuffle.

Dance thus becomes a central symbol of the saved Jew, in implicit opposition to both unsaved Jew and saved Gentile. Any time there are dancing Jews pictured in a Messianic brochure or in a painting, it seems intrinsically related to salvation. In Part II of "The Discipleship Manual," for example, which provides verses to witness to unsaved Jews, dancing Hasids dot the margins. These depictions of dancing Jews are everywhere. Two of the three pictures in the sanctuary of B'nai Mashiac in the early 1990s were of dancing Jews. Dancing Jews are on the front page of the congregation's songbook, and at "Messiah" 1990 at least half the paintings, drawings, and sculptures displayed dancing Jews. Dancing Jews are even part of God's communication. Lisa told me of a dream she had where members of the congregation were dancing by with me. She said she didn't know what it meant. Because this is the same woman who had a "word of prophecy" about my salvation, and this dream was subsequent to that word, I interpreted it as expressing her hope for my salvation.

What of the Messianic Gentile, whom doctrine delimits as, at best, a "spiritual Jew"? In singing Hebrew songs lustily, dancing Israeli dance steps, writing songs and leading songs, there need not be any barriers to feeling, to connecting, to constituting oneself as Jewish. In the ritual moment, a Gentile can be a Jew. In the ritual moment, salvation is Jewish. That is the power of the praise and worship.

HOLIDAYS

The greatest practice of Jewish ritual at B'nai Mashiach is during Jewish holidays. Celebrating Jewish holidays, and *not* celebrating Christian ones, confirms members' Jewish identity.

The emphasis on the Jewish holiday cycle comes directly from the American Jewish context. The American Jewish community finds its own distinctiveness in Jewish holidays versus Christian ones; celebrating Hanukkah rather than Christmas, Pesach (Passover) rather than Easter makes one a Jew. So if Messianic Jews are not supposed to assimilate, one of the major cultural resources for such identity are holiday observances.

Since Christmas and Easter are seen as hallmarks of "Gentile Christianity," these are not officially observed (although since the congregation contains a number of intermarriages, these might be celebrated with in-laws). The most popular holidays on the Jewish calendar are celebrated, since they are claimed to be "true Biblical festivals." A full slate of these festivals, including Rosh Hashanah, Yom Kippur, Sukkot, Hanukkah, Purim, Pesach, and Shavuot are observed, if not on the exact day of the festival, then on the nearest Friday night. The idea that Yeshua himself observed the festivals, as did the first-century Christians, makes these holidays seem both original and truer than Christian observances.

Holidays are also a special time in which Messianic Jews and Messianic Gentiles are encouraged to bring out their unsaved Jewish friends and relations. Yom Kippur is notable in this regard; it is the day when most unsaved Jews join the congregation in worship, attracted, in part, by the open services with no tickets required.

A Jewish reader might well imagine that Yom Kippur is possibly

the most difficult holiday to incorporate. For mainstream Jews, Yom
Kippur is the Day of Atonement, a day to pray, ask forgiveness for sins,
and be spiritually cleansed. For Messianic believers, who say they
already have a permanent atonement through Yeshua, what is the
purpose? Over time, Yom Kippur became primarily a day to rejoice
in the atonement of Messiah Yeshua; at B'nai Mashiac, celebration
rather than introspection is the theme. This emphasis took a while
to develop:

> [A Messianic song leader] was feeling a call years ago, on Yom Kippur, he
> was feeling an anointing of joy, suppressing it. . . . Eventually we began
> to go with that anointing. And only years later did we see that . . . God
> was calling us to walk in this. (B. Cohen, 1985)

This was the thrust of the three services the congregation held, at
night, the following morning, and in the evening.

One of the most interesting sections of the services was the *Al
Het*, the confession of sins that traditional Jews recite throughout
Yom Kippur. Once again, the Jewish context remained, but the
wording had been substantially altered. In the Messianic *Al Het*, traditional and Messianic lines were mixed together:

> For the sin we committed in Your sight in not looking to You, our First
> Love, and for the sin we committed against you through our lack of trust
> in Your Word [Messianic wording, especially the "first love" language].

> For the sin we committed in your sight unintentionally, and for the sin we
> committed against You publicly and privately [traditional Judaism].

> *We are thanking you O Lord, for your word teaches that you are slow to anger but
> quick to forgive us!!* [Messianic wording, replacing the traditional chorus
> that *asks* God's forgiveness].

This mixing puts Messianic content and a more positive frame on the
traditional Jewish confession of sins. One isn't asking God's forgiveness; one assumes it.

This message is explicitly repeated in prayers and sermonic
material:

> It's an appropriate time, when Jews are in synagogue. I remember when I
> went to the synagogue on Yom Kippur, I went and diligently sought God,

but I couldn't find Him until I had a broken heart to open my heart to God. . . .

You have a plan and a purpose for this nation, O God, which has been battered and broken over the years, now united again. Some Jews are not in the synagogue except for tonight, some are not in synagogue at all, some are in synagogue frequently. We lift up all of the nation of Israel, the greatest even to the smallest of them, religious and non-religious, we pray that a spirit of bitter weeping and mourning come upon them. They are seeking for the Messiah even though they don't know where. Touch the hearts of our friends and relatives, turn them to you, Lord.

Thank you for Messianic synagogues. Continue this mighty revival. Bring them to know You from the Scriptures, O Lord. *Praise* the Lord! [Big applause] (B'nai Mashiach Yom Kippur Service, September 28, 1990)

The mixed message continues. Jews are pictured as lost and confused. However, this is done in a context that honors Jewishness as well. This is a Yom Kippur service. The emotions of loyalty and peoplehood are evoked by the soft playing of "Hatikvah," the Israeli national anthem, in the background. The historical mention of being battered, broken, and then united also evokes the Holocaust-Israel story that shapes so many American Jewish lives (Lightstone 1995, 58). The Jewishness of Messianic Jews is highlighted even as it is contrasted with the emptiness of the unsaved Jewish life.

Hanukkah, another popular holiday, is problematic for Messianic believers for a different reason. The Books of Maccabees are not included in the Jewish and Protestant canons and even the tradition of the burning of oil for eight days is found only in rabbinic sources. How can Messianic believers claim this as a Biblical holiday? At least one Messianic Gentile to whom I spoke does not. Despite the congregational emphasis on the holiday, he sees it as a custom, like Christmas, and enjoys it without believing it to be very important. However, for some believers, the New Testament mention of Yeshua walking into the Temple at Hanukkah time (John 10:22–23) indicates his observance of the holiday.

Although the Gentile man was not terribly invested, the congregation as a whole certainly was. About three hundred fifty people showed up for the congregational Hanukkah celebration in 1990 on the Friday night of Hanukkah week. Decorations in the sanctuary mediated Christmas and Hanukkah messages; there was blue and white tinsel around the top half of the wall, pinioned by pink six-pointed stars. A big *dreidel* and *hanukkiah* cut out of paper hung on the left front wall.

On the left-hand side wall, a big blue banner said in red, on top, "Hanukkah, Festival of Lights"; underneath, in silvery writing, it said, "Yeshua, the light of the world." The intertextual play between these two statements points to the completion of both salvation and Jewishness, particularity and universality, in the Messianic movement.

During the service, a traditional Jewish Hanukkah song, "Mi Yi-malel," was sung by a congregational singing group. Though they introduced the song as "a traditional song done through synagogues all throughout the world in Hanukkah time," they changed the last line. "But now all Israel must as one arise, redeem themselves through God's own sacrifice" (obviously referring to Jesus) was sung, instead of the usual line, "redeem themselves through deeds of sacrifice." Investing Hanukkah with Christological meaning points out the superiority of Messianic Judaism.

Even greater emphasis is placed on the Messianic difference from the Gentile world, a pressing issue for Jews during the Christmas season. In several places during the evening, Jewishness was "proven" to be as good as or better than "Gentileness." Both in a saved and unsaved context, Jewish superiority was affirmed.

This global affirmation of Jewish pride might have indeed given Gentiles pause, except it was done by small children in a humorous way. A group of elementary school-aged children presented a musical skit called the "Eight Days of Hanukkah," sung to the tune "The Twelve Days of Christmas." There were eight posters, each lifted during another stanza of the song, which showed what was "given" on each day of Hanukkah in the song:

1. Warm bagel spread with cream cheese
2. Two matzoh balls
3. Three golden latkes
4. Four pounds of corned beef
5. Five kosher dills
6. Grandma's cooking
7. Seven Rabbis dancing [white bearded men]
8. Eight Fiddlers [on the Roof] fiddling

Now, such a satire is hardly unusual among elementary-school-age Jews. Indeed, many's the Christmas my friends and I sang that hoary seasonal favorite: "Deck the halls with balls of matzoh," or made jokes about "Hanukkah Harry" coming and leaving presents under the "Hanukkah bush." These satires are forms of resistance against the ubiquity of Christmas and the feeling each year of being "left out." Putting a pin in the Christmas balloon, mocking the high-toned Anglo-Saxon feel of the holiday by tainting it with Jewish categories was important to us.

However, such a satire remained private, at least in the circles in which I traveled. I can't imagine it ever being "sanctified" in a congregational event, with adults laughing and cheering, as it was in the Messianic Jewish congregation. In fact, the children performing the song appeared quite serious in the presentation; the adults seemed to get more enjoyment out of it. The enthusiasm with which this was received has to do with the precarious identity of Messianic Jews.

If American Jews feel alienated on December 25, how much more so Messianic Jews? Suddenly, they are a left-out segment of the Body of the Messiah, most of whom do commemorate Christmas. American Jews at this point can dismiss American Christians as "the other," but Messianic Jews can't quite do that. Moreover, they know that American Jews view Messianics as crypto-Christians, a threat to the fragile wall that separates the Jewish community from the seductive appeal of holly, mistletoe, and assimilation. Finally, they share with American Jews the haunting feeling that to abstain from Christmas is un-American, as the consumer hyperbole heats up, public buildings are decorated with lights and greenery, and office cubicles bear Santas and stockings.

One way of alleviating this multilayered tension is raising this typical Jewish satire of Christmas to a public, and thus sanctified, level, placing their overt loyalties with the Jewish community over against the Gentile community. As in other American Jewish satires of Christmas, the categories used revolve around food, rabbis, and fiddlers—the elements of nostalgic, cultural Judaism. Compared to the aristocratic tone of the "Twelve Days" (partridges in pear trees, maids a-milking), the Jewish gifts are deliberately vulgar and "earthy," thus providing the heart of the satire. The use of "vulgar Jewish ethnicity" transgresses the English Gentileness of the song; mocking the song at all shows an awareness of battling "Christmas consciousness." While the congregation is often ambivalent about a Jewish culture that values the material rather than the spiritual, here this physicality becomes a weapon to attack and vanquish the more sterile Christmas tradition.

Another way of coping with the ubiquitous presence of Christmas as an American holiday is to vaunt Hanukkah as an American holiday. As it celebrates the liberation of the land of Israel from oppressive rule, it is compared to the Fourth of July, with "fireworks" and "kosher hot dogs." Much as American Jews interpret Hanukkah in terms of American values (such as freedom of religion, a Constitutional concept no doubt foreign to the Hasmonean guerrilla fighters), here too Messianics seek to show that to be a good Jew is also to be a good American.

More explicitly, visitors and congregants are assured that being a Messianic Jew in no way catapults one into the Christmas tradition, in no way accelerates the disappearance of the Jewish people. Once again, adherents are assured, as they are on every holiday: "Messianic Judaism is still Jewish! That is the *whole point* of Messianic Judaism! To stay Jewish and remain a light to the nations—not to assimilate, but to stay Jewish!"

Hanukkah shows a strong adoption of the American Jewish ethic of the season. Unlike Yom Kippur, where unsaved Jewry is the focus, here Gentileness is clearly the assimilatory antagonist against which Jews must struggle. Although leaders in the congregation state time and time again that believing Gentiles are spiritual Jews, that their salvation is equally acceptable, holiday celebrations such as Hanukkah provide a rather different message.

LIFE CYCLE

Like holidays, life-cycle events have Jewish traditional practices with Yeshua-based spiritual content. Like holidays, life-cycle events often bring in large numbers of unsaved Jews with whom the Messianic community shares their faith. However, unlike holiday celebrations that are structured by leadership, the Jewish content of life-cycle events can be shaped by individuals and families, exercising the flexibility lauded by the Messianic movement.

The first Jewish life-cycle event impacting the lives of Messianic Jewish families is that of circumcision. "Circumcision is something someone will do once he has that relationship with God. That's why Abraham did that. Abraham circumcised himself and circumcised all the men in his household, because he had entered into that relationship with God and wanted to please God" (B'nai Mashiach adult education class, April 14, 1991). For baby boys, circumcision represents the continuation of God's covenant with Abraham, and God's promise of the Land of Israel to his descendants. Moreover, Messianic meanings are overlaid: Yeshua's new covenant of the circumcision of the heart (taken from Jeremiah 31:31–34 and Romans 2:29) is brought into the ceremony, to express a hope that the boy will one day spiritually fulfill the physical mark by accepting Yeshua (Rosen 1996, 12). Thus, Messianic circumcisions de-emphasize the communal dimension of traditional *b'rit milah* as a ceremony that decisively joins the newborn to the people of Israel, and emphasize the personal aspects of faith.

Finding a trained Jewish *mohel* (circumciser) to do a circumcision presents a different challenge to Messianics. Many *mohelim* will refuse to circumcise the boys born to Messianic Jews not only because they consider the Christian faith of the parents as decisively removing them from the Jewish community, but also because Messianics accept a child born of either a Jewish father or a Jewish mother as Jewish, which contradicts the traditional understanding that Jewishness is passed down only through the mother. In the past, this has led to some interesting intrigues to get baby boys circumcised. At the 1990 "Messiah" conference, I met a twenty-something athletic Messianic Gentile woman. During a break in the afternoon activities, we began to chat. She told me she belonged to a Messianic Jewish congregation in the South, and that a baby boy had just been born there. A *mohel* performed the circumcision. "He knew you were Messianic Jews?" I asked. She said he knew it, or at least she thought he knew it, but he didn't seem to mind. The attendees sang and danced but all in Hebrew and didn't mention Jesus. "He did the circumcision with the prayers and then we ate afterwards. He stayed for the food and seemed to have a good time." Whether or not this functionary knew of the family's beliefs, at least in Liberty area *mohelim* became so suspicious that any circumcision in the vicinity of B'nai Mashiach began to be questioned.[4]

Consequently, a small number of Messianic Jews have begun to train themselves as Messianic *mohelim*, offering their services not only to believers' boys but also to the unaffiliated unsaved, often in a Jewish-Gentile marriage (Rosen 1996, 12). This independence from the Jewish community may come as a relief to some Messianic Jews, who are ambivalent at best about their dependence on Jewish functionaries.

What of Messianic Gentile families? Once again, here they experience exclusion. Although some would like their child to be circumcised in a traditional manner, the Messianic *mohel* of B'nai Mashiach refuses to do so, stating clearly that the covenant of Abraham (and thus circumcision) applies only to the descendents of Abraham. Despite the vigorous assertions of spiritual and communal equality, the practices reserved only for Messianic Jews continue to make that group a somewhat privileged sector of the Messianic community (Kirsch 1996, 7).

After circumcision, or perhaps a naming ceremony for a girl, the next life-cycle event may well be baptism. When children accept the Lord, they are baptized in the "mikveh" (the swimming pool at the Messiah conference) by being fully immersed in water as a symbol of new birth. Many children make this declaration and are immersed at the age of five. This is considered a very important event. People often remember their "anniversaries in the Lord" and at the immersions I have seen, parents and friends jostled together to take videos and still pictures of their loved ones being immersed.

Some of the parents might decide to have a bar mitzvah or bat mitzvah for their child. At B'nai Mashiach, the bar mitzvah service is often structured the same way as a regular Messianic service, including praise and worship and a Torah reading of the child's choice. The "speech" that is made, if the child is saved, can include that child's testimony. For Messianic believers, this ceremony demonstrates a spiritual "coming of age," a chance to seek God on their own as adults (not responsibility for the *mitzvot* as is true in traditional Judaism) although as-yet-unsaved adolescents can also have a bar or bat mitzvah. (However, according to one young man, it just isn't considered as positive or powerful). Once again, the Jewish container is given a new meaning.

Weddings are also mainly Jewish in form, mainly Christian in content. While at B'nai Mashiach a *huppah* (wedding canopy) is used, the seven blessings are sung, and the wine glass is broken, the *ketubah*

(Jewish wedding contract) is not read. Instead, messages of Yeshua and his people as bridegroom and bride are discussed. In fact, the meaning of the wine glass is problematic, because its destruction traditionally represents sorrow at the destruction of the Second Temple that should permeate Jewish life, an interpretation that Messianic Judaism clearly rejects. At one wedding, Daniel said that "after a lot of study," he came to the conclusion that the real meaning of the glass breaking was the starting of a new life, and never even mentioned the Second Temple.

Because of the young age of the congregation, funerals of believers are uncommon. However, when one older Messianic Jewish woman who had been attending the congregation died, Daniel conducted the funeral in a non-sectarian funeral parlor. The coffin was open, and flowers as well as a large painting of the deceased was displayed. While this had to be done with the consent of the deceased's daughter, it gave a "Christian tone" to the room. Several people commented on the open casket. Still, there was a box of *kippot* available. When two men from the congregation entered and forgot to put them on, a woman from B'nai Mashiach fetched some for them, as if to emphasize, "This is what should be put on at a Jewish funeral."

As in other ceremonies, much of the form was Jewish, with the traditional psalms read at a Jewish funeral; Daniel even provided a slightly stumbling version of the *Kaddish* (the first I ever heard from a B'nai Mashiach member). There were changes, however. Within the frame of the service, Daniel made sure to talk about the deceased's spiritual salvation and the atoning work of the Messiah Yeshua (in fact he never used the word "Jesus" throughout the entire service). Despite one congregant who said that Daniel had spent time talking with the family about the religious views of the congregation, I remain unsure whether the woman's daughter or the few family members who attended ever realized that Daniel was a Messianic rabbi and that members who attended believed in Jesus. The daughter shook Daniel's hand after the ceremony. "Thank you, rabbi," she said gratefully.

OTHER OBSERVANCES

Food

Elective Judaism for many Messianic believers extends to the food they eat. "Biblical *kashrut*" is avoiding the unclean foods listed in the

Bible, but not being concerned with the special kosher slaughter of animals or the separation of milk and meat, which Messianic believers generally find to have no Biblical warrant. Biblical *kashrut* enables Messianic believers to refrain from eating pork and shellfish as a mark of both Jewishness and faith, but also to eat at Gentile homes and partake of everyday American food like McDonald's hamburgers. Unlike full *kashrut*, which restricts social intercourse between Jew and non-Jew, Biblical *kashrut* allows full interaction with Gentiles. It provides the gain of identity without the pain of exclusion.

This looseness enables Messianic believers to defend Biblical *kashrut* to Gentile Christians who believe that following any of the dietary restrictions is "Judaizing." Biblical *kashrut* is seen as acceptable, as long as it is part of a lifestyle, not a Law. One should not make unkosher Gentiles uncomfortable:

> There is a liberty in the law. . . . What if I'm in a Gentile's house, and want to witness to him and he sets down a plate of *hazzer* [pork] in front of me? Do I negate the witness of Yeshua because I don't want to touch something that's *treif* [not kosher]? (Yellin 1988)

In fact, one woman in the congregation tells a story of just such an event, when the members of one of the congregational singing groups, on a trip down South, ate pork breakfast foods so as not to offend a "good old boy."

The most common reason members give for keeping Biblical *kashrut* is that of a "proper witness" to unsaved Jews. Several people said that unsaved Jews would not listen to their evangelizing when the Jews discovered the Messianic believers did not keep kosher. For those unsaved Jews, this proved that the Messianic believers "went over to the other side." Thus, keeping Biblically kosher is once again seen as both identifying with the Jewish people and easing the witnessing process. One woman told me that if she ever lived among the ultra-Orthodox, she would keep rabbinically kosher, so that people would feel comfortable in her house.

Thus, the *stated* purpose of the "Messianic lifestyle," the explicit purpose that is acceptable to evangelical Christianity, is almost wholly outward-directed, geared to the audience that one expects to have. In fact, that is one of the formulas of success of Messianic synagogues; each should reflect the "Jewish lifestyle" of the Jewish populations in the area. As long as one does not "assimilate," the level of Jewish identity construction in ritual is definitely variable. Keyed into the pragmatic orientation of the movement, the appropriate amount of Jewishness is that which brings the most unsaved Jews to the Lord. Keeping a "Jewish lifestyle" is clearly a less important priority than one's "walk with the Lord."

However, there are some indications that, although this is the public rhetoric, soothing Gentile Christians who are afraid that Messianic believers are "Judaizing," the "testimony to unsaved Jews" is not the only explanation. Many Messianic believers during "testimonial times" talk about how they move in "believers' circles" too much of the time, and how they rarely see anyone who is unsaved, much less invite them to their homes. In that case, why follow Biblical *kashrut* at all? In fact, for those Jews who do keep kosher, Biblical *kashrut* is not acceptable, and Jews who *don't* keep kosher generally wouldn't mind eating pork and shellfish. Thus the public rhetoric, while "politically useful," is insufficient to explain the prevalence of certain customs.

This is borne out by several interviews in which Messianic believers say that while they began doing *kashrut* as a "testimony," they soon found other benefits for maintaining it, such as a personal discipline or a reminder of God's presence. One of the most common responses was that "they just felt the Holy Spirit leading them to it," a response that goes beyond the simple utilitarian maintenance of custom. As one Messianic rabbi put it, "Only demonic activity would tell us to disregard Biblical *kashrut* and the word of God" (Eisenberg 1988).

Clothing

The most common sartorial practice of Messianic believers appears to be wearing a *kippah* (skullcap) during services, donned by both Messianic Gentile and Messianic Jewish men. Occasionally these *kippot* will "proclaim their faith" in Yeshua, by saying in Hebrew around the rim "Yeshua ha-Mashiach." Another common practice, especially for women, is to wear identifying jewelry; Jewish stars are fairly prevalent, again among both Messianic Gentiles and Jews, while crosses are conspicuously absent. All of the members I asked about the *kippot* and stars said that they wore these objects not for any spiritual purpose, but to claim solidarity with Jews and for ease in witnessing to unsaved Jews.

The *tallit* (prayer shawl) is usually worn only by the leadership on the pulpit, as well as by the few visitors who think that such garb is appropriate. The reason for wearing it has nothing to do with the Biblical injunction to tie fringes on the corners of one's garment, the traditional Jewish purpose for wearing it; rather, Daniel explained to me that for him this was an imitation of the High Priest wearing special garb. Just as the *kippot* show identification with Jews, the *tallit* serves to identify congregational leadership. This is paralleled by Daniel's method of wearing the *tallit*; he leaves it folded up around his shoulders, looking more like a Roman Catholic stole than a traditional *tallit*. No one in the congregation wears *tefillin* (phylacteries), and only two men wear *tzitzit* on a regular basis, by tying fringes onto their belt loops rather than tying them onto the *tallit katan*, the traditional Jewish undergarment used for daily wearing of the fringes.

Why this choice of prayer accoutrements? The *kippah*, covering the head, is really the most problematic according to the New Testament, as Paul exhorted men not to cover their heads (1 Corinthians 11:4). However, those prayer accoutrements (*tzitzit* and *tefillin*) that are modeled to fulfill Biblical commands (Numbers 15:37–41; Deuteronomy 6:8) are not as popular. Why would Messianic believers stress the wearing of a headcovering, frowned upon by Paul, and ignore practices ordained by the Torah?

First and foremost, in the American Judaism of their youth, many Messianic Jews only knew of the *kippah* as the symbol of Jewish identity. The *tallit* is something that rabbis and cantors wore in synagogue—hence, it remains mainly confined to leadership. They may never have seen someone wear *tefillin*, which in any case might be too closely linked to the Orthodox community for them to feel comfortable in using them. Second, in a group that stresses spontaneity and bodily grace, the body is not perceived as something that should be externally wrapped and bounded, but internally guided and controlled. One member scoffed at the idea that the line in Deuteronomy, "You shall wear them upon your hand, they shall be frontlets between your eyes" referred to *tefillin* or any physical act; rather, its meaning was wholly spiritual, that whatever task one undertakes or thoughts one has, one should keep God in the forefront. (This person, however, was one of the only B'nai Mashiach members to wear *tzitzit*, taking Numbers literally if not Deuteronomy!) In general, congregational practice in this area remains a mirror of a liberal American Jewish norm.

Language

If one wants to symbolically connect oneself with a people, one of the easiest and yet most profound ways of accomplishing this is to use special terminology. Certainly, the spiritual code of B'nai Mashiach links adherents directly to the wider Spirit-filled evangelical community; words like "condemnation," "spiritual warfare," and "the anointing of the Lord" fill sermons, prayer, and conversation. However, the congregation also uses ethnic language to "name" their group and their affiliation. Both Hebrew and Yiddish are used by congregants to confirm their "Jewishness" (Saville-Troika 1989, 69) and also to eradicate the most "offensive" elements of Gentile Christianity.

Hebrew, used as the "holy tongue" among Jews and the "Bible language" among Protestants, is a language that conveys authenticity and authority in both of these cultures. Thus, Hebraisms allow Messianic Judaism to appear as it claims to be, "true Biblical Judaism." To this end, names such as Jesus, Paul, the New Testament, and words such as "pastor" and "baptism" are replaced by the Hebraisms of "Yeshua," "Rabbi Shaul," "B'rit Hadasha," and terms such as "Messianic rabbi" and "mikveh." For those whose Jewishness is so tied into expressive symbolism, these name changes are both significant and "really work"; people point to the names as evidence of the Jewish identity of the group. From a theological perspective, they "restore" the Jewishness of a Christianity clouded after many centuries of Gentile Christian distortion.

However, each word is not just a simple substitution, but evokes the absent "Gentilism" hidden under the Hebrew word. Certainly, anyone familiar with standard Christian terminology would hear in the word "tree" instead of "cross," and "B'rit Hadasha" instead of "New Testament," that underlying struggle with identity. And, because when there are a lot of Gentile visitors in the congregation, Daniel is sure to identify Yeshua as Jesus, this haunting characteristic of the underlying Jesus, the underlying cross, is occasionally highlighted explicitly from the pulpit itself.

Again, some other kinds of evidence support this incomplete erasure of Gentile Christian terminology. One woman spoke of her proclivity to cross out the name of Jesus when she sees it in a magazine or white it out in a Bible, and replace it with the word Yeshua. A visiting

Christian, presenting a marriage seminar, was apprised of the negative connotation of the word "Christian" to the Messianic audience,
and every time he used the word "church" to refer to B'nai Mashiach
a woman would hiss behind me, "It's a synagogue!" In the book *The
Calling*, the author can't leave old Hebrew Christian texts unchanged
in their quotations. In passage after passage the word "Yeshua" replaces the word Jesus, the term "Messianic Jew" replaces Hebrew
Christian, "Messiah" replaces Christ (Winer 1990, 3). Not allowing
original historical quotes to stand again shows a strong antipathy toward those very words. The words in their Gentile original, for some
Messianic believers, clearly evoke extreme discomfort.

Hebrew is also used to establish authenticity and authority in holiday and life-cycle observances. When Daniel uses Hebrew, in either
reading from the Torah or in a prayer, he demonstrates his qualifica-
tions to be considered a "real rabbi," for in the American Jewish context rabbis should know some Hebrew. While this reinforces Daniel's
authority, it also marks off the services as "real Jewish services" because of some use of Hebrew, confirming the Jewish identity of believers. Finally, some members of the congregation give their children Biblical/Hebrew first names, and some adults take on Hebrew
first names on their own. Again, this identifies the adherent not only
with the world of the Bible but also with their "Jewishness."

Yiddish words are also used, although not as frequently. When-
ever a Yiddish word is used in the congregation, titters are always
heard, titters that are never heard when Hebrew is spoken. Clearly
Yiddish has retained its powerful earthiness for listeners as a language
of the kitchen, of insults and of humor.

At B'nai Mashiach, the most common use of Yiddish is the word
kishkas (intestines), often to indicate the region where one should feel
the Holy Spirit operating, as in "deep down in your *kishkas*." The
Yiddish conveys the depth of the experience one should be having. It
also makes an important connection between the deepest part of the
"natural Jew," the *kishkas*, with the spiritual infilling of the Holy
Spirit, welding them together.

Yiddish has also been connected in the congregation with sexuality. At the dedication of their baby girl, Stewart and Lisa made
speeches. Stewart said, "We were wondering when to have children.
Lisa's parents dug a hole and planted a tree in the front yard. Then I
knew it was time to have a baby. Something clicked in my *kishkas*,

something about trees." There was a huge laugh. Daniel responded jokingly to this later: "You can plant as many trees in my yard as you want and it doesn't inspire me! [Laughter]. I'd be careful about that." Yiddish in this instance is again connected to humor and the body.

The Home

As part of the interview process and on some social occasions, I spent time in believers' homes. Those with any kind of Jewish artifact in their home were most likely to have Israeli artifacts, the choice of many American Jews as well. There were the usual assortments of Jewish kitsch from the Holy Land; camels, little brass liquor cups, olive wood carvings. On a more artistic note, some had highly colored artistic "primitives" of Jerusalem and Israel that are also quite popular among American Jews.

Besides artistic connections with Israel, another theme was "God hangings." Many homes had little Bible sayings framed and hung, or calendars with God sayings. The most astounding (and beautiful) artifact I saw was a full-size fabric wall hanging, sewn by Annie, that combined themes of Israel and the Bible.

Many of the artifacts blended Jewish and Messianic themes. For example, since there are "Messianic Jewish calendars" congregants can get the Jewish holidays listed along with Jewish-style Christological pictures and sayings. Holiday cards in different believers' homes included Hanukkah cards with mention of Yeshua, or Christmas cards with Jewish stars on them. Consonant with the congregational ethic, in no home did I see a cross, and on only some doorposts did I find *mezuzahs*. Gentileness tends to be eliminated; Jewishness is a choice.

The most common home observances are special Friday night dinners, lighting Hanukkah candles, and Passover seders. As is true of many American Jews, several congregants told me they observe holidays by showing up for the services run by the congregation, but don't necessarily do anything at home. Holidays (except for Rosh Hashanah and Yom Kippur) are generally not days to refrain from "servile work," and although some members say they try to take more time with the Lord on a Saturday morning, it does not seem to be uniformly observed as a day of rest. One of the congregational leaders helped someone move from the congregation on a Sabbath, another decided to put up his *sukkah* on the Sabbath Day.

Sukkah building is a fairly popular activity; I saw at least fifteen *sukkahs* that were erected by congregation members. The building of *sukkahs* is encouraged, in part, by the *Sukkah* hop, a night during Sukkot when a large section of the congregation, children and adults, go around the B'nai Mashiach neighborhood visiting people's *sukkahs* to dance, sing, and eat. This celebration emphasizes one of the cardinal rules of the Messianic Jewish lifestyle, "Don't forget to have fun." The recent popularity of *sukkah* building in American Judaism has much to do with the excitement the baby-boom generation found in "hands-on" Judaism; given the average age of B'nai Mashiac members, their interest in this activity is also to be expected. Once again, there is little in the pattern of Jewish behaviors that distinguishes Messianic believers from American Jews.

JEWISH GROWTH

In the past few years, much of the talk at Messianic Jewish conferences and now at B'nai Mashiach has focused on the increase of intensity and frequency of Jewish practices. B'nai Mashiach moved its service from Sunday to Saturday morning, the "real" Shabbat, creating controversy and losing members in the process. Other congregations associated with either the IAMCS or UMJC have added liturgy, trained Messianic cantors, and/or adopted a Messianic prayerbook.

There are several possible reasons for this shift. Some of the structural obstacles previously preventing greater Jewish content have been removed. The statement of reconciliation between the MJAA and the UMJC in 1993 removes "Jewish tradition" as a political football that divided these two movements; no longer does the MJAA have to see itself as "the party of reason," historically opposed to "the party of Jewish fanaticism" that the UMJC represented in the past. There seems to be a greater acceptance among evangelicals of the Messianic expression of Christianity and a greater appreciation of Messianic outreach capabilities (Anderson 1996, 51), which frees up those congregations dependent on Gentile good will to explore a greater level of Jewish ritual. Additionally, as more of the Messianic leadership is educated and ordained, not through Gentile seminaries, but through Messianic programs requiring courses in Judaism, increased knowledge can lead to increased practice. Finally, experience is also a factor: one leader remarked that twenty years of doing and learning about Jewish tradition has led to a mature, directed approach to integrating Jewish liturgy into Messianic services.

Others state that having more Jewish practices in Messianic synagogue life will bring in more unsaved Jews, who will thus perceive the movement as legitimately Jewish and be drawn toward salvation. At the 1995 "Messiah" conference, a *Jerusalem Report* article on Messianic Judaism was frequently cited by those advocating a greater return to ritual and liturgy. The *Report* correspondent pointed out a wide range of Jewish practice among Messianic Jews, from fairly traditional (and thus, seemingly sincere) to a group whose only evidence of Jewishness was a cross with a *tallit* draped over it (thus, seemingly duplicitous) (Beiser 1995, 28–29). Those in Messianic leadership leaning toward tradition used this article as evidence that the Jewish community would only be attracted to a Messianic Judaism with significant Jewish content. As Rick Smith, Messianic cantor of Beth Hillel in Atlanta, pointed out, "Liturgy is the history that is bound to our people, to the people of Israel, and when you ignore such a large part of history you are alienating the very people we are trying so desperately to reach" (Smith 1995). Those who disagree with the trend toward greater observance, such as Jackie Chazan, feel that Jews in general *aren't* attracted by more ritual, or else the Jewish synagogues would be filled. Adding more ritual is clearly the wrong direction. Her explanation is that this move toward tradition comes because the Spirit *isn't* moving right now to bring in the unsaved Jewish people, and so people mistakenly feel the need to "fill that lull."

Another reason for increased Jewish practice may be a greater need of tradition as a teaching tool, to keep the movement identified as Jewish. The Messianic movement is becoming more and more its own entity, institutionally separated from many aspects of "unsaved" Jewish life. The more Messianic schools, congregations, and literature proliferate, the more Messianic Jewish functionaries replace Jewish functionaries at life-cycle events, the less Messianic believers interact with the unsaved Jewish community. As the second generation grows to teenager and adulthood, having no knowledge of Judaism besides what takes place in Messianic synagogues, there is also a danger of this generation losing the sentimental attachment to songs and prayers that the first generation took for granted. There is a general fear of assimilation, paralleled, of course, in the wider Jewish community. However, while the Jewish community fears "melting" into the culturally Christianized secular milieu of Gentile society, Messianic Jews are more afraid of disappearing into the culturally Gentile evangelical subculture. David Rosenberg, a Messianic rabbi in New York, pointed out these dangers when he spoke about sobbing during the Mourner's *Kaddish* scene in *Schindler's List*. "How many of our children went . . . and missed the moment completely, had no emotional reaction to it whatsoever, because they had never seen it?" After a year of doing the *Kaddish* in his congregation, however, his son learned the necessary attachment to the prayer (Rosenberg 1995a). *Kaddish* was incorporated in weekly prayers as a way to emotionally connect with the Jewish people, to show honor to the deceased, strengthen Messianic synagogue–going among mourners who need to recite the prayer communally, and to impress unsaved Jews with the Messianic Jewish respect for tradition. Except for the last reason, all of these meanings of *Kaddish* are shared by American Jews, in contradistinction to the traditional interpretation that recitation will save possibly sinful parents from punishment after death (Donin 1980, 223–224; Millgram 1971, 155–156, 610 n. 24).

The inclusion of *Aleinu* in the worship at "Messiah" 1995 added to the Jewish daily liturgy because of its association with martyrs who chose death rather than baptism at the hands of a Christian mob, seems far more incongruous in the Messianic context (Millgram 1971, 455–457). The content, exalting the special destiny of the Jews over the Gentile multitude, has been modified in liberal Jewish circles because of its apparent ethnocentrism (*Gates* 1975, 615–621; *Kol* 1994, 444–445). This hardly seems a prayer likely to unify Jew and Gentile in the Messianic movement.

However, once again, the meaning the "Jew in the pew" gives to this prayer may well be quite different from the "official" version. One stands for the last time communally in the service, one bows and bends the knees at the appropriate spot, one joins in with the memorized Hebrew words and tune. When one hears the *Aleinu*, one knows the service is almost over. If the *Aleinu* was missing, its absence would be noted by even the most infrequent synagogue goer. The meaning of the words themselves for some worshippers may have less significance than the familiarity of the sound of the Hebrew words and music.

If this basic level of Jewish association with the *Aleinu* is accurate, Messianic congregations would have little difficulty incorporating the prayer wholesale. However, some precautions do appear to be taken by leadership. Although the prayer was sung in the Messianic

Torah service at "Messiah" 1995, the particularistic first paragraph asserting Jewish superiority was not translated, and the last line of the prayer, "On that day, may the Lord be One and His name One" was interpreted to mean that Father, Son, and Holy Spirit are one, and at the end of days, Jew and Gentile will be one. What could be seen as too particularistic a prayer for Messianic believers is carefully presented as an affirmation of the three-in-one Godhead and the unity of Jews and Gentiles in the Messianic movement, an ironic reversal from the traditional understanding. Its inclusion in Messianic services seems to have more to do with its expected place in a Jewish service than its traditional meaning or its history.

If one wants to save Jews, one must follow what the "folk" find significant, even if Messianic beliefs would clash with the official explanations of these prayers. If one wants to inculcate Jewish identity in the congregants and their children in order to feel like part of the people, it will do no good to create a Jewish identity that is out of step with the majority of American Jews. In these examples, Messianic leadership wants to use both of these prayers and is able to wed them to Messianic beliefs because of the altered significance given to the prayers by American Jews. Incongruous from an elite posture, adding this liturgy makes perfect sense given the associations of many American Jews.

As we have seen in this chapter, ritual plays an important role in managing the ambivalence present in Messianic Judaism. The very ability to create the types of ritual that characterize Messianic Judaism comes from the flexibility of elective Jewishness; the affective power of ritual blends the two cultures together, making Messianic Judaism "real" to its adherents.

It is this "reality" that the organized Jewish community attempts to fight. For anti-missionary organizations, Messianic Judaism is simply a fake perpetrated on an ignorant Jewish population. However, Messianic Judaism presents a notable challenge; the normative Judaism that institutional Jewry defends may itself be the illusion. Who and what is truly Jewish?

CHAPTER 7

The Saved *and* the Chosen?

[T]here is no universally recognized standard or authority in
Judaism. . . . If I want to be recognized as a Jew, I believe I must
know and live within the context of Jewish culture, however that
may be defined. I am married to a non-Jew; but that is not exclusively
a Messianic "ailment"; so are thousands of my fellow Jews. I (thus far,
anyway) do not keep kosher, but neither do most other Jewish people.
I believe in Jesus. Many Jews believe in Buddha, or Krishna, or nothing
at all. Who tries to stop them from being Jewish? Why should I be
treated differently?

L. Brandt, 1988:72

Messianic Judaism seeks to bridge both worlds, to be part of the "chosen" and part of the "saved." Messianic Judaism calls on Jews to accept
not only the Jewishness of Jesus but also to accept Christianity as part,
perhaps the only true part, of Judaism. It is thus the dangerous symbol,
the "theological transvestite"[1] that threatens to leach Christianity
into the Jewish home and synagogue under the name "Judaism." Such
a claim today offends most American Jews, who have an interest in
maintaining a firm line between Judaism and Christianity, especially
in an era of eroding sociological boundaries and accelerating assimilation. However, the Jewish community cannot dismiss Messianic
Jews as completely "Other," since those who are born Jews have a bio-
logical basis for belonging.

This partial inclusion, manipulated expertly by Messianic believers leads to the greatest challenge for the American Jewish community. As does any heretical group, the Messianic movement attempts
to prove its truths by critiquing contradictions found in the language
of the "establishment" group (Zito 1983). As Jews by birth, Messianic
Jews stake their claim as part of the wider Jewish community, con-
testing rejection by underlining the contradictions in contemporary

Jewish answers to "Who is a Jew?" and "What is Judaism?" Messianic Judaism thus holds an uncomfortable mirror up to the American Jewish community, a mirror that reflects fragmentation and uncertainty.

One can trace much of this fragmentation to the last two centuries of Jewish life. According to the traditional definition, a Jew is one who is either born of a Jewish mother or has been properly converted to Judaism. However, until the age of Enlightenment, being Jewish meant also to be in some kind of relationship with the Jewish religion. While Judaism has been sufficiently flexible in the past to accommodate a number of different visions (notably during the Second Temple period), for the past millennium Judaism has been decisively shaped by the acceptance of rabbinic and Talmudic authority.

Some view the weakening of that authority as the beginning of the modern period in Jewish life. As Judaism moved from the premodern world, the religious grounding that held Judaism together became less consequential. The Talmud and the rabbinical authorities were no longer as powerful as the ideology of personal freedom, a change abetted by the ruling powers who, moving swiftly toward nationalism, were no longer interested in ruling their populations by religious category. Jewishness became less a matter of ascription and more a matter of choice.

Out of this new freedom Jews discovered new ways to be Jewish, both religious and ethnic. The Reform movement, rejecting both Talmudic authority and Jewish nationalism, found the essence of Judaism as an ethical monotheistic faith. One could express a secular connection to the Jewish people through Zionism or other political and cultural organizations. There was no authoritative source, internal or external to Judaism, that limited such pluralistic fashioning of Jewish identity (Webber 1992, 246–251).

These trends, remarkable for the speed with which they altered the Jewish community, have accelerated further in the twentieth century. The state of Israel made secular Jewishness acceptable, and as some secular American Jews made Israel their "religion," they demonstrated unimpeachable Jewish loyalty without religious affiliation. The branches of Judaism themselves provide dazzling variety. Many Orthodox Jews, for example, believe in the Divine authorship of the Bible, the authority of the Talmud, the restriction of women from synagogue service leadership, and the practice of homosexuality as a

sin. Many liberal Jews in turn speak of the Bible as written by humanity, the Talmud as a guide rather than a standard of Jewish practice,
women as rabbis, and homosexuality as a lifestyle that can be sanctified through Jewish marriage (Greenberg 1996; Wertheimer 1993,
95–136).

Nothing in Jewish life has remained unaffected by pluralism—
even that touchstone of Jewish identity, being born Jewish. The Reconstructionist acceptance of patrilineal descent in 1968 was joined
by the Reform movement in 1983. Thus, in the American Jewish
community today are a number of individuals who would be considered Jewish by a large portion of American Jewry but not included as
Jewish by the rest, a confusion that is already leading to serious problems in life-cycle events and establishing Jewish families (Bulka 1984,
50; Cohen 1988, 5; Staub and Alpert 1988, 57–59).

Given the large variation within what is generally accepted in the
community as "Jewish" and "Judaism," is it possible to find a single
definition of either that includes all groups considered normative in
American Jewish life but excludes Messianic Jews and Messianic Judaism? Messianic Judaism challenges the normative Jewish community
to articulate its own boundaries. A seemingly simply task on the surface, it proves surprisingly difficult.

STATUS VIOLATION?

A partial acceptance of Messianic Jews has proven to be inescapable,
even by those organizations most set against the Messianic Jewish
movement. It is clear that despite Jewish protests to the contrary, Messianic Jews born Jewish are grudgingly recognized as such under Jewish law.

Conceding that some Messianics are indeed Jews by birth, some
Jewish authorities prevent their access to the Jewish community based
on the traditional exclusions of the apostate.[2] Even a statement created by the JCRC Task Force on Missionaries and Cults and signed by
representatives of the four major Jewish movements accepts the fact
that Messianic Jews are Jews by "status," although it strongly states that
their conversion to Christianity excludes them from all the privileges
of the Jewish community, including synagogue membership as well
as membership in Jewish communal organizations (*Meeting the Challenge* 1994). While one author argues that only a fundamental misun-

derstanding of Talmudic sources allows Jews to retain Jewish identity while accepting Christianity, and calls for a reclassification that would strip Jewish Christians of any Jewish identity under Jewish law (Friedman 1988/9), this opinion is at variance with the settled opinion of the majority. Jewish Christians, by their acceptance of another religion, have relinquished their communal ties to other Jews, but have not lost their fundamental Jewish identity in the eyes of God. It is their abandonment of Judaism, not their Jewishness, which is at issue.

The Israeli Supreme Court, refusing Messianic Jewish citizenship under the Law of Return, goes even further. Israel's Law of Return allows Jews and their non-Jewish spouses, children, and grandchildren to enter the country as automatic citizens. Those whose Jewish identities are otherwise uncertain (the Ethiopian Jews, for example) can be validated as Jews by being permitted to enter the country under the Law of Return. However, beginning with the case of Brother Daniel, and continuing with the Messianic Jews, born Jews who are also professing Christians have been denied entry under the Law of Return. Going beyond Jewish religious law, the Israeli Supreme Court has consistently ruled that accepting a Jew who chooses another religion violates the common-sense sociological boundaries of inclusion in and exclusion from the Jewish community (Tec 1990, 230). Thus, the Law of Return is a communal, not a theological arbiter of status.[3]

RELIGIOUS VIOLATION?

For those Jews accepting Jewish law as a standard of faith and practice, it is clear that Messianic Judaism can hardly be called "Judaism." Accepting Jesus as Lord and Savior, while acceptable for the Gentiles as inculcating respect for God and the Bible, is clearly understood as a religion that abandons absolute monotheism and is thus off-limits to Jews (J. Katz 1961, 165–168, 193). Rejecting the system of commandments in favor of salvation through human sacrifice also contradicts the very basis of rabbinic Judaism. For those who accept the authority of the Talmud, the Codes, and present-day rabbinic authorities, these lines remain carefully drawn. Even among Jews not particularly traditional, the belief in Jesus as God seems impossible for a monotheistic faith.

This exclusion rankles Messianic Jews, who seek to have not only their status but also their legitimacy in the community affirmed. They state that a two-thousand-year-old mistake is still a mistake; according to God's will as read in both the Old and New Testaments, the Jews were and are supposed to accept Yeshua. Even if one does not accept their religion as Judaism, they argue, is this an adequate basis for communal ostracism? After all, the American Jewish community is rife with well-accepted "heretical" Jews. Liberal Jews, who deny the Divine authorship of Torah and the authority of the Oral Law, wholly secular Jews, even Jews who follow Eastern religious beliefs are not systematically removed from Jewish life, but are in fact still welcomed into the community. Why, in the twentieth century, have the barriers fallen to include all Jews but themselves?

The acceptance of Reform Judaism as part of the community of Israel *is* an illuminating example of the flexibility of Jewish boundaries. Initially, Orthodox rabbis faced with the burgeoning Reform movement of the nineteenth century condemned its adherents in much the same way as Messianic Jews are censured today. Various rabbis in Germany and Hungary called reformers apostates (*meshummadim* and *mumarim*), deemed them worthy of excommunication, and forbade them communal privileges such as marrying an Orthodox Jew, having a Jewish burial, being counted in a minyan, being called up for Torah honors in a synagogue (all privileges that are presently forbidden to Messianic Jews). However, such sanctions were more a matter of wishful thinking than actual practice. The control of civil authorities over Jewish religious life put severe restrictions on the possibility of such a division. Moreover, faced with the twin dilemma of a rapidly growing liberal Judaism and a sharp rise in the number of Jews converting to Christianity, the rabbis eventually chose the lesser of two evils. Afraid that their rejection of Reform might lead erstwhile liberal Jews to embrace liberal Christianity instead, some rabbis began to distinguish between converts, who clearly intended to leave the community, and reformers, who were assumed to retain their communal identity despite their heretical ideas. The rapid rise of the Reform movement made them a majority in many communities; the ever-shrinking pool of Orthodox Jews could hardly tackle areas of community concern, such as growing anti-Semitism in Germany, without accepting Reform Jews as allies in matters of social concern (Bleich 1992; Ellenson 1987).

The legal responses of the Orthodox movement began to mirror this de facto recognition of the significant liberal Jewish presence in communities such as Germany. Reform Jews, as well as nonobservant Jews in general, were now interpreted as those who violate rabbinic law because of economic and social considerations, not because of deliberate ideological rebellion, and thus could still be considered part of the community. The temper of the times, with its laxity toward observance and its secular, materialistic outlook, created an entire generation the rabbis, basing themselves on Maimonides, classified as "children taken captive by Gentiles," a generation brought up ignorant of true Judaism and unaware of their violations. Such individuals were to be drawn back to Torah through love, not through sanctions (Bleich 1992, 91; Silber 1992, 73–74). Thus, by the end of the nineteenth century, while liberal Jews were still defined as sinners by the Orthodox rabbinate, they were rarely classified as "apostates" because of these mitigating circumstances. Even those calling for a separation of Orthodox synagogues and institutions from that of Reform, while not wishing to lend credence to a heretical system, still did not consider this to be a complete social or communal break with liberal Jewish individuals (Bleich 1992, 82).

Despite this softening of the Orthodox world, it is clear that liberal Judaism and Orthodox Judaism have little in common in their official religious languages, their behaviors, and their justifications of Jewish practices. Yet, despite the refusal of many Orthodox Jews to join non-Orthodox Jews in matters of religious policy, and the continuing struggle of the Orthodox rabbinate in Israel to keep non-Orthodox Judaism illegitimate, many Orthodox Jews remain willing to join with non-Orthodox Jews in matters affecting all Jews (for example, resettlement of immigrant Jews to Israel and anti-Semitism). Neither wrong belief nor wrong practice completely divide the Orthodox and non-Orthodox worlds, despite liberal Jewish acceptance of patrilineal descent that threatens to create two Jewish peoples, and in spite of intemperate statements that link liberal Judaism to Karaism (a medieval heretical movement) and to idolatry (Bleich 1983; Wertheimer 1993, 177). Present-day modern Orthodox rabbis, as did their predecessors a century ago, still cite the *halachic* ruling that liberal Jews should be forgiven their trespasses. Liberal Judaism, on the other hand, while increasingly chafing at the continuous delegiti-

mation of liberal Jewish organizations, rabbis, and rituals, more of-
ten seeks to maintain its ties with Orthodox Judaism as the bearers of
Jewish knowledge, the representatives of tradition, and, especially in
America, as the visceral reminder of the religion of generations past.

Turning from the massive, organized, public defection from
Torah-true Judaism that liberal Judaism represents for some Orthodox Jews, the existence of secular Jews in the community creates less
overt conflict. Those Jews, whom Larry Brandt refers to as "nothing
at all," compose 16 percent of all American Jews, over one million individuals, according to the 1990 National Jewish Population Survey.
Most of these secular Jews belong to no Jewish organization, religious
or otherwise; being Jewish is a status that they do not wish to activate
in any public way (Kosmin et al. 1991, 35). However, a small number
of these Jews have developed their own expression of Jewish identity:
Secular Humanistic Judaism, founded by Rabbi Sherwin Wine of
Birmingham, Michigan. Approximately ten thousand North American Jews (twenty-six congregations) are affiliated with the North
American Federation of Secular Humanistic Jews (Wertheimer 1993,
79), transforming Judaism into a religion glorifying the unlimited
potential of humanity rather than God (Wine 1978, 114–121).

Humanistic Jews indeed travel far from a traditional base. The
movement celebrates Jewish calendar and life-cycle events with
wholly secular content, expunging some prayers and fundamentally
altering others. There are now individuals training to become secular
Jewish leaders, performing rabbinic functions such as weddings for
secular humanist couples (Cherlin 1986). Rejecting religious conversion as the only avenue to the Jewish people, Humanistic Jews accept
as Jewish any person who identifies with the history, culture, and fate
of the Jewish people (Who 1989). This not only adds another definition to the overcrowded field, but, as one letter to the editor suggests
worriedly, could even allow "Jews for Jesus" to walk right into the
open Judaism that Humanistic Judaism has created (Roether 1989).

More recently, the Reform movement was faced with deciding
on the acceptability of Humanistic Judaism. When a Secular Humanistic congregation attempted to join the Union of American Hebrew Congregations (UAHC), it became a hotly debated issue among
the Reform rabbinate, some of whose members pointed out that the
Reform movement hardly required a creedal statement or belief in a

supernatural God for membership (Cohn 1992; D. Friedman 1992). While the bid for membership ultimately failed in 1994 (Edelstein 1994, 63), the willingness of even a minority of Reform rabbis and congregations to accept a secular Jewish congregation within their ranks is instructive. Judaism historically has been a praxis-centered religion, with some latitude on theological beliefs; today, this accepted latitude appears to include disbelief as well.

What of the clearest parallel to the Messianic Jewish case, that of Jewish Hindus and Buddhists? While acceptance of these individuals is overstated by the Messianic believers in order to make their point, there appears to be no concerted effort among most Jewish groups to exclude them from communal participation. In *The Jew in the Lotus*, Roger Kamenetz states that JUBUs (Jewish Buddhists) may comprise 6–30 percent of American Buddhist groups, far beyond their proportion in the population, many of whom practice Judaism and/or retain strong ethnic ties (Linzer 1996; Kamenetz 1994a, 7–9). Nor does communal ostracism necessarily follow. In a telling example, when a Jewish delegation of rabbis went to meet the Dalai Lama, the rabbis were concerned lest they would not be able to have a *minyan* (quorum) for prayers. When it was suggested that JUBUs could help make up the *minyan*, the idea was greeted with enthusiasm (Kamenetz 1994a, 30). One cannot imagine a similarly positive reaction to the inclusion of a Messianic Jew in a rabbinic prayer group.[4]

More commonly, self-identifying Jews seek to bring into or find within Judaism spiritual techniques learned in Eastern religions. A recent "Jew in the Lotus" conference at a Philadelphia synagogue attracted five hundred participants, including a large number of Jews involved in Eastern religions. Buddhist spiritual practices were seen as enhancing, rather than contradicting, the search for spirituality within Judaism (Anderson, Nov. 24, 1995). Some members of the Jewish Renewal movement have incorporated elements of Eastern worship and meditation in their own religious practices (Kamenetz 1994; Wertheimer 1993, 77–79). While some might consider them "fringe," few would exclude them from Jewish organizational life. Again, while Jews have borrowed from Christian practice over the centuries, it would be difficult to imagine a Jewish conference including workshops or classes demonstrating how use of a Christian rosary or being slain by the Spirit might enhance Jewish worship.

It is clear, then, that the present-day Jewish community contains a goodly number of "heretics" from one Jewish perspective or another,[5] even more than mentioned above if one includes the periodic Orthodox labeling of other Orthodox groups as "heretical." If one were to follow the great rabbi and philosopher Maimonides' definition, anyone who could not affirm one of his thirteen articles of faith, such as the resurrection of the dead, would be excluded from the Jewish community. If one were to follow a commonly accepted premodern definition, anyone who violates the Sabbath publicly is considered an ideological, deliberate heretic, not counted in the community of Israel. Both definitions would neatly decimate the American Jewish population (Lamm 1992, 150–158). Given the cost, it is not surprising that American Jews of all movements are loath to clearly identify boundary-crossers.

The exception, of course, is the Messianic Jews; the Jewish community is uniquely united in their condemnation of Messianic Judaism. The traditional allowances made by Orthodox Jews toward liberal Jews are not extended to Messianic Jews; unlike liberal Jews, Messianic Jews are not considered as "captive children" unintentionally violating Judaism. The core value of freedom of thought held by liberal Jews that enables them to accept secular Jews or Jews incorporating Eastern practices stops cold at Messianic Jewish theology; a Jew can believe almost anything but Jesus as Lord. Clearly, besides heresy, a more powerful dynamic is at work.

INNOVATION OR MASQUERADE?

An excellent example of the special treatment accorded the Messianic movement is the Jewish community's criticism of Messianic ritual, which they assert is merely a cover luring in unsuspecting Jews to evangelical Christianity. While it is true that one of the primary reasons Messianics practice Jewish ritual is to attract Jewish unbelievers, Messianics also claim that practicing Jewish ritual expresses their Jewish communal identity. Examining the latter justification, the Messianics are not the only ones to legitimate their Jewishness with religious ritual. Because ethnicity has been wrapped in a religious container, one of the only ways to express Jewish ethnicity is through religious language. One speaks of giving *tzedakah* even when the giving is in a wholly secular context, or of *tikkun 'olam* (repairing the world) for liberal political activity far from the original Kabbalistic meaning of uniting the Godhead. In Hebrew school, children are taught what Jews do on Shabbat and holidays, even though few families may celebrate either. The religious standard is still held up as the demarcator of Jewish identity.

This would explain the use of Jewish ritual by groups who transform the meaning of the very rituals they use. The presence of the ritual confirms the Jewish ethnic orientation of the group, but the original meaning of the ritual has been altered to express the core values, not of traditional Judaism, but of the group utilizing the ritual. Even small portions of the ritual or liturgy are sufficient to give the value expressed a "Jewish flavor" (Webber 1992, 260 n. 12).

The best example of such transformation has been the Passover seder, which has been celebrated as a feminist cry for women's liberation (Broner and Nimrod 1992), an interracial event upholding the American dream of equality (Fein and Saperstein 1996), and an Israeli-Palestinian gathering highlighting the suffering of the oppressed (New Jewish Agenda 1984). Liberal Jewish seders regularly transform the meaning of the traditional service from emphasizing the saving acts of God to the courage of humanity, as in the Reconstructionist Haggadah, which sharply elevates the role of humanity in the Passover story (Kaplan et al. 1941). Other holidays, such as Hanukkah, also reflect prevailing American values or secular Zionist achievements rather than a rabbinic religious message (Joselit 1992).

Just as Jewish religious forms express Jewish ethnicity or secular values in a number of transformed rituals, so too when Messianic believers sought to express ethnic continuity, they chose to infuse forms of Jewish life with a new, Christological meaning. However, unlike the general acceptance of or indifference toward alterations performed by other Jews, Messianic Jews are accused of using Jewish elements in their worship deceptively, warping the very essence of the Jewish ritual. At a rabbis' meeting I recently attended, where I shared some of the views in this chapter, attendees were alternately horrified and amused at my comparisons between "legitimate innovation" and masked Christianity. Once again, accepting Jesus places Messianic Judaism outside the boundary lines.

However, the reasons for this exclusion go far beyond the strictures of Jewish law, beyond the possible idolatry that Jesus represents.

Given the acceptance of some forms of Eastern worship and the understanding of the secular character of much of the American Jewish
community, given the far-reaching alterations liberal Judaism has
made in traditional Jewish belief and practice, given the almost universal Jewish practice of sanctifying American values through Jewish
ritual, it seems clear that what has provoked the ban against Messianic
Jews is not merely a flouting of *halachic* boundaries of belief or behavior. Rather, Jews who accept Jesus are understood to have committed
far more than the worship of a strange god; they have committed betrayal. Because for many the point of practicing Judaism at all is as a
"cultural totem," demarcating Jewish identity in contrast to the
Christian community (Schwartz 1995, 50), the Messianic use of such
practices to dismantle the very boundary between the Jewish and
Christian peoples sabotages the whole project of Jewish ritual.

COMMUNAL VIOLATION?

Several factors are involved in denying Jewish Jesus-believers a place
in the Jewish people. Historically, the long period of Christian persecution of Jews still resonates with the Jewish people, despite the great
strides that have been made in Jewish-Christian relations. Jews who
accept Jesus, therefore, are still perceived by many as becoming traitors to their heritage. Even today, one finds the most organizationally
alienated American Jew basing her Jewish identity as a victim, vulnerable to an anti-Semitism that is still perceived as an inescapable corol-
lary of serious Christian faith (Liebman and Cohen 1990, 49; Ribuffo
1989, 153). According to Marshall Sklare, not only fear but conde-
scension has kept a largely secularized Jewish population from examining Christian claims. Christianity has been viewed, by the American Jewish community at least, as an inferior, overly emotional and
superstitious religion compared with the intellectual rigors of traditional Judaism (Sklare 1993, 32). Jews who accept Jesus threaten that
automatic dismissal of Christianity.

Endangering that dismissal opens the floodgates. Jews have long
lived in countries with vast Christian majorities and tiny Jewish minorities; the United States is no exception. Given this population distribution, the Jewish community has struggled to maintain a distinctive identity under constant threat of assimilation. Although a Jew can
be liberal, secular, even Buddhist, these choices do not necessarily

lead to losing one's Jewish identity. However, in the insightful essay of Stuart Charmé, accepting Jesus is different. "[T]o embrace the *radioactive core of goyishness*—Jesus—violates the final taboo of Jewishness and brings immediate condemnation. Belief in Jesus as messiah is not simply a heretical Jewish belief, as it may have been in the first century; it has become the equivalent to an act of ethno-cultural suicide" (Charmé 1987, 28).

The type of "uncivil Christianity" Messianic Judaism represents only makes that suicide more certain in the eyes of the Jewish community. One might even imagine, for example, a group of Jewish converts quietly mingling Jewish and Quaker practice being considered harmless and even interesting, its members perhaps still permitted to take part in Jewish communal organizations as long as no one tries to convert unsaved Jews. However, conservative Protestantism has always made Jews nervous; the evangelical Christian proselytizes a Jew with the fierce devotion with which a hungry child contemplates his birthday cake. From the perspective of the cake, it is a rather daunting prospect.

Even worse is the nature of this particular birthday boy. For liberal Jews, especially, evangelical Christians are uniformly perceived as the Religious Right, understood as a group monolithic in thought, a threat to personal rights for women and minorities and to the separation of church and state, loosely associated with Southern rednecks, snakehandling, and preachers proclaiming that Jews will burn in hellfire. Evangelicals oppose the sanctified liberal values that have become Judaism for many American Jews. When this unattractive spiritual imperialism is given a Jewish face, when a Jew puts her trust in one who sounds and behaves like a Jew, only to discover the evangelical Christian beneath, it is experienced as a deep treachery, a type of religious "Invasion of the Body Snatchers." According to the Jewish community, resisting Messianic Judaism prevents the subversive disappearance of the Jewish people.

It is on this basis that Messianic Jews have been forcibly removed from American Jewish institutional life. There is an assumption that any Jew who accepts Christianity also accepts Christendom, fully divorcing herself from any Jewish identification and raising children with no Jewish identity. To become Christian is to eradicate Jewishness. Indeed, until the last century, most Christian denominations wouldn't have it any other way. "As regards the complete loss of personal Jewish status . . . nothing short of total personal alienation will bring it off. . . . If the apostate is to be expelled, he must first reject not only Judaism—as a religion—but Knesset Israel—Jewry as a people" (Lichtenstein 1963, 276).

However, unlike apostates of ages past, Messianic Jews enthusiastically embrace a form of Jewish identity, careful to inculcate this identity in Messianic synagogue, home, and day school. They claim solidarity with Israel and Jews worldwide. They are still loyal to the Jewish community, they assert—it is the Jewish community that has summarily rejected *them*.

If they do have a sense of genuine communal connection, this introduces an uncomfortable "gray area" in the black-and-white thinking concerning Jewish converts. Messianic Jews would challenge the notion that accepting Jesus means wanting to abandon Jewish membership. They distinguish belief in Christianity from joining a Gentile community, separating two terms ("Gentile" and "Christian") that are usually accepted as synonyms in American Jewish life.

Of course, the obvious question still remains: do they have a genuine communal connection to the People of Israel? This book has demonstrated that the Messianic attachment to Jewish peoplehood is certainly conflicted and at many points questionable. Some in the Jewish community would argue, with merit, that any group that consigns most Holocaust victims to Hell and considers the past two thousand years of Jewish history an unfortunate rabbinic distortion of true faith can hardly consider themselves as belonging to the Jewish people. To find Jewish history "bifurcated" by the Jesus-event, and to lose interest in the living culture of Jews that follows the events of the New Testament, seems inherently Christian, outside the pale of correct constructions of Jewish history (Krauscz 1993, 271). Their acceptance of Yeshua, especially, can be seen as a historical abandonment as much as a theological abandonment:

> That historical memory, alive in action, thought, feeling, language: That is essential to the responsibility of the Jew as Jew. . . . It may be seen in the extraordinary fusion achieved by the word "baptism," as Primo Levi uses it to describe the tattooing on his arm on his arrival at Auschwitz. . . . The transformation of Primo Levi to Haftling 174517 is thus linked to centuries of Christian anti-Semitism and the will to baptize Jews and the "Jewish problem" into nonexistence. (Goldstein 1993, 104–105)

By accepting Yeshua, Messianics no longer seem to share the common history, common destiny, and sense of mutual responsibility that is the glue of Jewish communal life.

Despite the visceral estrangement that many Jews feel when encountering these aspects of Messianic ideology, there are certainly no standards to establish legitimate or illegitimate configurations of Jewish historical consciousness among American Jews. One does not need to have a historical awareness of medieval Judaism or approve the Talmud to be considered part of the Jewish people; both the Reform movement and Zionism in earlier times neatly passed over the rabbinic era to find inspiration in the prophets and warriors of Biblical Israel. One does not have to find Christianity and anti-Semitism synonymous to be considered a good Jew. And, while "damnation" seems an especially repugnant repudiation of common fate, especially when applying eternal hellfire to Holocaust victims who already were burned in the crematoria, even the rabbis of the Talmud considered the possibility of eternal consignment to *Gehinnom* (Gehenna), a place of torment and fire, for those who reject the resurrection of the dead or lead the masses to sin, even one who publicly shames his neighbor (Raphael 1996, 145). While most rabbinic texts refer to *Gehinnom* as a temporary assignment, and almost all Jews today would reject the concept of Hell entirely, there still exists within Judaism the possibility of damnation.

Moreover, the situation is far more complex than mere repudiation. As Messianics distance themselves from certain areas of communal connection, they avidly cling to others, especially the history of Zionism. While one can contest their claim to continued Jewish identity, the mere existence of that claim and the complexity of that claim obstructs the path to their easy exclusion on the communal basis of complete alienation from Jewishness.

This purported solidarity increases their acceptability from a surprising source—Orthodox Judaism. Michael Wyschograd, an Orthodox Jew and co-author of the widely used anti-missionary *Judaism and Jewish Christianity*, now suggests that it is better for a Jew converted to Christianity to keep some of the commandments than to abandon all forms of Jewish practice (Wyschograd 1995a). Answering respondents' fears that such an approach panders to the Messianic Jewish movement and takes the acceptance of Christian belief (essentially idolatry) too lightly (Borowitz 1995; Charry 1995; Novak 1995),

Wyschograd, basing his views on key Talmudic texts, emphatically affirms: "In my view, a Jewish idol worshipper is better off not eating pork than eating it" (Wyschograd 1995, 233). The power of *mitzvot* observance, Wyschograd believes, will itself pull the believer in Jesus back to Judaism. While discounting those Jewish Christians who only use Jewish symbols to draw new converts into Christianity, eventually to assimilate them in the larger Christian population, he lauds the Torah-observant Jewish Christian communities he has heard exist in Israel who observe the commandments for their own sake. One might imagine that the congregants of B'nai Mashiach, who have no intention of assimilating into churches and attempt to teach their children a "Jewish lifestyle," while not Torah-observant in the strictest sense, might also meet with Wyschograd's approval. While Messianic Judaism is definitely not accepted as Judaism, Wyschograd finds that Jewish Christianity might be seen as an avenue for Christians born Jewish to be more observant Jews—a startling notion!

While Wyschograd encourages the practice of *mitzvot* among Jewish converts as an avenue to return them to the Jewish people, at least two older sources even suggest that Messianic Jews may never have left. A Hasidic rabbi of the nineteenth century, Rabbi Zadok ha-Kohen of Lublin, suggests that anyone who calls himself Jewish remains part of the Jewish community. He reasons that since a Jew is to commit martyrdom rather than convert to Islam, even though Islam is not an idolatrous religion, false belief must not be the issue but abandoning Jewish identity is. Biblical Jews who worshipped idols never identified themselves, nor were they identified by others, as anything but Jewish (Lamm 1992, 172). In a far earlier ruling, Rav Yosef Caro cites a medieval ruling by French scholars concerning a traveling apostate who both worshipped in churches and claimed Jewish identity in Jewish homes. Rather than cut him off, these scholars concluded that he genuinely believed he was a Jew and should be treated as such. His Christian worship should be understood as though he was either pressured to perform it or was innocent of its idolatrous import (Rabinovitch 1992, 187).

While these are clearly exceptional rulings under very different historical circumstances, one can see how the neat division between Jew and Christian is complicated, even in Jewish law, when a group mixes Christian belief with Jewish identification.

This confusion is amply demonstrated by the recent situation in which a synagogue president of a Conservative congregation in Utica, New York, declared his belief in Yeshua. While he was forced to resign the presidency, he remained a member of the congregation because he was still a Jew by birth, and was reportedly supported in this by the congregational rabbi. Is synagogue membership based on one's status as a Jew or one's beliefs? Is it necessarily abandoning Jewish identity to believe in Jesus? The issue is not a simple one to resolve; it was taken up by the United Synagogue's and the Rabbinical Assembly's committees on "Law and Standards" to define the Conservative movement's position (Kahn 1996).

THE JEWISH CHRISTIAN FUTURE

These complications will soon not be confined to the Messianic movement. Even though Messianic Judaism may appear to be an aberrant crossing of the firm boundary between Judaism and Christianity, in decades to come Messianic Judaism may be known simply as the first movement, not the only movement, to express a distinctive Jewish-Christian identity. The greater acceptability of the "Other" through religious dialogue, increasing social interaction, and rising rates of intermarriage may lead to other forms of Jewish Christianity besides the evangelical variety described in this work.

Many have noted the most surprising and troubling finding of the National Jewish Population Survey of 1990: more Jews since 1985 are marrying non-Jews than are marrying other Jews (Kosmin et al. 1991, 14). Christians are now the spouses, parents, grandparents, and in-laws of Jews. As social integration of Jews in Christian neighborhoods and friendship circles has become family integration of Jews and Christians, the instinctive Jewish fear of Christians has begun to fade, and the reflexive refusal to investigate Christianity as a theological option may also weaken in turn (Liebman and Cohen 1990, 52–54).

Jewish synagogues and organizations, in order to retain the next generation of Jews, encourage intermarried families to raise their children as Jews. Thus, while seeking to maintain some form of boundary between Judaism and Christianity, liberal synagogues also invite intermarried families to take part in synagogue life.

However, Reform Judaism may have been more successful with

the latter than with the former. As more and more non-Jews enter Reform synagogues as members, the Reform synagogue faces complex boundary issues. Should non-Jews teach religious school? Become president of the congregation? Be called up to Torah honors? Be a part of a Torah-passing chain at bar and bat mitzvahs, which symbolically represents the passing down of Jewish values from generation to generation? The answers to these questions on the part of a significant number of Reform congregations is "Yes" (Cohen 1991; *Defining* 1990). Ironically, those synagogues most accepting in their outreach would eject a Messianic Jew (Jacob 1987, 107–108), but could permit a non-Jew with the same theological beliefs a place in the congregation and even in Jewish ritual. The confusions that can result in such outreach have even led to a Reform resolution suggesting that children attending church school should not be permitted to enroll in Jewish religious school, because they were personally confusing Jewish and Christian beliefs and in turn confusing the other children (Anderson Dec. 1, 1995, 45).

While Jewish leadership generally opposes the idea of raising children "in both religions," arguing that the end result would be confusion and torn loyalties to parents, the notion remains popular among families themselves, who want to fully include both parents in raising the children. Shoppers in recent holiday seasons can find both greeting cards and children's books that demonstrate the growing popularity and acceptability of celebrating both sets of holidays in the home. How-to books share experiences to show that one can raise a happy, well-adjusted child in both traditions (Gruzen 1990).

Those raised as either Jewish or Christian are given religious options different from children of an inmarriage. When children of intermarriage are raised in one religion, most still have a permanent sense of belonging to two cultures, two religions. Some, even though brought up in one religion, may as adults shift to their "other half." Thus, children raised in an interfaith marriage are ripe for other religious options, ones that might allow them to bring together the two halves of their identity as one. Organizations such as Pareveh: Alliance of Adult Children of Jewish-Gentile Intermarriage provide resources, newsletters, and personal help to those engaged in such a search (Goodman-Malamuth and Margolis 1992, 10–13, 69–73).

The Messianic movement is well situated to take advantage of the needs of intermarried families, providing them a place where both their faith and cultural needs are fulfilled. Perhaps a forerunner of a liberal Messianic movement might be found in the "Interfaith Chavurah" of Hartford, Connecticut, which attempts to sanctify the interfaith experience. With a rabbi as lead clergyperson and a minister and priest on staff, the interfaith synagogue seeks to make synagogue-going an ecumenical experience (Wertheimer 1993, 79–80).

There remains an important dissimilarity between the Messianic approach and Jewish openness toward Christians and Christianity: for American Jews, the assumption remains that Christianity is distinct from Judaism. However, the same is not always true when churches adopt Jewish practices. In the church world, Jewish ritual serves to remind Christians of the Jewish roots of their faith, linking them back to their own origins in Christianity and the early church. Many churches regularly celebrate some form of Passover Seder at the time of Jesus' Last Supper, some with Christological content, others led by a rabbi or using traditional Jewish materials. Some churches, most notably the Seventh-Day Adventists, have long accepted the Jewish Sabbath as the Christian Sabbath as well. Recently, a Methodist congregation built a *sukkah* to commemorate Sukkot (Swartz 1994).

Not only individual churches, but church organizations are involved in adding Jewish forms to worship. The Catholic Order of the Beatitudes, having a thousand members worldwide, practices a traditional Jewish Friday night service welcoming the Shabbat (Halevi 1996). Further Jewish-Catholic permutations may develop. In his book *Jewish Identity*, Elias Friedman calls for a distinct Hebrew-Catholic identity among Jewish converts to Catholicism, somewhat parallel to the evangelical-Jewish identity of Messianic Jews.

Out of the Christian community has arisen a mirror image of Messianic Judaism, the "B'nai Noach" (Children of Noah). During the first years of "Jews for Jesus," Meir Kahane tried to organize a countergroup that would demonstrate the absurdity of their claims, calling it "Christians for Moses" (Baker 1973). In fact, the B'nai Noach are the real "Christians for Moses." Several thousand former Christians, including clergy, have renounced their belief in Jesus, but are not converting to Judaism. Accepting that God made them Gentile for a reason, they study the seven Noachide laws that apply to righteous Gentiles with ultra-Orthodox rabbis and celebrate Jewish holidays. While difficulties remain in the movement, including the creation of appropriate prayers and rituals for the B'nai Noach, the Bar Ilan Center in Jerusalem has begun to offer Noachide studies for Gentiles, and annual Noachide conferences since 1993 have brought together those who share Noachide beliefs (Hanke 1995; Niebuhr 1991). This innovation allows for a separation between Christian and Gentile, allowing some Gentiles to be appended to the Jewish community without becoming Jewish themselves. The simple Jewish/ Christian dichotomy is now being complicated from the Jewish as well as the Messianic side.

We are becoming the "other"; the "other" is becoming "us."

THE BOUNDARY DILEMMA
A Rabbi's Response

> Jews for Jesus, the Black Hebrews, Brother Daniel . . . and indeed the whole Christian church all argued that they were/are the living Jews of their generation. We deny their claim based on the absence of fidelity on their part to what we claim is the authentic tradition. Remove the conception of tradition . . . affirm the right of Jews to formulate Judaism as they see fit without regard to the past and there is no basis for argument with anyone's Jewish claim.
>
> Liebman 1988: 103

The American Jewish community has a strong desire to see itself as an authentic heir to Jewish life in centuries past, a community embodying the unique values that has made Judaism distinct among the nations. In contrast, it seeks to present Messianic Judaism in the light of an inauthentic interloper, masking its Christianity behind a pretense of Jewishness.[6]

However, using history and theology to articulate this communal position, certain weaknesses become obvious. The persecutory history that makes Christians "other" need not be determinative of future estrangement, as Messianics point out, and becomes less and less relevant in an era of increasing intermarriage and increasing acceptance of Jews and Judaism by Christian communities. To make religious ideology the touchstone of Jewish acceptability by excluding

Messianic Jews for wrong belief threatens to exclude a large number of Jews who have no religious belief, or whose religious beliefs can be judged as heretical. "Correct" historical or communal attachment is a matter of strong intra-Jewish disagreement. Even being born Jewish is a matter of dispute. Who, in fact, truly belongs in the Jewish community? Far from retaining an essential Jewish core that Messianics abandon, American Jews cannot even agree on what that core is.

This is not to deny that American Jewish pluralism has distinct advantages. The Jewish community's embrace of diversity has led to a highly inclusive structure, allowing most who identify themselves as Jewish a place in the polity. This leads to larger numbers and increased communal strength. Allowing for such pluralism also provides a certain flexibility in changing circumstances. As is often mentioned, if there were not Pharisees as well as Sadduccees when the Second Temple was destroyed, Judaism would not have survived. Even the very search for Jewish identity in a changing world has led to a veritable publishing industry in Jewish self-examination, which paradoxically strengthens Jewish identity as it laments its demise. (One might include this book as the most recent entry in that extensive list.) And, up until the last half-century, pluralism existed in boundaries of Jewish life that were both clearer and less conscious. One was Jewish if born of a Jewish mother. Religious or secular, this was an inescapable identity, counterposed to that of the Christian / the "goy" / the Gentile. One tended to live in Jewish neighborhoods, have Jewish friends, choose a Jewish spouse, eat Jewish foods, practice some Jewish ritual. One who married a non-Jew was understood to have taken a decisive step away from the community; one who converted completed the leave-taking process.

However, this sense of givenness has given way. Communal boundaries taken for granted for centuries are eroding, and while the community fears the rate of intermarriage, most agree that it will be difficult to reverse such a powerful trend. Ritual boundaries are eroding as philoJudaic Christians and Messianic believers do Jewish practices with Christological content and Jews in intermarried families blend Jewish and Christian ritual. These boundaries, once firm enough to keep Jews "in the fold," are firm no longer. As with other ethnic and religious groups, the American "melting pot," while not an ideal, is becoming a reality.

In this homogenization of culture, it would seem that only ideological differences serve as effective boundary markers. The divergent
values liberal and conservative Christians hold have divided denominations; people who sing the same hymns and share the same church
history no longer share the same frame of reference (Wuthnow 1988,
132–172). While American Judaism has been more comfortable
seeing itself as a religion of "deed" rather than of "creed," this emphasis may need to change.

Until now, according to Jewish communal expectations, the
amount of ritual indicates the strength of Jewish identity. Quantifi-
able Jewish ritual has dominated sociological research on Jewish continuity; what Jews do has classified them as "more" or "less" Jewish,
more or less in touch with the "golden thread" that binds Jews to their
ancestors and to each other (S. Cohen 1988; Goldscheider 1986). For
example, the 1990 National Jewish Population Survey assumed individuals had a stronger Jewish identity if they had regular synagogue
attendance, fasted on Yom Kippur, visited Israel, practiced Jewish
holidays, did not put up a Christmas tree, and lit Shabbat candles
(Kosmin et al. 1991, 35–36). If ritual is the sole measure of Jewishness, the Messianic believers I knew in the congregation would
score favorably, certainly outstripping the average "Jew by religion"
in their attendance at services and possibly even doing other Jewish
practices. If *doing* Jewish is *being* Jewish, ironically, Messianic Jews are
more Jewish than many born Jews. It would seem that "deed" alone,
focus on a collection of behaviors without investigation of intention,
is not an accurate measure.

Jewish leadership, in fact, is called upon to articulate its "creed"
more and more often. In this era of unprecedented choice, the question for a young Jewish person is no longer, "How much Jewish observance will I do?" but rather, "Why be Jewish at all?" A compelling
and coherent answer to this question is needed to retain Jews in the
community in an era of strong competition, not just from other religious groups, but from general secular culture, which is now far more
"given" than one's Jewishness.

However, it remains an open question whether American Judaism
as a whole can provide satisfactory answers. Here, pluralism can be
a disadvantage. Given the prevalence of the instant sound bite, explaining the complexity and diversity of Jewish expression to a young

Jew can be perceived as tedious and indecisive. The inability to articulate a common Jewish identity was less important when the community retained its next generation as a matter of course; it is far more
dysfunctional when the community is by no means assured of that
outcome. When the only shared core value within American Judaism
is that Jews do not believe in Jesus, it is clearly an insufficient response.

As a rabbi, I seek some way of intelligently drawing the boundaries of Judaism and Jewishness, to respond to the challenge that Messianic Judaism represents to the Jewish community. What Messianic
Judaism teaches me as a rabbi is the importance of clarity and consensus for the future survival of Judaism, the need to know who we are as
well as who we are not.[7] A continued identity based on a loose ethnic
configuration and habitual custom, while it has served us well thus far
in the United States, will not provide the motive energy to engage the
next generation. It is high time that together we figured out who we
are.

An Academic's Response

> We adamantly reject the version of Jewish history that suggests that
> there has always existed a normative, halakhic Judaism that has sur-
> vived unchanged despite the challenges of Jewish heretics in every
> generation. A careful look at Jewish history reveals the fact that Jews
> have been divided in every generation. Every period of our history has
> been witness to competing interpretations of Judaism, whose advocates
> condemned one another. It has never been possible, in advance, to
> determine which groups would emerge victorious to tell the tale.
>
> > J. Staub and R. Alpert, 1988:62–63

I can only smile at the earnest platitudes and foolish quest of my rabbi-
self above, marked by the conventional lament of the "ever-dying
people" that has served as a rallying cry for centuries of Jewish life
(Rawidowicz 1974). To believe that "Jewish authenticity" is something that can be defended from a "false Judaism" is to make the assumption that there is an "genuine Judaism" present carrying within
it the essence of "genuine Judaism" past, a line of unbroken continuity that Messianic Judaism violates. Indeed, such an assumption is
highly questionable.

There has always been change in Judaism—in the case of the transformation from Temple cult to synagogue-centered Judaism, enormous change. However, the era of Enlightenment and emancipation introduced a new kind of alteration, as individuals and groups self-consciously utilized elements of tradition to achieve unprecedented variation in Jewish life. New Judaisms emerged, each a different solution to the challenges of modern society (Neusner 1987).

This self-awareness is not limited to liberal Judaisms, which unreservedly declare their use of traditions to profoundly reshape the context from which those traditions are taken (Magnus 1992, 335). Even Orthodoxy, which claims an unbroken connection to rabbinic Judaism, engages in a type of self-conscious selectivity unknown to premodern adherents of Torah, having to choose which elements of Jewish life remain applicable, which elements of secular life are permissible, broadly innovating despite its self-definition as the conservator of tradition. These Judaisms may bear external similarities to premodern Judaism, but the philosophies that guide their adherents—autonomy, historical consciousness, egalitarianism—are very different principles than those that guided their ancestors (Neusner 1987, 115–147). Indeed, as Jonathan Boyarin points out, the belief among some Lubavitch Hasidim that Rabbi Schneerson will be resurrected as Messiah brings these ostensible guardians of true Judaism very close, in some respects, to Christianity (Boyarin 1996, 168).

This phenomenon of invented tradition is certainly not limited to Judaism, but affects any traditional group attempting to create continuity with the past while facing the dilemmas of modernity (Clifford 1988, 277–346). Understanding the nature of socially constructed reality, any group claiming to represent unbroken authenticity has constructed a "necessary fiction" (Hardison 1981, 36), necessary to the group's functioning, but fiction all the same. For a group as wedded to ritual and tradition as Judaism, such a necessary fiction can breed a profound uneasiness. We recognize the unsteady character of our modern constructions, while at the same time claim to maintain the chain of tradition that links us to the earliest days of Judaism. To be challenged on the truth of the latter proposition, to be told that contemporary Judaism is something fundamentally Other than the idealized world of premodern Judaism, threatens to destroy the sense of generational continuity which for many Jews is the source of Transcendent fulfillment.

In order to show that they are as acceptable as the next Jew, Messianic believers shout that the uniform of authenticity, which the Jewish community clutches about itself to ward off the cold winds of change, has been blown off long ago. "At least we believe in God!" declares the Messianic Jew to the secular Jew. "At least we believe the Torah is God's word!" declares the Messianic Jew to the liberal Jew. By examining the most extreme case, one of the only groups of Jewish origin that have clearly been cited as out of the pale, one can see that in fundamental ways most American Jews, if not all, are "out of the pale." We are not "pure"; we self-consciously search, we innovate, we profane, we cover core secular values with Jewishness. We weave Judaisms out of the traditions of our forebears and the values of contemporary society, actively constructing identities while calling this creativity "Jewish continuity." We not only forge our generational link in the chain of tradition, but periodically refashion the entire chain, fastening its far end to the places most relevant to us—the prophets, the mystics, the warriors, the peacemakers (Plaskow 1992, 34). We are all, from a Jewish perspective somewhere, heretics.

As the American Jewish community looks at Messianic Judaism, we see ourselves as in a carnival funhouse mirror. At first, we startle, frightened, at the unfamiliar figure in the glass, the small, impossibly squat body, the vast head. Some of our usual features have disappeared, others are exaggerated almost beyond recognition. This is not us. And then, just as suddenly, we get an eerie prickle of acknowledgement; yes, this is us, after all. We move cautiously up and down, side to side, watching the mirror magnify our flaws, stretching our visage in strange ways. We laugh, but the laugh is as much uneasiness as delight. There we are, stripped of normality, stripped of defenses. Fascinated yet agitated, we turn away from the mirror, seeking in a nearby window the reassuring reflection of our face and body as it always was, every feature back in place, hiding again the disturbing truths revealed.

The enemy is us.

NOTES

1. Studying the Messianic Jews

1. The American Jewish community tries to avoid using this term, understanding that it gives credence to the Messianic claim of practicing and believing Judaism, a claim which the Jewish community rejects. My use of the term is simply for clarity's sake; I refer to the group with the same nomenclature it refers to itself. On my part, this does not imply any recognition of Messianic Judaism as "real Judaism." I generally refer to adherents as "Messianic believers" or "Messianics," unless a distinction needs to be made between an adherent of Jewish birth and an adherent of Gentile birth. Then I refer to them, respectively, as "Messianic Jew" and "Messianic Gentile," again following the group usage.

2. What exactly constitutes evangelical Christianity is a matter of some debate. For the purposes of this work, I find James Davidson Hunter's definition most helpful. "At the doctrinal core, contemporary Evangelicals can be identified by their adherence to (1) the belief that the Bible is the inerrant Word of God, (2) the belief in the divinity of Christ, and (3) the belief in the efficacy of Christ's life, death, and physical resurrection for the salvation of the human soul. Behaviorally, Evangelicals are typically characterized by an individuated and experiential orientation toward spiritual salvation and religiosity in general and by the conviction of the necessity of actively attempting to proselytize all nonbelievers to the tenets of the Evangelical belief system" (Hunter 1983, 7).

3. Reconstructionism is one of the four major branches of Judaism. Founded by Mordecai Kaplan, it emphasizes maximal Jewish observance combined with a liberal social ethic, emphasizing the centrality of "Judaism as a civilization." It can be classified, along with the Reform, the Conservative, and to some extent the Modern Orthodox movement, as part of "liberal Judaism." Laura Levitt's definition is a useful one: "These specifically 'religious' Jewish communities are committed to certain liberal principles, including the social contract, a faith in rationality, and liberalism's commitment to a kind of universal discourse" (Levitt 1996, 367).

4. It is important to note that different congregations in the Messianic Jewish movement have different ways of presenting their Jewish identity, from almost "Orthodox" to almost nonexistent at the extremes (although their Christian theological beliefs appear rather consistent). Thus, different groups may develop alternative methods for creating and maintaining the complex Messianic Jewish identity. However, because B'nai Mashiach has set much of the style for the con-

gregations included within its congregational arm (see chapter 2), B'nai Mashiach, although not definitive for the entire Messianic Jewish movement, can be seen to represent a goodly number of Messianic Jewish congregations.

2. What Is Messianic Judaism?

1. Stephen G. Wilson (Wilson 1995, 143–168) attempts a rough typology of these groups, based on varying fragments of evidence from the patristic period. The Ebionites, described by Irenaeus and Epiphanius, seem to have accepted a low Christology, not accepting Jesus as Lord, but as a prophet and exemplar of following the Law. They themselves accepted circumcision and purification laws, among other commandments, and rejected Paul's antinomian stance. Their major religious text was the Gospel of Matthew, and they seem to have had a critical approach toward the Hebrew prophets. The *Kerygmata Petrou* (Proclamation of Peter), describing the beliefs of a Jewish Christian group that may or may not be identical with the Ebionites, speaks of Moses as the prophet for the Jews and Jesus as the prophet for the Gentiles, allowing both groups a path toward salvation. A second Jewish Christian text, *The Ascent of James*, presents James, Jesus' brother, as leader of the early church, opposed by Paul. While adhering to the Law, followers accepted the substitution of baptism for sacrifice after the destruction of the Second Temple. A third group, the Nazarenes (described in Epiphanius), appear to have accepted the most "orthodox" Christianity—Jesus as the son of God, both the Hebrew Bible and the New Testament as their Scripture, and acceptance of Paul's mission to the Gentiles. They were, however, distinct from Gentile Christians in their continued adherence to aspects of the Law. Wilson also mentions Christian Judaizers, who variously seem to have admired or adopted various Jewish practices.

While any identification of Jewish Christian groups remains tentative, all seemed to retain some adherence to the Torah. According to these groups, Jesus did not come to abrogate the Law, but in fact to reform it, either through reinterpretation of rabbinic principles or though more radical changes to the Torah itself. Despite these alterations, the centrality of Torah observance for Jewish Christians remained unchanged, both as a God-given mandate and at least as a partial path to salvation. Therefore, some Jewish Christians kept the Law while permitting Gentile Christians among them not to; others insisted that all who were of their fellowship, Jew or Christian, needed to keep the Law. Moreover, in contrast to the growing orthodoxy of the Church, some Jewish Christians apparently viewed Jesus neither as God nor as the Son of God, but as a human who attained prophetic or semi-divine status through his merit and the visitation of the Holy Spirit (Segal 1992, 340–348).

2. See the essays included in *Jewish Christians and Christian Jews: From the Renaissance to the Enlightenment*, ed. Richard H. Popkin and Gordon M. Weiner (Dordrecht, The Netherlands: Kluwer Academic Publishers, 1994).

3. For example, Leopold Cohn was on the executive committee of the first conference in 1903 and served on the constitution and by-laws committee in 1914 (Winer 1990, 93). Planning meetings for the Alliance were held at the headquarters of the Presbyterian Church and at the Williamsburg mission to the Jews in 1914 (Winer 1990, 7). In addition, the HCAA raised money for a Chair of Jewish Studies and Missions at Moody Bible Institute. The Alliance sponsored the chair until the 1930s, and even after that time the Chair was filled with Alliance-approved candidates (Winer 1990, 25).

4. By 1978, in the publication *The American Messianic Jewish Quarterly* (*AMJQ*), only the names of the "Advisory Board" (prominent Gentile Christians associated with various conservative Christian denominations) were listed, no longer institutional affiliations, and by 1980 this listing had moved to the last page, in tiny print under the description of the MJAA, and was called the "Board of Reference." Additionally, the regular inclusion on page 2 of the quarterly of the statement "Having no resources of our own, we depend entirely upon the voluntary contributions of Christian people" (*AMJQ*, Spring 1976, 2) had been entirely dropped by the Summer 1976 issue.

5. Other organizations under the MJAA umbrella include the Young Messianic Jewish Alliance (YMJA), serving the teens and twenties population, and the International Relations Committee (IRC), which serves as a public relations and educational arm of the movement on contemporary social and political issues. One of their projects was to raise money for Ethiopians who have been classified as Falash Mora, those Ethiopians claiming Jewish ancestry but having converted to Christianity, whom the Messianic movement claims as fellow Messianics. The MJAA also sponsors a "Russia project" to spread the word about Messianic Judaism to Russian Jews, which includes concerts, congregation planting in St. Petersburg, Moscow, and Minsk (among other cities), establishing a Messianic Bible school, and providing humanitarian aid.

6. Another variant, not accepted by or accepting of Messianic Judaism, is the "N'tzarim" based in Ra'anana, Israel, who believe that Yeshua was a human Messiah, not God, come to bring Jews back to authentic Orthodox practice. Hence, "N'tzarim" are often members of Orthodox synagogues and refer to Messianic Judaism as "Messianic Christianity"!

3. The Messianic Jewish Self

1. "Filling" may be related to a feminization of the believer submissive to an active, male God (Chodorow 1989 181–182; Erikson 1968, 261–294; Meyer 1980, 123–124) as well as echoing ubiquitous consumer language that describes "filling" our material lack (O'Neill 1985, 102–103).

2. According to the congregation, if only one grandparent is Jewish, the grandchild is Jewish. Many American Jews, even those accepting patrilineal descent, would

not consider that same grandchild Jewish, especially if (as is likely) that grandchild was raised as a Christian.

3. Linzer (1996, 97–103) shows that Jewish Buddhists of the same generation reported the same problems as well as positive aspects in their Jewish upbringing; these issues are hardly limited to Jewish Christans alone.

4. In the 1960s a common accusation of children against parents was that of hypocrisy in politics and lifestyle, and thus it should be no surprise that it pops up in religious critiques as well. Kenneth Keniston calls this "the institutionalization of hypocrisy" when a group, often during rapid social change, highlights the gap between the ideals of the society and real behavior (Gerlach and Hine 1970, 167–168).

5. With the resurgence of interest in Jewish spirituality in the 1990s, the ethnic character of much that passed for religious Judaism in the last thirty years has become apparent. Present-day articles and books speak about God, while contrasting this theological focus with earlier decades of neglect. According to David Wolpe, the result of this neglect was the belief that "God was not real," but simply a Hebrew name in a Hebrew blessing that itself was not understood. Because of its associations with Christian fundamentalism, Wolpe asserts, we have become reluctant to even say the very Jewish phrase "God loves you." (Wolpe 1992). Even Orthodox Jews, held by liberal Jews as the surviving remnant of "old-time religion," do not necessarily share a belief in God. Half of the women newly come to modern Orthodoxy interviewed by Lynn Davidman said they were not certain about their belief in God (Davidman 1991, 102–106). In an informative parallel, Samuel Heilman discovers that more than half of "centrist Orthodox" Jews do not strongly reject the notion that God plays an insignificant role in everyday life, despite the statement in a central code of Jewish law, *Sefer Ha-Chinuch* (25:1) that excludes communal standing to those Jews denying God's active Providence (Heilman and Cohen 1989, 90–95). Not even the supposed reservoir of Jewish faith and tradition is immune to the a-theistic orientation at the heart of much of American Judaism. However, it is important to note that "spirituality" has begun to influence even the most staid institutions of liberal Judaism. Healing services, a new emphasis on contemporary music and dance in Shabbat worship, and increased God-talk from pulpits personalize the Divine for congregants. B'nai Jeshurun, a synagogue in Manhattan, is an outstanding example of the success of this approach.

6. "[T]he development of a postwar American Jewish culture within the framework of middle-class consumerism made the rejection of that world the rejection of Jewishness itself" (Prell 1998, 137).

7. The congregation's understanding of salvation includes the following points: "(a) You have made a public confession of your faith in the Messiah Yeshua (Jesus); (b) You have accepted Him as your personal Savior and Redeemer; (c) You believe in His deity, atonement for sin, and resurrection from the dead; (d) You declare your adherence to Scriptures of the Old and New Covenant as the supreme rule for faith and life" ("Messianic Jewish Alliance of America: Application for Membership" in the "Messiah" 1991 conference booklet).

8. This experience of tapping into a Higher Power is a very old concept, rooted in American society from at least the nineteenth century. In *The Positive Thinkers*, Donald Meyer indicates that from Christian Science to Norman Vincent Peale there has been a "positive thinking" emphasis on surrendering control to a Higher Power that will fill all one's needs (Meyer 1980, 116–122). Seeking wholeness and abundance, such ideology was a response to the bureaucratized world of the twentieth century, which limited personal empowerment. The solution was to completely relinquish the middle term of political change, and look to the disgruntled individual to change him/herself by going directly to a Transcendental Power source. This is congruent with popular Protestantism: "The sociology of Protestant culture was to be essentially the psychology of Protestant individuals" (Meyer 1980, 314). Surrendering control to a Higher Power has a venerable history.

9. Kathleen Boone understands this reluctance to integrate Jesus' message as an inheritance from dispensationalism to contemporary fundamentalism. Because the present dispensation of grace begins with Jesus' death and resurrection, his words and teachings are part of the superseded dispensation of law. Jesus' teachings are far less important than his resurrection, which brought grace and hope to the world; in fact, Paul's writings explaining this event are of greater importance. Certainly what Boone describes is true of Congregation B'nai Mashiach, in which Paul's letters are used in sermons, taught, and discussed far more often than the words of Yeshua himself (Boone 1989, 51–52).

10. This was later confirmed to me by a former member whose gay brother had previously been part of the congregation. He was counseled and prayed over to change his sexual preference, but to no avail.

11. For evangelical Christianity, R. Marie Griffith's *God's Daughters* (1997) is the latest entry in a long series of excellent works that specifically address the construction of gender in evangelical/fundamentalist Christianity, exploring the ways in which Christian men and women live an ideal that adherents consider more stable, orderly, and attuned to the will of God than the mores of secular individuals. In Judaism, Debra Kaufman's *Rachel's Daughters* (1991) and Lynn Davidman's *Tradition in a Rootless World* (1991) explain how newly Orthodox Jewish women find new peace, purpose, and even feminist values expressed in traditional feminine roles. Both demonstrate that conservative religion can provide welcome shelter from the gender role confusions found in American culture during the last twenty-five years.

12. The middle-class Covenant Fellowship Susan Rose observed similarly cultivated women's femininity by glorifying their roles as wives and mothers, praising their strength in supporting their men through prayer rather than in leadership. Even those women who say they espoused feminism in their pre-evangelical life find a relief in returning to traditional values (Rose 1990).

13. I find it significant that JAPness is taken as an accurate reflection of Jewish reality, but Jewish male effeminacy is understood by the congregation purely as an anti-Semitic canard. Thus, in this interpretation, Jewish women really *are* materialistic and shallow, but Jewish men are certainly not unmanly!

14. In 1991, the number of Messianic Gentiles was estimated by leadership at 25 percent, and Jewish families (at least one spouse Jewish) at 90 percent. Using simple math, if all the members were married (which they aren't), the percentage of couples would be 60 percent Jewish-Jewish, 30 percent Jewish-Gentile, and 10 percent Gentile-Gentile. If this reflects the actual proportions of the married couples, the percentage of "mixed couples" is consonant with the percentage of all Jews (22 percent) married to non-Jews (Kosmin 1991, 13). However, this proportion seems to have changed somewhat with a new influx of Gentile members into B'nai Mashiach.

15. The newly formed International Federation of Messianic Jews includes in its platform "Recognition of the Gerim (righteous Gentiles) as co-workers deserving full membership." It is possible that, with time, Messianic Gentiles who have taken on full Jewish practices will be accorded a special status, akin to a convert, within Messianic Judaism as a whole. It may already be that way in "Torah-observant" Messianic Jewish congregations that offer the possibility of conversion to Judaism.

16. See chapter 6 for the attempt of Messianic Gentiles to secure Jewish status for their male children through ritual circumcision.

17. According to an essay by Timothy Huckabay found at the "Menorah Ministries" Website (www.menorah.org/conver.html), conversion under false pretenses occurs among Gentile believers (not necessarily those in Messianic congregations) who feel that through conversion to Judaism they can best evangelize Jews, and even make *aliyah* to Israel in order to accomplish this mission. While the writer quotes a "Jews for Jesus" archivist and cites his own conversations with members of the Messianic movement to discourage this practice, saying that the truth of Jesus cannot be spread through a fundamental lie, he also states that there are some evangelicals who have no problem with the practice.

18. However, there is evidence that this salvation/damnation belief is softening in evangelical circles as well (Hunter 1987, 34–40).

19. These direct responses to my questions about Hell were not usually the first I received. Often, when I asked the question, many people responded with, "I would never approach someone like that, be saved or be damned, because that would turn them off." They would deflect the issue to one of style, not substance, reassuring me that they weren't like hellfire Bible thumpers. I'm not sure if that was out of discomfort with the question or that the style of witnessing was at the forefront of their minds.

20. This has since changed to Saturday morning, as the congregational services have shifted.

4. Community

1. I have even heard this said outright by a Messianic rabbi, who stated that the Jews are "our enemies" because "they are against our own Messiah." In fairness, he also

states "I love my brothers in the body of Messiah. Sometimes they act like enemies of the gospel for Jewish people." Still, there seems to be a difference between *being* an enemy (Jews) and *acting* like an enemy (believers) (Rosenberg 1995).

2. A Liberty anti-missionary worker insists that this version of events is a complete fabrication—Shlomo Carlebach, far from being pleased, had tears in his eyes at the sight of Jesus-believing Jews performing his songs. Here, I am more interested in the implications of the narrative than its "truth."

3. This phrase alludes to a rather distasteful passage in the New Testament, Revelation 2:9; the "Jews who are not" belong to the synagogue of Satan!

5. History, Prophecy, and Memory

1. During "Messiah" 1990, significantly, the Holocaust *was* discussed. As mentioned above, Hitler's definition was used to defend Messianic Jews' "Jewishness"; the speaker proclaimed, "This should answer the question if either your father or mother is Jewish, are you Jewish? You are Jewish!" Trying to establish their own historical link to the Holocaust, the speakers counted 1.75 million German Jewish "believers" affected by Hitler in 1933. Sixty percent of professionals who lost their jobs were "Jewish believers." This really stretches the definition of believers; in the congregation nominal Lutherans and Catholics would hardly be considered "believers." However, given the difficulty of identifying with the unsaved Jews of the concentration camps, as discussed above, the claim to a large number of Holocaust victims of their own helps Messianic Jews to feel a part of the tragedy that so defines American Jewish life.

2. This is a rewording from a humorous "prayer" given during the film *Fiddler on the Roof* by the town rabbi: "May God bless and keep the Czar . . . far away from us!"

3. While religious Zionism understands the founding of Israel as the beginning of the redemption process, and a prayer to that effect is regularly recited in some American synagogues, this is not often consciously articulated in American Jewish discourse. More prevalent is the notion that Israel's existence after the Holocaust and its survival of Arab wars in miraculous, but it is a miracle without a specific theological framework.

6. Practices, Rituals, and Life Cycles

1. There is no scholarly consensus on the use of the term "ritual." For example, both Tambiah (1985, 128) and Bird (1995, 23–25), in keeping with classic ritual theory, seek to distinguish ritual from other activity on the basis of certain content and form, such as repetition. In reaction to such reification of terminology, Bell

(1992, 74) takes as "ritualized" behavior that which is distinct and privileged in a social system, regardless of specific content or form. The ritual activity analyzed in this chapter certainly fits both conventional understandings of ritual and Bell's focus on "ritualization."

2. For example, many Conservative Jews accept patrilineal descent for determining Jewish identity, even when the Conservative leadership is against it. See Mayer (1992), 179–180.

3. While there is flexibility in ritual law in Messianic Judaism, there is none in moral law. Murder, stealing, and sexual immorality are not really considered "options." In fact, as David often said, those who continue to backslide in these moral areas may not have been saved in the first place. This separation of obligatory moral law as contrasted to optional ritual law is not only stressed in church life, but in American Jewish life as well, where "being a good person" takes precedence over ritual observance (Sklare 1993, 208–212).

4. At present, Messianic believers turn to other Messianic believers to perform life-cycle events and provide most Jewish ritual items. However, even today, to take part in life-cycle rituals, to obtain religious objects, to authenticate themselves as Jews, Messianic believers have to get past the rabbinic gatekeepers.

There are Messianic Jews who have been married by a Conservative Jewish rabbi, Messianic Jewish children who have been circumcised by Orthodox Jewish *mohelim*, even Messianic Jewish sons and daughters who have had bar and bat mitzvahs in regular synagogues. Even today, Torahs must be purchased from Judaica purveyors in the United States and Israel for use in Messianic synagogues. Indeed, according to several accounts I heard, there are Messianic believers who are members of normative Jewish synagogues, attend worship frequently, or join local congregations for special celebrations. One Messianic rabbi's wife takes her children regularly to Purim services at a local Jewish synagogue.

In order to do this, Messianic believers must keep mum about their faith in Yeshua, a silence which the American Jewish community understands as deceptive and unethical. Sometimes, the Jewish functionaries remain uninformed as to the convictions of the Messianic believers, as in the case of the rabbi who married the Messianic Jews. Since the movement at that time was practically non-existent, they had a choice of being married by a minister or a rabbi, and since both partners were born Jewish, the minister was unacceptable to both families. When I asked incredulously whether the rabbi knew of their beliefs, as the rest of the family did by that time, the woman replied no, and continued angrily, "And he didn't ask. He didn't ask about God. All he cared about was whether I kept kosher."

In other instances, less believably, it is claimed that the Jewish functionaries *did* know the people they were dealing with were Messianic Jews, and that they didn't want to make an issue of it. Sometimes this slant on the Messianic Jewish relationship with the Jewish community is taken to lengths that invite disbelief. In a roundabout manner, I discovered that one of the singing groups from B'nai Mashiach used to perform in local synagogues. I asked one of the members, "You did concerts in synagogues? Did they know your beliefs?" He said, "Well, we didn't advertise it. The people who hired us knew our views, of course, but the other members of the congregation didn't necessarily know it, and we didn't do witnessing or anything." This doesn't correspond with the Jewish Community Relations Council records that tell the story of alarmed synagogue programmers calling after the concert, when they discovered that these tuneful Jews were actually Messianic Jews. Even the Mossad, I was told, is secretly comfortable about Messianic Jews coming to live as citizens in Israel, as long as the ultra-Orthodox don't make an issue of it and force their hand.

These assertions, that either the Jewish community is at fault for not knowing or silently approves, enable the Messianic believers to get what they need from the Jewish community. Although they took great pains not to mention their connection with Jesus, each Messianic believer preferred to believe that either the Jewish community member was at fault for not investigating their views or that the member accepted their Jewishness (as long as they weren't overt about their belief in Yeshua). This reasoning permits the Messianic believer to rationalize away the charge of deception, which is used frequently by Jewish anti-missionary organizations. Moreover, the second explanation, while less plausible, has its advantages as well; it creates the picture of a cadre of sympathetic but silent Jews who really don't have a problem with Messianic Judaism. These rationales permit Messianic believers to continue feeding their Jewishness from available Jewish institutions while sidestepping the hostility the American Jewish community often feels toward them. In that way, their links with authentic Jewish life can be maintained and thus, they feel, their own authenticity as Jews can be bolstered.

7. The Saved *and* the Chosen?

1. In an intriguing article, Susannah Heschel (1997) draws upon queer theory to explain modern Christian theological resistance to the Jewishness of Jesus. Jesus can be seen as a "theological transvestite," a figure belonging to both the Jewish and Christian worlds, who calls into question the separate identities of Judaism and Christianity. Fearful that accepting Jesus might mean accepting the validity of the rabbinic Jewish tradition that nurtured him, liberal nineteenth- and twentieth-century Protestants denigrated first-century Judaism (most notably, the Pharisees) and claimed that Jesus' religious vision came in spite of his Jewish environment, not because of it. In the same way, Messianic Judaism serves that ambiguous role for American Jews.

2. An apostate is one who is considered to have left Judaism for another religion. This can be distinguished from the heretic, who claims to be part of the religion, even representing the truest part of that religion. However, it is also clear that a heretic may claim membership in a group that already considers her an apostate, as is the case for a Messianic Jew (Charmé 1987, 17–18).

In Jewish law, apostates remain Jewish by status, although they lose communal privileges. This stance owes much to Rashi, through an ingenious rendering of Sanhedrin 44a ("Though he sinned, he remained an Israelite") removing it from its original context of affirming a Jew's exalted place despite sinfulness and applying it specifically to the case of an apostate (J. Katz 1958). However, the implications of this decision have varied. In some rulings, as in the case of Jewish marriage remaining valid even when one partner turned apostate, the Jewishness of the convert was considered ineradicable despite the suffering that such a ruling could cause. However, rabbinic rulings and custom also initiated practices clearly at odds with the supposition of inalienable Jewish status, including disinheriting apostates, charging them interest (something not done with other Jews), ignoring, rather than mourning, an apostate's death, and requiring an apostate returning to Judaism to immerse in a ritual bath, just as a proselyte would (Jacobs 1975; J. Katz 1961, 70–80).

3. Popular Israeli opinion seems more tolerant on this matter than the court system. According to a 1988 Israeli public opinion survey asking who should be permitted into Israel under the Law of Return (financed by the Messianic movement, although conducted by the Dahaf Research Institute), 61 percent of Israelis would support entry under the Law of Return of a person born of a Jewish mother, who believes that Yeshua is the Messiah, and was baptized in the framework of a Messianic Jewish congregation. Remarkably, almost half (49 percent) would even permit a person born of a Jewish mother and who was baptized in the framework of a Christian church to enter under the Law of Return. These results are even more striking when it is understood that those Israelis defining themselves as religious or traditional also were somewhat supportive of the Law of Return being applied to Jesus-believing Jews; in the case of the person belonging to the Messianic Jewish congregation, these numbers are 50 and 57 percent respectively; in the case of the person being baptized in the Christian church, the numbers drop to 26 and 48 percent respectively (Dahaf 1989, 79–90).

4. In my discussions with Jews, one boundary Messianics seemed to cross that "regular" Jews did not was the belief that human beings are born good, with a pure soul. Two men pointed out that while Messianic believers understood that Yeshua was necessary to save from sin, such an idea of "original sin" isn't Jewish. This anthrocentric border is intriguing. However, what would one do with Jewish Buddhists, since Buddhism rejects not only the notion of the soul but even of the "self"?

5. For example, in a letter to the editor (Yuter 1991) an Orthodox rabbi responds to a Reform rabbi this way: "The Hebrew Christians believe, in error, that the Messiah has come; Reform Judaism rejects the belief in a personal Messiah, which is to my mind an even greater deviation from Torah theology."

6. Part of the attractiveness of excluding the Messianic movement is the "Jewish togetherness" it engenders. Apart from external anti-Semitic or anti-Israel threats,

in no place do Jews from ultra-Orthodox to secular find such solid common ground except for repulsion of Messianic Jews. Besides rejection reflecting ideological issues, one cannot forget how communally useful such opposition is. "True irony . . . is based upon a sense of fundamental kinship with the enemy, as one *needs* him, is *indebted* to him, is not merely outside him as an observer but contains him *within*, being consubstantial with him" (Burke 1989, 257–258).

7. For an equally positive assessment of the impact of missionaries on the American Jewish community, see Sarna 1987.

BIBLIOGRAPHY

Albanese, C. L. 1981. *America: Religions and religion*. Belmont, Calif.: Wadsworth Publishing Company.

Anderson, A. E. 1996, August 8. Messianic explosion. *Jewish Exponent* (Philadelphia), 1, 51.

———. 1995, December 1. When religions collide. *Jewish Exponent*, 45.

———. 1995, November 24. Seeking spirituality. *Jewish Exponent*, 17–18.

Ariel, Y. 1991. *On behalf of Israel: American fundamentalist attitudes toward Jews, Judaism and Zionism, 1865–1945*. Brooklyn, N.Y.: Carlson Publishing.

Back, K. 1972. *Beyond words*. New York: Russell Sage.

Baker, D. L. 1973, March 30. Christians for Moses. *Christianity Today* 17:46.

Bakhtin, M. M. 1981. *The dialogic imagination*. Ed. Michael Holquist. Austin: University of Texas Press.

Barron, B. 1992. *Heaven on earth?* Grand Rapids, Mich.: Zondervan Press.

Beckford, J. A. 1983. The restoration of "power" to the sociology of religion. *Sociological Analysis* 44: 11–32.

Beiser, V. 1995, January 26. For the love of Jesus: The ominous rise of Messianic Judaism. *Jerusalem Report* 5: 26–31.

Bell, C. 1992. *Ritual theory, ritual practice*. New York: Oxford University Press.

Bellah, R., R. Madsen, W. M. Sullivan, A. Swidler, and S. M. Tipton. 1985. *Habits of the heart*. New York: Harper and Row.

Biale, D. 1992. Zionism as an erotic revolution. In *People of the body: Jews and Judaism from an embodied perspective*, ed. H. Eilberg-Schwartz, 283–308. Albany, N.Y.: SUNY Press.

———. 1986. *Power and powerlessness in Jewish history*. New York: Schocken Books.

Bird, F. B. 1995. Ritual as communicative action. In *Ritual and ethnic identity*, ed. J. N. Lightstone and F. B. Bird, 23–52. Waterloo, Ontario: Wilfrid Laurier University Press.

Bleich, J. D. 1992. Rabbinic responses to nonobservance in the modern era. In *Jewish tradition and the nontraditional Jew*, ed. J. J. Schacter, 37–115. Northvale, N.J.: Jason Aronson, Inc.

———. 1984. Parameters and limits of communal unity from the perspective of Jewish law. In *Halacha and contemporary society*, ed. A. S. Cohen, 151–166. New York: Ktav Publishing House, Inc., Rabbi Jacob Joseph School Press.

Boone, K. 1989. *The Bible tells them so.* Albany, N.Y.: SUNY Press.

Borowitz, E. B. 1995. Apostasy from Judaism today. *Modern Theology* 11: 173–179.

Bowen, J. R. 1992. On scriptural essentialism and ritual variation: Muslim sacrifice in Sumatra and Morocco. *American Ethnologist* 19(4): 656–671.

Boyarin, D. 1997. *Unheroic conduct: The rise of heterosexuality and the invention of the Jewish man.* Berkeley: University of California Press.

Boyarin, J. 1996. *Thinking in Jewish.* Chicago: University of Chicago Press.

Brandt, L. 1988. Response. *Mishkan* vols. 1–2, nos. 8–9: 70–74.

Breines, P. 1990. *Tough Jews.* New York: HarperCollins.

Broner, E. M., and N. Nimrod. 1992. The women's haggadah. In *The Telling* [1993], 193–216. San Francisco: HarperSanFrancisco.

Bulka, R. P. 1984. *The coming cataclysm.* New York: Mosaic Press.

Burke, K. 1989. *On symbols and society.* Ed. J. R. Gusfield. Chicago: University of Chicago Press.

Carlson, J. 1992. Syncretistic religiosity: The significance of this tautology. *Journal for Ecumenical Studies* 29: 24–34.

Chamberlain, R. 1995. The forgotten history of Messianic Judaism. Tape. "Messiah" 1995, no. 50.

Charmé, S. L. 1987. Heretics, infidels and apostates: Menace, problem or symptom? *Judaism* 36: 17–33.

———. 1984. *Meaning and myth in the study of lives.* Philadelphia: University of Pennsylvania Press.

Charry, E. T. 1995. Christian Jews and the law. *Modern Theology* 11: 187–193.

Cherlin, L. 1986. Celebrating the life cycle. *Humanistic Judaism* 16: 44–47.

Chernoff, D. 1989. *Yeshua the messiah.* Havertown, Penn.: MMI Publishing Co.

Chodorow, N. 1989. *Feminism and psychoanalytic theory.* New Haven: Yale University Press.

Christian leaders deplore Messianic Jewish activities. 1985, February 19. *Connections,* 5.

Clifford, J. 1988. *The predicament of culture.* Cambridge: Harvard University Press.

Cohen, B. 1985a, April 22. Messianic Judaism, part II: A believer's identity and calling in the scriptures. Tape.

———. 1985, April 14. Messianic Judaism, part I. Tape.

Cohen, D. N. 1991, November 15–21. Reform grapple with the role of non-Jews in the synagogue. *The Jewish Week,* 6.

Cohen, S. 1988. *Unity and polarization in Judaism today: The attitudes of American and Israeli Jews.* New York: The American Jewish Committee.

Cohn, J. D. 1992. Communications: Humanistic congregation. [Letter to the editor]. *CCAR Journal* 39: 65–66.

Conway, C. 1984, October 1. 900 protest effort of Messianic Jews. *The Philadelphia Inquirer.*

Cox, H. 1995. *Fire from heaven: The rise of Pentecostal spirituality and the reshaping of religion in the twenty-first century.* New York: Addison-Wesley Publishing Company.

Cucchiari, S. 1990. The lords of the culto: transcending time through place in Sicilian Pentecostal ritual. *Journal of Ritual Studies* 4: 1–14.

Dahaf report on Israel public opinion concerning Messianic Jewish aliyah, The. 1989. *Mishkan* 10: 79–90.

Danziger, M. H. 1989. *Returning to tradition: The contemporary revival of Orthodox Judaism*. New Haven: Yale University Press.

Davidman, L. 1991. *Tradition in a rootless world*. Berkeley: University of California Press.

Defining the role of the non-Jew in the synagogue: A resource for congregations. 1990. Cincinnati: Union of American Hebrew Congregations. Commission on Reform Jewish Outreach of the Union of American Hebrew Congregations and the Central Conference of American Rabbis.

Donin, H. H. 1980. *To pray as a Jew*. New York: Basic Books.

Douglas, M. 1970. *Natural symbols*. New York: Pantheon Books.

Edelstein, A. 1994. Jews who choose Jesus. *Moment* 19: 30–39, 62–63.

Eichhorn, D. M. 1978. *Evangelizing the American Jew*. Middle Village, N.Y.: Jonathan David Publishers.

Eisenberg, S. 1988. "Keeping kosher: Biblical or rabbinic?" Tape.

Ellenson, D. 1987. The Orthodox rabbinate and apostasy in nineteenth-century Germany and Hungary. In *Jewish apostasy in the modern world*, ed. T. M. Endelman, 165–188. New York: Holmes and Meier.

Ellwood, R. S., Jr. 1973. *One way: The Jesus movement and its meaning*. Englewood Cliffs, N.J.: Prentice-Hall.

Endelman, T. M., ed. 1987. *Jewish apostasy in the modern world*. New York: Holmes and Meier.

Erikson, E. 1968. *Identity, youth and crisis*. New York: W. W. Norton and Co.

Evearitt, D. J. 1989. *Jewish-Christian missions to the Jews: 1820–1935*. Ann Arbor, Mich.: University Microfilms.

Feher, S. 1998. *Passing over Easter: Constructing the boundaries of Messianic Judaism*. Walnut Creek, Calif.: AltaMira Press.

Fein, L., and D. Saperstein, eds. 1996. *A common road to freedom: A Passover haggadah*. Washington, D.C.: Religious Action Center of Reform Judaism.

Finkelstein, J. 1979. Beit ha-sefer ha-adom ha-katan: The little red schoolhouse. *The American Messianic Jewish Quarterly*, 17–19.

Fishman, S. B. 1992. The faces of women: An introductory essay. In *Follow my footprints: Changing images of women in American Jewish fiction*, ed. S. B. Fishman, 1–62. Hanover, N.H.: University Press of New England.

Flake, C. 1984. *Redemptorama: Culture, politics, and the new evangelicalism*. Garden City, N.Y.: Anchor-Press/Doubleday.

Frankel, E. 1990. The promises and pitfalls of Jewish relationships. *Tikkun* 5: 19–22, 95–98.

Friedman, D. 1992. Communications: Humanistic congregation. [Letter to the editor]. *CCAR Journal* 39: 66–67.

Friedman, E. 1987. *Jewish identity*. New York: The Miriam Press.

Friedman, J. 1994. The myth of Jewish antiquity: New Christians and Christian-Hebraica in early modern Europe. In *Jewish Christians and Christian Jews*, ed. R. H. Popkin and G. M. Weiner, 35–56. Dordrecht, The Netherlands: Kluwer Academic Publishers.

Friedman, T. 1988/9. Who is not a Jew?: The *halachic* status of an apostate. *Conservative Judaism* 41: 53–60.

Fruchtenbaum, A. G. 1983. *Hebrew Christianity: Its theology, history and philosophy*. San Antonio, Tex.: Ariel Ministries.

Gans, H. J. 1979. Symbolic ethnicity. In *On the making of Americans*, ed. H. J. Gans, N. Glazer, J. R. Gusfield, and C. Jencks, 193–220. Philadelphia: University of Pennsylvania Press.

Gates of prayer: The new Union prayerbook. 1975. New York: CCAR.

Gerlach, L. P., and V. H. Hine. 1970. *People, power and change: Movements of social transformation*. Indianapolis: Bobbs-Merrill.

Glazer, N. 1972. *American Judaism*. 2d ed. Chicago: University of Chicago Press.

Goldscheider, C. 1986. *Continuity and change: Emerging patterns in America*. Bloomington: Indiana University Press.

Goldstein, L. J. 1993. Thoughts on Jewish identity. In *Jewish identity*, ed. D. T. Goldberg and M. Krausz, 79–92. Philadelphia: Temple University Press.

Goldwyn, R. 1987, October 9. Robertson talks back. *The Philadelphia Daily News*.

Goodman-Malamuth, L., and R. Margolis. 1992. *Between two worlds: Choices for grown children of Jewish-Christian parents*. New York: Pocket Books.

Gordet, R. 1989. Kingdom Now, Dominion theology, and Messianic Judaism. Tape. "Messiah" 1989, CF 526.

Greenberg, E. J. 1996, January 12. A faithful commitment. *The Jewish Week*, 208, nos. 26, 37.

Griffith, R. M. 1997. *God's daughters: Evangelical women and the power of submission*. Berkeley: University of California Press.

Gruzen, L. F. 1990. *Raising your Jewish/Christian child: How interfaith parents can give children the best of both*. New York: Newmarket Press.

Gutwirth, J. 1987. *Les Judéo-Chrétiens d'aujourd'hui*. Paris: Les Éditions du Cerf.

Halevi, Y. K. 1996, January 11. The Church repents. *The Jerusalem Report*, 34–38.

———. 1993, February 25. For the love of Jesus. *The Jerusalem Report*, 14–15.

Hanke, K. E. 1995. *Turning to Torah: The emerging Noachide movement*. Northvale, N.J.: Jason Aronson, Inc.

Hanna, J. 1988. *Dance, sex and gender*. Chicago: University of Chicago Press.

———. 1979. *To dance is human: A theory of non-verbal communication*. Chicago: University of Chicago Press.

Hardie, M. 1995, Spring. Messianic Jewish congregation gives to Jewish National Fund for water project. *The Messianic Times* 5: 2.

Hardison, O. B., Jr. 1981. *Entering the maze: Tradition and change in modern culture*. New York: Oxford University Press.

Harris-Shapiro, C. 1994. Messianic Jews as mirror. *Reconstructionist* 59: 36–43.

Heath, D. 1992. Fashion, anti-fashion and heteroglossia in urban Senegal. *American Ethnologist* 19: 19–33.

Heilman, S. 1977. Inner and outer identities: Sociological ambivalence among Orthodox Jews. *Jewish Social Studies* 39: 227–240.

Heilman, S., and S. Cohen. 1989. *Cosmopolitans and parochials: Modern Orthodox Jews in America.* Chicago: University of Chicago Press.

Henry, M. 1996, May 9. Messianics looking to sink roots of another kind. *Jewish Exponent* [reprint from *Jerusalem Post*], 8.

Herberg, W. 1960. *Protestant-Catholic-Jew.* New York: Doubleday and Co.

Heschel, S. 1997. Jesus as theological transvestite. In *Judaism since gender,* ed. M. Peskowitz and L. Levitt, 188–199. New York: Routledge.

Hofstadter, R. 1970. *Anti-intellectualism in American life.* New York: Knopf.

Hunter, J. D. 1987. *Evangelicalism: The coming generation.* Chicago: University of Chicago Press.

———. 1983. *American evangelicalism.* New Brunswick, N.J.: Rutgers University Press.

Jacob, W., ed. 1987. *Contemporary Reform responsa.* New York: CCAR.

Jacobs, L. 1975. *Theology in the responsa.* London and Boston: Routledge and Kegan Paul.

Joselit, J. W. 1992. "Merry Chanuka": The changing holiday practices of American Jews, 1880–1950. In *The uses of tradition: Jewish continuity in the modern era,* ed. J. Wertheimer, 303–326. New York: Jewish Theological Seminary.

Kahn, G. 1996, April 12. Conservative bodies debate membership of a 'Messianic Jew.' *The Forward,* 1, 3.

Kamenetz, R. 1994a. *The Jew in the lotus.* New York, HarperCollins Publishers, Inc.

———. 1994. Has the Jewish Renewal made it into the mainstream? *Moment* 19: 42–49, 79–82.

Kaplan, M. M., E. Kohn, and I. Eisenstein, eds. 1941. *The new haggadah.* New York: Behrman House.

Katz, J. 1961. *Exclusiveness and tolerance.* New York: Schocken Books.

———. 1958. Though he sinned, he remained an Israelite. [Hebrew] *Tarbiz* 27: 203–217.

Katz, S. T. 1984. Issues in the separation of Judaism and Christianity after 70 C.E.: A reconsideration. *Journal of Biblical Literature* 103: 43–76.

Kaufman, D. R. 1991. *Rachel's daughters: Newly orthodox Jewish women.* New Brunswick, N.J.: Rutgers University Press.

Kaufman, G., and L. Raphael. 1984. Shame as taboo in American culture. In *Forbidden fruits: Taboos and tabooism in culture,* ed. Ray Browne, 57–66. Bowling Green, Ky.: Bowling Green University Popular Press.

Kaye/Kantrowitz, M. 1982. Some notes on Jewish lesbian identity. In *Nice Jewish girls,* ed. E. T. Beck, 28–44. Trumansburg, N.Y.: The Crossing Press.

Kirsch, R. 1996, July/August. Letter to the editor. *The Messianic Times* 7: 7.

Klein, J. W. 1980. *Jewish identity and self esteem.* New York: American Jewish Committee.

Kol haneshamah: Shabbat vehagim. 1994. Wyncote, Penn.: The Reconstructionist Press.

Kosmin, B., S. Goldstein, J. Waksberg, N. Lerer, A. Keysar, and J. Scheckner. 1991.

Highlights of the CJF 1990 national Jewish population survey. New York: Council of Jewish Federations.

Krauscz, M. 1993. On being Jewish. In *Jewish identity,* ed. D. T. Goldberg and M. Krauscz, 264–278. Philadelphia: Temple University Press.

Kravitz, B. 1996. *The Jewish response to missionaries.* Los Angeles: Jews for Judaism International Inc.

Kuhn, M. H. 1964. The reference group reconsidered. *Sociological Quarterly* 5: 5–22.

Lamm, N. 1992. Loving and hating Jews as halakhic categories. In *Jewish tradition and the nontraditional Jew,* ed. J. J. Schacter, 139–176. Northvale, N.J.: Jason Aronson, Inc.

Lapides, L. 1987. Do we need the Fellowship of Messianic Congregations? *Mishkan* 6–7: 121–134.

Lasch, C. 1978. *The culture of narcissism.* New York: W. W. Norton and Co.

Leventhal, B. R. 1988. Theological perspectives on the Holocaust, part II. *Mishkan* 8–9: 79–134.

Levitt, L. 1997. *Jews and feminism: The ambivalent search for home.* New York: Routledge.

———. 1996. Rethinking Jewish feminist identity/ies: What difference can feminist theory make? In *Interpreting Judaism in a postmodern age,* ed. S. Kepnes, 361–378. New York: New York University Press.

Lichtenstein, A. 1963. Brother Daniel and the Jewish fraternity. *Judaism* 12: 260–280.

Liebman, C. S. 1988. *Deceptive images: Toward a redefinition of American Judaism.* New Brunswick, N.J.: Transaction Books.

———. 1973. *The ambivalent American Jew.* Philadelphia: Jewish Publication Society.

Liebman, C. S., and S. M. Cohen. 1990. *Two worlds of Judaism.* New Haven: Yale University Press.

Lightstone, J. N. 1995. The religion of Jewish peoplehood: The myths, rituals, and institutions of the civil religion of Canadian Jewry. In *Ritual and ethnic identity,* ed. J. N. Lightstone and F. B. Bird, 53–62. Waterloo, Ontario: Wilfrid Laurier University Press.

Lindsey, H. 1989. *The road to holocaust.* New York: Bantam Books.

Linzer, J. 1996. *Torah and dharma: Jewish seekers in Eastern religions.* Northvale, N.J.: Jason Aaronson, Inc.

Lipson, J. L. 1990. *Jews for Jesus: An anthropological study.* New York: AMS Press.

Litvin, B., ed. 1965. *Jewish identity: Modern responsa and opinions.* New York: Phillip Feldheim.

Loyd, L. 1981, April 19. Love thy neighbor? *The Philadelphia Inquirer.*

McDonald, S. S. 1976, December 19. Jews for Jesus. *The Philadelphia Inquirer.*

McGuire, M. 1982. *Pentecostal Catholics.* Philadelphia: Temple University Press.

Magnus, S. S. 1992. Reinventing Miriam's well: Feminist Jewish ceremonials. In *The uses of tradition: Jewish continuity in the modern era,* ed. J. Wertheimer, 331–348. New York: Jewish Theological Seminary.

Marsden, G. 1980. *Fundamentalism and American culture*. New York: Oxford University Press.

Mayer, E. 1992. The coming reformation in American Jewish identity. In *Imagining the Jewish future: Essays and responses*, ed. D. Teutsch, 175–190. Albany, N.Y.: SUNY Press.

Meeting the challenge. 1994. New York: Jewish Community Relations Council. Photocopy.

Merrell, F. 1985. *A semiotic theory of texts*. Berlin: Mouton de Gruyter.

Messianic Jewish Alliance of America. 1990. *Operation Joshua: Worldwide campaign for the right of Messianic Jews to make aliyah*. Booklet.

Meyer, D. 1980. *The positive thinkers*. New York: Pantheon Books.

Millgram, A. 1971. *Jewish worship*. Philadelphia: Jewish Publication Society.

Mirsky, N. 1978. *Unorthodox Judaism*. Columbus, Ohio: Ohio State University Press.

Mittelman, R. 1987. *The Meknes mellah and the Casablancan ville nouvelle: A comparative study of two Jewish communities in transformation*. Ann Arbor, Mich.: University Microfilms.

Myerhoff, B. 1980. *Number our days*. New York: Simon and Schuster.

Neitz, M. J. 1987. *Charisma and community*. New Brunswick, N.J.: Transaction Books.

Neusner, J. 1987. *The death and birth of Judaism*. New York: Basic Books, Inc.

———. 1981. *Stranger at home*. Chicago: University of Chicago Press.

New Jewish Agenda, ed. 1984. *The Shalom Seders: Three Haggadahs*. New York: Adama Press.

News and notes. 1996, July/August. *The Messianic Times* 7: 23.

Niebuhr, R. G. 1991, March 20. Tennessee Baptists turn to Judaism for new inspiration. *The Wall Street Journal*.

Novak, D. 1995. Response to Michael Wyschograd. *Modern Theology* 11: 211–218.

Oberman, H. A. 1984. *The roots of anti-Semitism*. Trans. J. I. Porter. Philadelphia: Fortress Press.

Ochs, C. 1991. What Jews can learn from Christian spirituality. *Proceedings of the Center for Jewish-Christian Learning* 6: 24–29.

O'Neill, J. 1985. *Five bodies*. Ithaca, N.Y.: Cornell University Press.

Open letter to the Supreme Court of Israel, An [advertisement]. 1990, May 5. *Jerusalem Post*, 4.

Ophir, A. 1996. The poor in deed facing the Lord of all deeds: A postmodern reading of the Yom Kippur *Mahzor*. In *Interpreting Judaism in a postmodern age*, ed. S. Kepnes, 181–220. New York: New York University Press.

Plaskow, J. 1992. A response. In *Imagining the Jewish future: Essays and responses*, ed. D. A. Teutsch, 29–34. Albany, N.Y.: SUNY Press.

Polkinghorne, D. E. 1988. *Narrative knowing and the human sciences*. Albany, N.Y.: State University of New York.

Poloma, M. 1982. *The charismatic movement: Is there a new Pentecost?* Boston: Twayne Publishers.

Prell, R. 1998. Cinderellas who (almost) never become princesses: Subversive representations of Jewish women in postwar popular novels. In *Talking back: Images of Jewish women in American popular culture*, ed. J. Antler, 123–138. Hanover, N.H.: Brandeis University Press.

———. 1992. Why Jewish princesses don't sweat: Desire and consumption in postwar American Jewish culture. In *People of the body: Jews and Judaism from an embodied perspective*, ed. H. Eilberg-Schwartz, 329–360. Albany, N.Y.: SUNY Press.

———. 1989. *Prayer and community: The havurah in American Judaism*. Detroit: Wayne State University Press.

Pruter, K. 1987. *Jewish Christians in the United States: A bibliography*. New York: Garland Publishing.

Quebedeaux, R. 1983. *The new charismatics II*. New York: Harper and Row.

———. 1978. *The worldly evangelicals*. New York: Harper and Row.

Rabinovitch, N. L. 1992. All Jews are responsible for one another. In *Jewish tradition and the nontraditional Jew*, ed. J. J. Schacter, 177–204. Northvale, N.J.: Jason Aronson, Inc.

Raphael, S. P. 1996. *Jewish views of the afterlife*. Northvale, N.J.: Jason Aronson, Inc.

Rausch, D. 1993. *Fundamentalist-evangelicals and anti-Semitism*. Valley Forge, Penn.: Trinity Press International.

———. 1982. *Messianic Judaism: Its history, theology and polity*. Lewiston, N.Y.: Edwin Mellen Press.

———. 1979. *Zionism within early American fundamentalism*. Lewiston, N.Y.: Edwin Mellen Press.

Rawidowicz, S. 1974. Israel: The ever-dying people. In *Studies in Jewish thought*, ed. N. Glatzer, 210–224. Philadelphia: Jewish Publication Society.

Ribuffo, L. 1989. God and Jimmy Carter. In *Transforming faith: The sacred and secular in modern American history*, ed. M. L. Bradbury and J. B. Gilbert, 141–159. New York: Greenwood Press.

Roether, R. 1989. Letter to the editor. *Humanistic Judaism* 17: 3–4.

Rose, S. D. 1990. Gender, education, and the new Christian right. In *In gods we trust*, 2d ed., ed. T. Robbins and D. Anthony, 99–118. New Brunswick, N.J.: Transaction Publishers.

Rosen, K. 1996, Spring. Circumcision is a covenant. *The Messianic Times* 7: 12.

Rosenberg, D. 1995a. Cantorial instruction. Tape. "Messiah" 1995, no. 60.

———. 1995. Jewish self-hatred. Tape. "Messiah" 1995, no. 35.

Royce, A. P. 1982. *Ethnic identity*. Bloomington, Ill.: Indiana University Press.

Rubin, T. I. 1990. *Anti-Semitism: A disease of the mind*. New York: Continuum.

Ruether, R. R. 1974. *Faith and fratricide*. New York: Seabury Press.

Sandeen, E. 1970. *The roots of fundamentalism*. Chicago: University of Chicago Press.

Sarna, J. D. 1987. The impact of nineteenth-century Christian missions on American Jews. In *Jewish apostasy in the modern world*, ed. T. M. Endelman, 232–254. New York: Holmes and Meier.

Saville-Troika, M. 1989. *The ethnography of communication.* 2d ed. New York: Basil Blackwell.

Schaffer, M. D. 1985, October 30. Messianic leader in city is denied Jewish burial. *The Philadelphia Inquirer.*

Schiffman, M. 1990. *Return from exile.* Columbus, Ohio: Teshuvah Publishing Co.

Schmid, R., and J. F. Kess. 1986. *Television advertising and televangelism.* Amsterdam: John Benjamin Co.

Schneider, S. W. 1992. Detoxifying our relationships. *Lilith* 17: 15–19.

Schwartz, T. 1995. Cultural totemism: ethnic identity primitive and modern. In *Ethnic identity: Creation, conflict, and accommodation* [3d ed.], ed. L. Romanucci-Ross and G. A. De Vos, 48–72. Walnut Creek, Calif.: AltaMira Press.

Segal, A. F. 1992. Jewish Christianity. In *Eusebius, Christianity and Judaism,* ed. H. W. Attridge and G. Hata, 326–351. Detroit: Wayne State University Press.

Sevener, H. 1989. Trends in Jewish evangelism. *Mishkan* 10: 67–70.

Silber, M. K. 1992. The Emergence of Ultra-Orthodoxy: The invention of a tradition. In *The uses of tradition: Jewish continuity in the modern era,* ed. J. Wertheimer, 23–84. New York: Jewish Theological Seminary.

Silberling, K. 1995, Winter. Women in leadership. *The Messianic Times* 5: 6.

Silver, G. 1984, November 14–20. Overbrook Park under siege. *Welcomat* (Philadelphia), 1.

Sklare, M. 1993. *Observing America's Jews.* Hanover, N.H.: Brandeis University Press.

———. 1974. Introduction. In *The Jews in American society,* ed. M. Sklare, 1–30. New York: Behrman House.

Sklare, M., and J. Greenblum. 1972. *Jewish identity on the suburban frontier.* 2d ed. Chicago: University of Chicago Press.

Sobel, B. Z. 1974. *Hebrew Christianity: The thirteenth tribe.* New York: John Wiley and Sons.

Soleau, J. K. 1997. Moments of transformation: The process of teaching and learning. *Journal of the American Academy of Religion* 65: 809–830.

Smith, R. 1995. Messianic Jewish Liturgy. Tape. "Messiah" 1995, no. 56.

Staub, J., and R. Alpert. 1988. *Exploring Judaism: A Reconstructionist approach.* Wyncote, Penn.: The Reconstructionist Press.

Stern, D. H. 1991. *Messianic Jewish manifesto.* Jerusalem: Jewish New Testament Publications.

Swartz, C. 1994. When Jews celebrate with Christians. *The Reconstructionist* 59: 44–48.

Tambiah, S. 1985. *Culture, thought and social action: An anthropological perspective.* Cambridge, Mass.: Harvard University Press.

Tec, N. 1990. *In the lion's den.* New York: Oxford University Press.

Thumma, S. 1991. Negotiating a religious identity: The case of the gay evangelical. *Sociological Analysis* 52: 333–347.

Wacker, G. 1988. Playing for keeps: The primitivist impulse in early Pentecostalism. In *The American quest for the primitive church,* ed. R. T. Hughes, 196–219. Urbana, Ill.: University of Illinois Press.

Waters, M. C. 1990. *Ethnic options: Choosing identities in America.* Berkeley: University of California Press.

Webber, J. 1992. Modern Jewish identities: The ethnographic complexities. *Journal of Jewish Studies* 43: 246–267.

Weber, T. P. 1983. *Living in the shadow of the second coming.* Chicago: University of Chicago Press.

Weigert, A. J. 1991. *Mixed emotions.* Albany, N.Y.: SUNY Press.

Wertheimer, J. 1993. *A people divided.* New York: HarperCollins Publishers, Inc.

Who is a Jew? 1989. Resolution, Second Biennial Conference of the International Federation of Secular Humanistic Jews. *Humanistic Judaism* 17: 2, 5.

Wilson, S. G. 1995. *Related strangers: Jews and Christians, 70–170 C.E.* Minneapolis: Fortress Press.

Wine, S. T. 1978. *Humanistic Judaism.* Buffalo, N.Y.: Prometheus Books.

Winer, R. 1990. *The calling.* Wynnwood, Penn.: MJAA Publishing, Inc.

Wohl, H. 1979, October 25. Beth Yeshua's bid meets resistance. *The Main Line Times,* 1.

Wolf, R. 1995, Winter. Women in leadership. *The Messianic Times* 5: 6.

Wolpe, D. 1992. Why God is a hot topic. *Jewish Spectator* 57: 6–9.

Woocher, J. S. 1986. *Sacred survival: The civil religion of the American Jews.* Bloomington, Ind.: Indiana University Press.

Wuthnow, R. 1988. *The restructuring of American religion.* Princeton: Princeton University Press.

———. 1978. *Experimentation in American religion.* Berkeley: University of California Press.

Wyschograd, M. 1995a. Letter to a friend. *Modern Theology* 11: 165–171.

———. 1995. Response to the respondents. *Modern Theology* 11: 229–241.

Yancey, W. 1984, October 1. *The social characteristics of the Jews in Overbrook Park.* Photocopy.

Yellin, B. 1988. Is the Torah for today? Tape. "Messiah" 1988.

Yerushalmi, Y. H. 1982. *Zakhor: Jewish history and Jewish memory.* New York: Schocken Books.

Yuter, A. J. 1991, October 23. Reform is told about religious authenticity. [Letter to the editor]. *Jewish Post and Opinion,* 3.

Zipperstein, S. J. 1987. Heresy, apostasy, and the transformation of Joseph Rabinovich. In *Jewish apostasy in the modern world,* ed. T. Endelman, 206–231. New York: Holmes and Meier.

Zito, G. V. 1983. Toward a sociology of heresy. *Sociological Analysis* 44: 123–130.

[handwritten note:] Jewish Christians and Christian Jews: From the Renaissance to the Enlightenment ed Richard H Popkin & Gordon M. Weiner (Dordrecht The Netherlands; Kluwer Academic Publishers 1994)

ACKNOWLEDGMENTS

This book owes much to a great many people. To my dissertation advisor, John Raines, who first encouraged me to publish, to my editor, Micah Kleit, and Beacon Press, who saw the potential hidden in an obese manuscript, and to innumerable friends, colleagues, and teachers who made their impact in a phone conversation or over a cup of coffee. I especially thank those various segments of the local Jewish community who heard me speak on this topic and responded with thoughtful insights and questions. I want to thank my parents, Hal and Eve Harris, for their continued encouragement through these many years. My husband Jon has been of incalculable help on this project as a sounding board for new ideas, emotional support, computer *maven*, and, for the past four years, babysitter. My son Aryeh has been of help in refraining from coloring on my manuscript and often rearranging my priorities. Most of all, I thank the members of Congregation B'nai Mashiach who made this book possible. It was their openness and their willingness to tell their stories that enabled me not only to publish a book, but also to think deeply about my own faith and identity.

Since this story was written, B'nai Mashiach and the Messianic movement have continued to create congregations and controversy. In 1997, the Federation of Jewish Men's Clubs, a Conservative Jewish organ, took up the "menace" of the "Hebrew Christians" as a year-long project. Jewish anti-missionary groups busily present programs and respond to family problems. Meanwhile, Messianic Judaism flourishes, growing congregations, retaining second-generation Messianic believers as the new young leadership of the movement, and gaining more popularity in evangelical circles. B'nai Mashiach remains, as of this writing, continuing in vibrancy and eager expectation of the Last Days.